Post-capitalist Futures

Post-capitalist Futures

Political Economy beyond Crisis and Hope

Edited by
Adam Fishwick and Nicholas Kiersey

First published 2021 by Pluto Press
345 Archway Road, London N6 5AA

www.plutobooks.com

Copyright © Adam Fishwick and Nicholas Kiersey 2021

The right of the individual contributors to be identified as the authors of this work has been asserted in accordance with the Copyright, Designs and Patents Act 1988.

British Library Cataloguing in Publication Data
A catalogue record for this book is available from the British Library

ISBN 978 0 7453 4082 1 Hardback
ISBN 978 0 7453 4083 8 Paperback
ISBN 978 1 7868 0723 6 PDF eBook
ISBN 978 1 7868 0725 0 Kindle eBook
ISBN 978 1 7868 0724 3 EPUB eBook

This book is printed on paper suitable for recycling and made from fully managed and sustained forest sources. Logging, pulping and manufacturing processes are expected to conform to the environmental standards of the country of origin.

Typeset by Stanford DTP Services, Northampton, England

Simultaneously printed in the United Kingdom and United States of America

Contents

Introduction: The Endings of Capitalism beyond Crisis
and Hope   1
Adam Fishwick and Nicholas Kiersey

1 Critical IPE and the End of History   26
   Owen Worth

2 Dialectical Ends and Beginnings: Why Barbarism at the
   End of Capitalism Means Barbarism beyond Capitalism   47
   Bryant William Sculos

3 A New Wheel to Keep Capitalism Moving? The Artificial
   Womb in Feminist Futures and the Capitalist Present   67
   Catia Gregoratti and Laura Horn

4 Development Alternatives: Old Challenges and New
   Hybridities in China and Latin America   86
   Paul Bowles and Henry Veltmeyer

5 'Property Belongs to Allah, Capital, Get Out!' Turkey's
   Anti-capitalist Muslims and the Concept of Alternatives
   to Capitalism   108
   Gorkem Altinors

6 Socialist Governmentality and the Problem of the
   Capital Strike, or, a Defence of Fully Automated Luxury
   Communism   126
   Nicholas Kiersey

7 Belaboured Markets: Imagining a More Democratic
   Global Economic Order   152
   Jonathon W. Moses

8 Post-capitalism and Associated Reactions: Mapping
   Alternative Routes and Transcending Strategic Certainty   174
   David J. Bailey

9	Mapping Post-capitalist Futures in Dark Times *Adam Fishwick*	196
10	The Distance Between Two Dreams: Post-neoliberalism and the Politics of Awakening *Japhy Wilson*	216

Afterword: Living in the Catastrophe 239
Adam Fishwick and Nicholas Kiersey

Notes on Contributors 249
Index 252

Introduction: The Endings of Capitalism beyond Crisis and Hope

Adam Fishwick and Nicholas Kiersey

Envisioning how capitalism might end has recaptured the academic imagination. Mapping out the potential of systemic collapse and the possibilities that might emerge within it represent two increasingly prominent, but rarely reconciled strands of academic work. Work on the nature of crisis – and various elements of the economic, political and ecological crisis in which we find ourselves – is now a cornerstone of the international political economy literature (Streeck 2014, 2016; McNally 2010; Harvey 2017; Moore 2015). But understanding the utopian projects that might overcome these – and the avenues by which they are foreclosed – is less well developed in the field, despite widespread interest elsewhere (Hudis 2012; Mason 2015; Srnicek and Williams 2015; Frase 2016; Gibson-Graham 2006; De Angelis 2017). Drawing out the concrete connections between these two sets of ideas – between the dystopian collapse and the utopian alternative – remains missing or incomplete. For example, van der Linden (2017) writes '[Harvey] longs for "a more fairy-tale-like ending" and sees, without well-founded reasons, "many grounds for hope" … [but] he offers no serious assessment of strategic possibilities, of potential agents of change, or of concrete steps that could realize his ideal' (van der Linden 2017: 187). Combining the 'fairy-tale-like ending' with the contemporary dynamics of crisis and collapse, while incorporating those logics that prevent such a process, are the focus of the volume that we introduce here.

Our aim – in this chapter and in the wider volume it will accompany – is to draw out the multiplicity of contemporary crises and 'utopian' alternatives that may be arising in various forms, building upon an understanding of the current moment of crisis as a piecemeal re/decomposition of global capitalism. In what follows we develop a reading of what we term the 'end(ings)' of capitalism that reflects what we perceive as the multiple, intersecting conditions of crisis that manifest beyond the spectacularism of catastrophe (Lilley et al. 2012) and, instead, are to be located in crises' continual, unstable remaking of conditions for capitalism's renewal. From here, we construct our critical reading of post-capitalism that we situate directly within this process of re/decomposition, in which we seek to draw out the multiple fissures that these crises create, the agents of change that emerge and the multiple societal dynamics that seek to foreclose their lived and imagined futures. In this way, our reading of the current conjuncture is a hopeful one – our contributions will unpack the political and prefigurative possibilities that emerge in-against-beyond capitalism, but they will do so by situating these in the conflictive dynamics of the present – in a *political economy of post-capitalism*. As Kim Stanley Robinson recently argued: 'Dystopia has done its job, it's old news now, perhaps it's self-indulgence to stay stuck in that place any more. Next thought: utopia. Realistic or not, and perhaps especially if not' (2018). Challenging the 'self-indulgence' of dystopia, therefore, is the starting point for our thinking on a way to reconcile the utopian visions that are circulating in our current moment.

The questions we look to address in the volume are: how, through a careful reflection on the current intersecting moments of contemporary crisis, can we map out the fissures that may be emerging? And how can the fissures that they may produce – or may already be producing – provide openings for us to identify emergent 'agents of change'? How can we situate these agents in a political economy of post-capitalism, in which the conditions for capitalism's renewal are under continual contestation? And in what ways can we situate utopias in the interceding contradictions of the contemporary crises of capitalism? Even if dystopias are 'self-indulgent', we must situate our thinking in the concreteness of the living present.

Following the onset of the Covid-19 pandemic, locating our thinking in the dystopias of the present has become even more urgent. The deepening inequalities on which this new crisis has shed renewed light, alongside the Black Lives Matter protests that have spread throughout the globe under these renewed crisis conditions, only make this more important. Many of the contributions to this volume were written and developed before the unexpected catastrophe of Covid-19 emerged. Yet, as editors, we believe the arguments presented in these works, which focus on the different dynamics and intersections of capitalist crisis and the challenges they produce for moving beyond capitalism, remain just as prescient. We turn to draw out some of these implications in an editorial Afterword at the end of the volume, as well as reflecting on some of the themes we address in this introductory chapter. Notably, we consider the question and interrelation between crisis and catastrophe as we enter a period that may well be more catastrophic than many of us could have ever imagined.

In what follows, we outline these contemporary engagements with crisis and our multiple end(ings) of capitalism, starting from those visions of the multiple crises of the present as creating new fissures for moving towards an uncertain jump into the future. Using this notion of the multiplicity of crises and the emergent alternatives, we begin to develop an understanding of the political economy of post-capitalism, one in which the interceding dynamics of crisis foreclose and reopen fissures that produce a re/decomposition of global capitalism. Our use of end(ings), here, is deliberate as a means of expressing uncertainty and multiplicity of possible endings for capitalism as necessarily contested and contingent.

THE END OF THE WORLD AS WE KNOW IT (AND AS WE DON'T)

'It's easier to imagine the end of the world than the end of capitalism', a quote attributed to Frederic Jameson, opens up our critical lens on the catastrophist vision of the ending of capitalism. It critically engages a popular consensus that not only does an end to capitalism have to come about in catastrophic form, but that a catastrophic ending is the only one we can comprehend (Lilley et al. 2012). Reflecting on the centrality of 'catastrophism' to environmental politics, Lilley (2012) argues for its inherent limitations:

> Those who believe that the system will crumble from crises and disasters lose sight of the ways that capitalism uses crises for its own regeneration and expansion. Likewise a focus on spectacu-

lar catastrophes typically overlooks the prosaic catastrophes of everyday life that are the sediment upon which capitalism is constructed. (Lilley 2012: 2)

As Lilley argues, crises are endemic to capitalism and cut through the day-to-day existence of our lives, providing unending sources for capitalism's own recomposition and rebirth and offering little more than 'shortcuts' to a better future (Lilley 2012: 12). Moving beyond the limits of this catastrophism enables us to look past the inevitability of decline to identify the means through which crises allow capitalism to reconstitute itself through new modes of dispossession and accumulation, new sites of value-extraction and exploitation, and the forceful reassertion of power across the various levels of the political. Moreover, it also provides a starting point to unpack the grounds of a political economy of post-capitalism.

It is this catastrophism that pervades, for example, the recent work of Wolfgang Streeck (2014, 2016) on the understanding of the end of capitalism. For Streeck (2014), and in a different way for Wallerstein et al. (2013), the problem is simple. Capitalism has entered a phase in which its long-standing disorders have become terminal. Falling growth rates, rising indebtedness and heightening inequality – combined with anti-democratic tendencies that have emerged across the globe in the aftermath of crisis and recovery – provide evidence, for Streeck (2016), that capitalism as a social system is no longer viable. This diagnosis of a terminal decline, however, rests on the assumption that collapse will unfold in spectacular form or be foreclosed by a reordering of the nation-state to contain and supplant it.

This vision is predicated on exactly the kind of catastrophism Lilley et al. decry. It is, Streeck argues, important that: 'instead of imagining [capitalism] being replaced by collective decision with some providentially designed new order, we allow for capitalism to collapse by itself' (Streeck 2014: 46). His 'social system in chronic disrepair' is, in essence, a collapsing global economic order riven by the immense contradictions he identifies that have, for now, destroyed any political capacities that could stabilise it once again (2014: 47). It is, in turn, this understanding of crisis that has led to a more recent articulation of what he characterises as the 'interregnum' of these capitalist crises. In this continuation of his earlier claims, Streeck (2017) argues that the catastrophic crisis of global capitalism must be addressed by a re-energising of the nation-state for only this, he claims, can mitigate the debilitating societal impact of the crisis. Admittedly, while he is clear that, 'even a post-globalist, neo-protectionist policy ... would be unable to guarantee stable growth, more and better quality employment, a deleveraging of public and private debt, or trust in the dollar and the euro' (Streeck 2017: 16), he insists that, in the face of 'cosmopolitan identitarianism' and societal 'dissolution', the only viable 'agent of change' is the nation-state (2017: 18). Yet this call for a renewal of the twentieth-century social compromise neglects the ways in which previous dynamics of crisis, and the role of national compromise, provided the institutional mechanisms for capitalism to remake itself from within during its earlier crises. Similarly, it neglects the multiplicity of crises, to which we will now turn.

Streeck's and others' understanding of the terminal crises faced by capitalism, therefore, provide us with something of a dead end. As Tooze (2017) argues, the often oddly uncritical advocacy of 'national' societies as the progressive exit relies on the thinking of catastrophism:

> But if hope and wishful thinking are an opium of the masses, then the promise of a disillusioned realism, a realistic accounting of the real no less, isn't without its ideological temptations either. Most obviously it can feed fatalism. But it can also do the opposite: sweeping historic gloom goes hand in hand with rebirth, a promise commonly vested in the nation. (Tooze 2017)

Leaving the contradictions of global capitalism to their inevitable end or managing crisis through a redirection of the prevailing impulses towards nationalism present us with little option beyond a social system that reproduces, as Lilley argues, the sediment of its rebirth. Such a depiction, moreover, serves to de-antagonise the unfolding of contemporary crisis by relocating social conflict to the institutional forms of the nation-state. Readings of the inevitability of capitalism's end, rather than the multiplicity of its end(ings) lead us away from identifying the intersecting, contradictory dynamics of de/recomposition that lie at the heart of crisis as a living, everyday dynamic and, therefore, of the simultaneous possibilities of contestation, recomposition, transformation and defeat that constitute a political economy of post-capitalism. Instead, drawing out the specificities of the current intersecting crises of global capitalism enables us to envision the complex dynamics of class, gender and race through which it plays out. And, in turn, this provides for thinking about post-capitalism as embedded in and overwritten by these distinctive logics as intrinsically contestable crises.

Crisis, therefore, is not a singular moment of collapse, but a living reality that weaves its way through the very fabric of contemporary capitalism. For McNally (2010), this current crisis is one wedded to the long trajectory of neoliberal transformation. Neoliberalism, he argues, has been – contrary to prevailing understandings – a period of 'global slump', a remaking of the global economy as a means of sustaining global capitalism through similar dynamics to those earlier noted by Streeck: indebtedness, inequality and stagnating wages and demand (McNally 2010: 3–5). This slump, he argues, is a transformative moment where '[the] present is history', whereby the collective struggles to overcome and to sustain the faltering logics of accumulation that underpin it will define the future we will encounter (2010: 9). Thus, unlike Streeck, for McNally decline is not an inevitable collapse of contradictions and the present moment is not one in which the inevitability of that collapse forecloses possibilities of transformative change. Alternatively, it is a moment in which struggle and contestation return to the fore in shaping the unfolding trajectory of what is emerging from within the living present.

The tendency of crisis – and the current modalities of intersecting capitalist crises – represents not an end to capitalism in and of itself, but new and contested terrain on which it is attempting to reconstitute itself in new terms around class, gender and race. It is, as argued by Lorey (2015), a new moment in the (re)constitution of the self under conditions of heightening and multiple forms of insecure and precarious life (Lorey 2015; Fisher, 2009). These, of course, are historically significant in the wider constitution of global capitalism (Federici 2018; Bhattacharya 2018), but the newly precarious modes

Introduction

of existence manifest these new axes of the crises of global capitalism as it seeks to reconfigure – in its own process of surviving – the terrain of social reproduction (McNally and Ferguson 2014). In enabling such a dynamic: 'the key development has been the massive expansion of the global labour reserve as a result of the most accelerated and extensive processes of primitive accumulation in world history' (2014: 9). This central facet of contemporary crisis is, then, critical in the recomposition of capital. It is a new phase in the cycle of dispossession, primitive accumulation and expansion to redress renewed crisis that is creating new terrains for capital accumulation and, simultaneously, for their contestation.

DEBATING POWER AND LEGITIMACY, AT THE END(ING) OF CAPITALISM

There are of course many different ways of approaching this question of the relative significance of the (re)constitution of the capitalist self, in the context of contemporary capitalism's expanding dynamics of primitive accumulation. However, a quick review of the positions that various anti-capitalist scholars have adopted on these questions suggests the prevalence of at least two poles of thought. At one pole, we can observe scholarship where the focus is less on the role of capitalist subjectivity, and more on the idea of a kind of neoliberal return to sovereignty. Here then, at the end(ing) of capitalism, power is said to have been reconstituted as something like an autonomous force or logic, with profoundly anti-democratic or even authoritarian characteristics. At the opposite pole, we find an argument that the end(ing) of capitalism is a more or less prolonged and uncertain conjuncture of crisis wherein governmental bodies have become preoccupied not only with the management of the capitalist self, but with the orientation of human life more broadly. We turn now to a brief outline of each position. As should become clear, however, our purpose here is not to 'pick a side' in the debate. To the contrary, our goal in identifying this theoretical tension is to suggest that it may constitute a productive lens through which the reader might wish to assess the following chapters.

Clustering around the first pole, advocates of the authoritarian neoliberalism hypothesis (see Bruff 2014; Burak Tansel 2017) contend that the economic difficulties of the last decade mean that prospects are likely poor for any capitalist elites who may be hoping for a re-legitimisation of capitalism. Rather than accept this, however, and confront the failings of some forty years of neoliberalism, elites today are instead doubling down on the logic of the market, and turning to techniques of propaganda and distraction to ensure their purchase on political power. Indeed, the recent electoral success around the world of 'strongman'-style leaders, such as Donald Trump, Boris Johnson, Erdogan, Duterte and Bolsonaro, all of whom have displayed tendencies towards economic nationalism and the demonisation of foreigners, suggests that it may yet be too early to deem this strategy of securing the rights of capital a failure.

A political project advocating government through the application of market-based principles to an ever-expanding domain of everyday life, neoliberalism of course became a prominent ideology in the 1970s, in the wake of a number of disastrous crises which had undermined the reputation of the Keynesian post-war model (for a detailed discussion of this point, see Slobodian 2018). Already tacitly authoritarian in its prescriptions for quotidian life, neoliberalism nevertheless enjoyed several decades of relative popularity in the West, coming to be seen by many as the natural model for equitable and democratic government (Dardot and Laval 2014). Riding the coat-tails of this ideological success, the 1990s saw an electoral shift to the centrist liberalism of the so-called 'Third Way', which was able to achieve a number of socially progressive policy goals despite remaining largely committed to the 'business as usual' of financial deregulation, privatisation, and cuts to social services. With the 2008 financial crisis, however, the project seems to have suffered a precipitous loss of prestige, and the political hegemony of centrist liberalism appears to have run aground.

Yet it would be incorrect to say that authoritarian neoliberalism was born on the coat-tails of Trump or Bolsonaro. It was already apparent at the outset of the Obama administration that nations in the so-called Western 'core' of the global economy were becoming relays for austerity and were, thus, 'internalizing the interests of transnational capital at the expense of labour' (Bieler and Morton 2018: 239). Addressing the European context specifically, Bieler and Morton discuss a number of legal mechanisms introduced since the outbreak of the crisis, empowering European institutions to fine countries that do not live up to the standards of the European Union's (EU's) Stability and Growth Pact. While policies such as these are, of course, ratified by the national parliaments, they trade off significant amounts of economic sovereignty once they are locked into supranational structures. The upshot, Bieler and Morton aver, has been a certain 'depoliticization' of economic governance in Europe. As they note, citing Ian Bruff, henceforth labour movements working in such contexts will find it difficult to articulate any real front against austerity, as the threats that most affect them are emanating from a supranational level and are, thus, effectively 'insulated' from any kind of dissent (Bieler and Morton 2018: 241).

Insofar as it helps us to identify the hidden stakes of what we might term, with Cahill (2014), 'actually existing neoliberalism', we find this focus on the authoritarian dynamics of contemporary neoliberal government to be instructive. At the very least, it's a welcome corrective to any number of constructivist attempts at explaining the 2008 crisis and its aftermath as the result of nothing more than cognitive error. Blyth (2013), for example, appears to suggest that the crisis was essentially an accident. To be sure, the 1999 repeal of the Glass–Steagall Act made possible a panoply of new, complex financial instruments, but the core issue was the 'epistemic hubris' of the US bankers who failed to see the obviously mounting risk in their portfolios (Blyth 2013: 91). Whereas Mirowski (2013), for his part, even as he discusses the cynical strategies of the 'Neoliberal Thought Collective', with its intentional deliberations over where and when to use esoteric and exoteric discourses, never broaches the possibility that the will to engage in such calculation might be driven by anything other than a political imaginary.

Nevertheless, it is clear that, by suggesting we live now in something of a post-democratic age, the question of the subject of capitalism is not an analytical priority for critics of authoritarian neoliberalism. Weakened by decades of neoliberal attack, they contend, the traditional institutions of representative democracy stand before us corrupted and broken. For this reason, the traditional instrumentalism of the liberal approach to political power, which posits the state as the primary locus of the political, will no longer suffice. Discourses of legitimation may still circulate in the public sphere, but function now only in the most overtly cynical, propagandistic manner, as the expression of raw capitalist elite self-interest (Bieler and Morton 2018: 68–71). So, how then are we able to fight capitalism, today? Guided by their belief that we are confronted by, and subordinated to, an insulated, authoritarian mode of elite power, critics of authoritarian neoliberalism are not sanguine about the possibility of leveraging the traditional institutions of representative democracy. For this reason, they say, the left is advised instead to adopt a more tactically 'disruptive' posture. That is, to turn to non-traditional sources of leftist energy and welcome to the fold a wider range of 'everyday' expressions of anti-authoritarianism and refusal than might traditionally be considered as political (see for example, Bailey et al. 2016).

Critically, the subject here is seen as one that is active and intentional in its disruptive activities, despite its subordination. These activities of this subject run a wide gamut, from the more obviously performative antics of the Yes Men (see Terranova 2010), to those of the black bloc-style and other direct-action militant groups, already well known from their interventions in the cities of Berkeley and Charlottesville (Jones 2017). Equally, such activity can also take the form of a more strategically oriented 'exodus', predicated on the creation of autonomous forms of social reproduction that attempt to create islands of non-capitalist life, albeit inevitably within the context of capitalism itself (Holland 2011; Arditi 2014). As Bruff and Burak Tansel express it, however, the point is less to prescribe an ideal range of tactics, and more that we must learn to take into account a 'broader range of resistances', from the struggles of indigenous peoples, to those who seek refuge from gender or citizenship-based discrimination, to those who seek to defend 'black lives' from militarised policing (Bruff and Burak Tansel 2019: 242).

There are, however, other ways of approaching the questions of power and subjectivity, at the end(ing) of capitalism. Turning now to our second pole, we find a literature inspired, if not by Marx, then at least by a certain Foucauldian reading of Marx. Now, of course, for some Marxists, Foucault might appear an unlikely ally in this kind of conversation. If one surveys scholarship on authoritarian neoliberalism, for example, it's not unusual to see him described as Bieler and Morton do, as a theorist solely of 'fetishized self/other differences', which have no specific internal relation to capitalism (2018: 66). For Bruff, similarly, because Foucault saw 'power relations' as always, in the final instance, 'the singular source of all human practice', he externalised discourse from material forces and, in so doing, reduced society to the status of a mere relay of power (Bruff 2009: 341).

To us, however, a Foucauldian approach does not necessarily need to be read in opposition to the authoritarian neoliberal approach just described. Consider, for example, the parallels between Foucault's theory of governmentality, itself in many ways a critique both of the anarchist theory of the state and the instrumentalism of what is commonly taken as Marx's own theory of the state. Commenting on Marx's theory of social change in *Capital*, vol. I, Foucault observes that what many Marxists comprehend as the effects of capitalism are actually presented by Marx as its causes, and vice-versa. Thus, for Foucault, Marx shows us:

> How, starting from the initial and primitive existence of these small regions of power – like property, slavery, workshop, and also the army – little by little, the great State apparatuses were able to form. State unity is basically secondary in relation to these regional and specific powers; these latter come first. (Foucault 2012)

For Foucault, then, Marx's concept of power is actually local, multiple and productive, much the same as it is in his own theory of governmentality. The upshot is that the works of Marx and Foucault bear strong affinities to each other on the subject of power. Affinities which, moreover, open up interesting possibilities for our debate on post-capitalism.

It may be important to recall that, for Foucault, power is articulated through bodily desire. Or, more specifically, through the experience of pleasure (Foucault 2000: 120). The technologies upon which 'wide' governmentality as a general model of power is founded emerge first with the confessional technologies of Christian pastoral care

(Foucault 2007: 183–5). The development of these technologies is significant, as Konings (2015) explains, insofar as they augur the historical passage from idolatrous religion to generative faith – that is, the innovation of a mode of governance premised on the use of icons. Confession, in this sense, does not so much instil a new 'truth' in the subject as solicit an affectively mediated relation with an ultimately unknowable god. Thus, citing Judith Butler, Konings provides us with the crucial punchline of the whole debate: we should not presume that the subject of capital internalises ideas in a linear or passive-cognitive fashion. Rather, like the confessional subject of Christianity, the subject of capital is called on to act in a space of freedom. It is an adaptively reflexive subject, drawing on emotional, autonomously held memories to 'feel out' its response to change.

The point we wish to make here, in this discussion about power and legitimacy at the end(ing) of capitalism, is that an approach to capitalist power grounded in the concept of desire might prompt us to look again at the idea that the end(ing) of capitalism is being subtended solely by an authoritarian neoliberal state, the rationality of which is itself determined solely by material interests, and the 'cold logic' of the marketplace. To be sure, this is not to suggest that the institutions of the state have no bearing on the question, or that they are not operating according to a neoliberal logic. Rather, the point is simply to suggest that, by situating liberal technologies of government within 'capital', critics of authoritarian neoliberalism are effectively bracketing the role of desire at the point of capitalism's constitution and, ultimately, in its potential reconstitution. In other words, their theoretical framing suppresses the possibility that capital might itself be a confessional phenomenon. Such oversights are indeed unfortunate for, as Spinozist Marxists like Pierre Macherey (2015) and Frédéric Lordon (2014) have shown, the idea of an expropriation of active 'biopower' is by no means inconsistent with Marx's understanding of the concept of living labour, as the source of capitalism's surplus.

In drawing attention to this approach, our goal is not to deny the significance or importance of research carried out by critics of authoritarian neoliberalism. To the contrary, we think these research questions are essentially complementary. Earlier in this chapter, we spoke of new dynamics of accumulation at the end(ing) of capitalism. To see how the (re)composition of the capitalist subject might be considered an example of this, one need only think of the intensifying place in capitalist production of the value of life itself, or the 'productive power of subjectivity' (Read, 2003: 153). As Lazzarato puts it, attempts to re-float capitalist valorisation in the wake of the 2008 crisis are to no small degree caught up with the radical externalisation of the risks of capitalist chrematistics onto the crowd. For Lazzarato, this shift bespeaks a machinic turn in the nature of capitalism. Value, he explains, is today drawn from the interface between conscious and non-conscious labour, thereby exceeding any quantifiable relation to the value of the labour time necessary for its manufacture (2014: 43–5). If such operations of colonising new aspects of social life are in any way successful, then this suggests another vector of capitalist longevity.

One example of such a non-obvious method of capitalist re-valorisation is the rise of the so-called gig economy. As Callum Cant (2019) observes, workers for platform-based courier service companies like Deliveroo are often lured in by the promise of high wages, only then to find themselves stuck: caught between their own status as 'independent contractors', and thus as the sole responsible agents for the upfront investment in their own gear, not to mention its maintenance and insurance, and the surge pricing mechanism of the platform. The result is that, for extended periods of their time on the job, gig workers may earn below minimum wage. Moreover, as critics like Sarah Mason (2018) have noted, the merging of piecemeal work with networked hand-held devices and 'gaming' aesthetics effectively links the self-esteem of ride-share workers to their ratings within apps like Uber and Airbnb. In this sense, the gig economy workers of our online era are encouraged on multiple fronts to 'stay loyal' to their platforms. As the expression of a mode of power, the picture that emerges is one that is messy and unclear. In London's terms, it is less self-evidently an authoritarian mode than it is a sort of cynical version of voluntary servitude, where real and authentic joys and freedoms are still possible for the worker, so long as they are willing to trade for those joys 'an unlimited commitment' of our very selves; the total economisation of our capacities for life (Lordon 2014: 38).

To summarise, this Foucault-inspired approach to the end(ing) of capitalism shows that there may be more to the resilience of capitalism today than a focus on mere authoritarianism might let on. It is an approach that allows us to think about a newly emerging role of the non-signifying, and the autonomic, in capitalist valorisation. As in Marx's own time, we have a mode of capitalism that is emerging and reproducing itself from the *bottom-up*. Moreover, clearly, it is being facilitated by means of technologies that secure the voluntary participation of workers. Elites and organic intellectuals no doubt play a role in the reproduction of this capitalist order, but this is a cynical mode of capitalism that is more than capable of sustaining itself, even as neoliberal elites and planners stumble and blunder in their efforts to create any kind of long-term fix. The upshot, as Beggs (2013) observes, is that while capitalism as a system will most likely continue, so long as it is able to guarantee the extraction of surplus value from commodified labour, it does not necessarily follow that the elites and planners of capitalism are rational, or have a perfect roadmap of 'the preconceived needs of the economic system'. The short-sightedness of these elites, and their potential for making grave mistakes, cannot be understated as we reflect on capitalism's long-term prognosis.

To flesh out this point briefly, it may well be worth remembering the great turn of the 1970s, where we saw the first neoliberal governments begin to take power. As Dardot and Laval (2014) suggest, this turn was the result neither solely of 'economic changes internal to the capitalist system' nor was it merely an 'ideological revenge' of Milton Friedman. The neoliberal programme was first able to gain traction, they contend, only insofar as it was able to present itself as the solution to a *political* problem – namely, the 'excess of democracy' as perceived by many liberal and neoconservative intellectuals, in the late 1960s. What those intellectuals could not see, or refused to see, was the fact that these same demands were themselves in no small measure the result of contradictions inherent in the Fordist regime of valorisation. Nevertheless, with this focus on excessive democracy, the authoritarian genealogy of neoliberalism is made strikingly clear. And it is in

Introduction

this precise sense, we wholeheartedly agree, that neoliberalism has *always* been authoritarian. The point, however, is that this tendency is not reducible to its status as a rational philosophy or masterplan of capitalism, or that it is incapable of mistakes, or overplaying its hand. Whereas what the Foucauldian approach outlined here offers us is an ability to explain simultaneously both the basis of capitalism's ability to articulate and re-articulate itself, as a technology of desire, even in spite of neoliberalism's myriad errors and misjudgements, while also avoiding the tautology of having to claim that capitalist thought is necessarily reducible to the reason or logic of capital itself. For this reason, as we will now suggest, it may well be the case that the left should not give up the fight for some of those traditional, statist avenues of resistance.

DISORDER, DOMINATION AND DISRUPTION

So as capitalism begins to reconstitute itself through these multiple axes, what of the possibility of post-capitalism and, more importantly, the political economy of post-capitalism? Some of the most prominent ideas around the passage to post-capitalism posit this as residing in the transformative potential of technology (Mason 2015; Srnicek and Williams 2015). For Paul Mason (2015), technology presents a significant opportunity for an emergent post-capitalism that will supplant capitalism as an 'adaptive system which has reached the limits of its capacity to adapt' (Mason 2015). He argues that a triple transformation led by technological change over the last two decades has produced conditions whereby work is no longer necessary, scarcity is over and collaborative production (based on the example of Wikipedia) is supplanting competition (Mason 2015). Srnicek and Williams (2015), and the wider 'post-work' movement (see, for example, Frayne 2015), offer a more sophisticated understanding of the possibility of post-capitalism via technological revolution. They argue that a left political programme aimed at full automation can provide the basis for a post-work society in which work and income are delinked, opening an uncertain future where human capacities are targeted at demands beyond capitalist production (Srnicek and Williams 2015: 176). They argue explicitly against what they term the 'folk politics' of prefigurative, utopian projects of 'post-capitalism' and towards an overarching 'universalist' societal transformation driven by the potentialities of new technologies in the present.

Yet these ideas have been increasingly problematised. The notion of technological change as the dimension along which we can delineate the possibilities of post-capitalism, imagined as a post-work society, neglects some of the important dimensions of capitalist crisis and its role in the reconstitution of capitalism already outlined. As argued by Pitts and Dinerstein (2018), the proposal that post-work – the removal of the imperative to work under capitalist social relations – and universal basic income (UBI) will enable the development of a post-capitalist society misses the specificities of capitalist 'forms' taken by those institutions that would regulate such a society. Based on a thorough critique of post-work and UBI, they argue that this idea is a false resolution that 'temporarily defers the contradictions of class antagonism without resolution through the antagonism itself' (Pitts and Dinerstein 2018: 481). This is a crucial contribution that reflects the understanding of capitalist crisis explicated earlier, inasmuch as the terrain of capitalism's end(ings) is not a space that can be neutrally reconstituted with its institutions easily converted to the ends of constructing a post-capitalist utopia, but one in which that reconstitution itself must be viewed through the lens of ongoing antagonism.

Thus far, we have suggested the possibility of a productive tension between two somewhat different perspectives on power and legitimation, at the end(ing) of capitalism. We have tried to make it clear here that both of these perspectives have important contributions to make. With its focus on parallel economies and piecemeal disruptions of everyday life, the essential contribution of the critique of authoritarian neoliberalism is its insistence on hope. In this sense, it is a perspective clearly aligned with what Hardt and Negri (2009) term 'exodus'. That is, seeing possibilities for resistance among ordinary people, it encourages us to abandon traditional state-focused hegemony in favour of material ruptures wherein imaginative cyber-nomadic potentialities can take flight. What we have also tried to point to, however, is a Foucauldian approach, which simultaneously poses a version of capitalism that is perhaps more immanent to our affective lives, and thus more resilient to everyday modes of resistance than we might hope, but also a version of the capitalist state that is perhaps less rationally governed than it might first appear to be.

For us then, the complexities of global capitalism are such that both approaches will be required at once. Some have referred to this as 'left-wing convergence' (see Prichard and Worth 2016; Kiersey and Vrasti 2016). On the one hand, the exodus approach possesses a tried and trusted capacity for viral, network-based auto-generation that more traditional hegemonic models lack. On the other, politically significant degrees of rupture will likely be impossible to accomplish without the embrace of some measure of state capacity. The question, therefore, is to balance the goal of provisioning for the movements of exodus, and all the creative, disruptive subjectivities they can generate, with that of a state-oriented hegemonic strategy (a detailed discussion of this question can be found in Arditi 2014). Indeed, such concerns have been at the centre of recent left-'exit' debates in Europe (see, for example, Panitch 2015). While we are clearly not as nostalgic for the nation-state as Streeck, or so naïve as to think that the capitalist state can be easily reformed, we are equally keen to avoid a retreat into performativity – a tendency emblematic of a despondent society that has succumbed to the grip of what Mark Fisher (2009) termed 'capitalist realism'. For these reasons, we do think it is important to reflect on both the role of popular affect in sustaining capitalist necessity to such a seemingly improbable degree, and the need for the state to take up the margin of freedom remaining to it within capitalism, to create 'non-reformist' time and spaces for democratic production to flourish, and for movements to be able to mobilise and build capacity, and to hold the state accountable to this goal (Gorz 1968).

To conclude, a central idea for us in this conversation is that capitalism derives its surplus value from work in 'the commons' (Gibson-Graham 2006; De Angelis 2017). Not only does this way of seeing capitalism begin very firmly from the idea of diverse and multiple modalities of life and alternative sites of contestation to and against capital (see Gibson-Graham 2006, in particular), but it also maps out the conditions from which an alternative political economy

– an organisation of economic activity and social relations – might emerge. Perhaps the most comprehensive effort made to do this – to explore precisely how the mechanisms of the commons, rooted in the specific economic conditions that underpin them, appears in Massimo De Angelis (2017). Here he explicates the dynamics of an autopoietic commons, which persists in-against capitalism via self-reproducing 'commoning' social practices. He argues that it is a critical mass of such commoning that will produce a 'tipping point' at which the multiplication of these commons will spread without friction as they become viewed as the best form of societal organisation (De Angelis 2017: 291). However, while he does explicitly acknowledge the multiple barrier points to multiplication, his vision of multiplication seems too reliant on a quantitative expansion of the presence of commoning practices, which, in a way, acts to invert the logic of the catastrophist 'end', with an emergent new beginning driven by an expansionary logic of the global commons.

Consequently, we must begin to delineate the parameters of a political economy of post-capitalism that simultaneously acknowledges the reconstitution of capitalism in the continual 'disorders' of its demise and the terrains through which alternative utopian forms, mobilised by a diverse array of 'agents of change' may begin to emerge *in antagonistic relations of social conflict.* As argued elsewhere, the unfolding of crisis is shaped through the contested dynamics of disruption and domination (Huke et al. 2015). To do this, then, we turn now to an overview of the contributions to this volume. As the reader will see, the assembled chapters share a common frame of reference, identifying the intersection between the fissures emerging through the unfolding of crisis not as a spectacular collapse – as in 1929, 2008 and other more localised economic crashes – but in the various continuing crises of everyday life that are inflected by the persistent re/decomposition of global capitalism. The outcomes of this process, to borrow from Pitts and Dinerstein (2018), is that the social form is continually reconstituted, but in a manner that is contested and in which the possibility of opening up alternate modes of social life becomes possible. These are unknown and unknowable, but traceable through the identification of the various 'utopian' alternatives that emerge and are foreclosed in that moment, both in the

Introduction

actors engaged in the process and the fissures that open and re-close. It is, then, these dynamics of crisis, reconstitution and transformation, but also of defeat, that comprise the dynamics of our political economy of post-capitalism and on which our chapters will build.

TOWARDS POST-CAPITALIST FUTURES

In chapter 1, Worth provides an invaluable overview of what it means to speak of a critical tradition in International Political Economy (IPE), drawing on an extensive body of work to identify how the need to engage with emancipatory or transformative perspectives is essential in bringing about its own 'end of history'. Here then, he argues that combining the theoretical constructs of Gramsci's 'war of position' and Luxemburg's 'dialectical materialism' can provide a fruitful avenue for thinking in and past the current conjuncture. Specifically, these approaches can provide a practical framework through which academic work in critical IPE can contribute to the continuing confrontation with neoliberalism today, both in dismantling the wider hegemonic project and constructing tools for rebuilding anew.

In chapter 2, Sculos develops an important argument around the 'psycho-social' factors from which alternate forms of post-capitalism might emerge, centring on the tension between socialism or barbarism. In doing so he raises the uncomfortable but central paradox, namely: can the subjects produced by capitalism be the same subjects that ultimately come to transform it? Drawing on the work of Fromm, he highlights the necessary, and immensely complex task, of constructing a 'productive' social character, with a disposition to cooperative communities that might provide the foundations for the movements and post-capitalist futures that are yet to emerge.

In chapter 3, Gregoratti and Horn critically engage the radical imaginaries of xenofeminism and feminist calls for 'full surrogacy now' to unpack how we might understand the limits that really existing capitalist social relations impose on technological solutions to contemporary crises of social reproduction. In doing so, they argue for a Marxist feminist account of socially reproductive labour to understand the opportunities and limits of artificial womb technology. Drawing on feminist science fictions, too, they ask that we consider the 'contending and contradictory objectives, desires and subjectivities embodied in living labour' as the starting point of any technological imaginary for women's liberation in, after and beyond capitalism.

In chapter 4, Bowles and Veltmeyer draw on the rich tradition of Critical Development Studies to provide an account of two contemporary alternatives to capitalism – in China and in the hybrid new forms of social and economic organisation that emerged in recent decades in South America. In doing so they move away from celebratory accounts of success and, instead, examine the challenges and limitations of what 'development' is and who it is for. They present the various hybridities that are produced and exist on the boundaries between capitalism and forms of post-capitalism, exploring the lessons that can be drawn but also emphasising the challenges these 'islands' face in the crises of the present.

In chapter 5, Altinors examines the case of Turkey's 'anti-capitalist Muslims' and their imaginaries of a post-capitalist future. His chapter interrogates the relationship between Islam and capitalism in Turkey, drawing on the experience of the Gezi Park protests to develop a non-Eurocentric account of what an alternative to capitalism – a post-capitalist future – might look like in this context. As he argues, the specifics of Islamic capitalism, as it emerged in Turkey, have given rise to a specific constellation of Islamic anti-capitalism.

In chapter 6, Kiersey explores the normative implications of post-structural IPE's libertarian framework of time and contrasts it with that of a number of thinkers associated with neo-Marxism (Hardt and Negri, Mark Fisher). Using the Anthropocene or, as McKenzie Wark terms it, 'the metabolic rift' of capitalist modernity, as his case, he advances an argument based on what Michel Foucault termed socialist governmentality. Specifically, he argues that, in times of crisis, the task of emancipation today presupposes a confrontation with a vertically integrated and vindictive power called capitalism.

In chapter 7, Moses explores the current international regime – or world order – in which global capitalism exists untethered from the needs and demands of much of its population. He examines several alternative regimes, drawing on the wider critical IPE literature, to explore how regulation and democratic control are central for futures beyond the (neo)liberal capitalist world order. Specifically, he draws out crucial elements of recent Nordic experiences, such as how to provide workers the capacity to 'exit', to provide a useful pathway for thinking about the modalities of regulation necessary to improve the lives of the global population.

In chapter 8, Bailey elaborates the need to embrace the uncertainty of the current conjuncture and, consequently, move beyond what he describes as the twentieth-century certainties that have encountered continual barriers to moving beyond capitalism. Here, he emphasises the importance of navigating – via Hardt and Negri – the current debates on left strategy between horizontal prefigurativism and vertical left populism. In doing so, he draws on the work of three important theorists – Luxemburg, Fanon and Gago – all of whom begin from a position of 'structural weakness' and, in distinctive but complementary ways, begin to conceptualise and traverse the uncertain pathways to post-capitalism.

In chapter 9, Fishwick explores the forms through which pathways towards post-capitalism might emerge, situating his argument through the work of George Ciccariello-Maher and his 'decolonised dialectics'. In doing so, he foregrounds the violent dynamics of exclusion that characterise capitalism as a means to conceptualise how this might present the grounds on which prefigurative practices can generate a forceful rupture with the crises of the present. He argues that these paths exist beyond any inclusive technological utopianism and Western-centric universalisms in a multiplicity of agency rooted in diverse particularisms.

In chapter 10, Wilson uses the idea of the 'dream' to make sense of the construction of radical praxis, drawing on the work of Mladen Dolar to unpack the political significance of his call to remain in the 'impossible' space between dreams and awakening. To do this he critically engages the limitations of the post-neoliberal experience in Ecuador. Specifically, he argues that the government programme of Rafael Correa produced a return to another dream that failed to resolve the destructive consequences of neoliberalism. Instead, it was only spontaneous mobilisations and uprisings that embraced the impossible space.

REFERENCES

All URLS were last checked on 12 December 2020.

Arditi, Benjamin (2014) 'Post-hegemony: Politics Outside the Usual Post-Marxist Paradigm', in Alexandros Kioupkiolis and Giorgos Katsambekis (eds) *Radical Democracy and Collective Movements Today*. London: Routledge, pp. 17–44.

Bailey, David, Monica Clua-Losada, Nikolai Huke, Olatz Ribera-Almandoz and Kelly Rogers (2016) 'Challenging the Age of Austerity: Disruptive Agency after the Global Economic Crisis', *Comparative European Politics* 16(1): 9–31.

Beggs, Mike (2013) 'Dollar diplomacy', available at: https://jacobinmag.com/2013/07/dollar-diplomacy

Bhattacharya, Gargi (2018) *Rethinking Racial Capitalism: Questions of Reproduction and Survival*. London: Rowman and Littlefield International.

Bieler, Andreas and Adam Morton (2018) *Global Capitalism, Global War, Global Crisis*. Cambridge: Cambridge University Press.

Blyth, Mark (2013) *Austerity: The History of a Dangerous Idea*. New York: Oxford University Press.

Bruff, Ian (2009) 'The Totalisation of Human Social Practice: Open Marxists and Capitalist Social Relations, Foucauldians and Power Relations', *British Journal of Politics & International Relations* 11(2): 332–351.

Bruff, Ian (2014) 'The Rise of Authoritarian Neoliberalism', *Rethinking Marxism* 26(1): 113–129.

Bruff, Ian and Cemal Burak Tansel (2019) 'Authoritarian Neoliberalism: Trajectories of Knowledge Production and Praxis', *Globalizations* 16(3): 233–244.

Burak Tansel, Cemal (ed.) (2017) *States of the Discipline: Authoritarian Neoliberalism and the Contested Reproduction of the Capitalist Order*. New York: Rowman and Littlefield.

Cahill, Damien (2014) *The End of Laissez-Faire? On the Durability of Embedded Neoliberalism*. Cheltenham: Edward Elgar.

Cant, Callum (2019) *Riding for Deliveroo: Resistance in the New Economy*. Cambridge: Polity Press.

Dardot, Pierre and Christian Laval (2014) *The New Way of the World: On Neoliberal Society*. New York: Verso.

De Angelis, Massimo (2017) *Omnia Sunt Comunia: On the Commons and the Transformation to Postcapitalism*. London: Zed Books.

Introduction

Federici, Silvia (2018) *Witches, Witch-Hunting and Women*. Oakland, CA: PM Press.
Fisher, Mark (2009) *Capitalist Realism: Is There No Alternative?* Ropley: Zero Books.
Foucault, Michel (2000) 'Truth and Power', in James D. Faubion (ed.), *Power: The Essential Works of Michel Foucault 1954–1984*. New York: The New Press.
Foucault, Michel (2007) *Security, Territory, Population: Lectures at the Collège de France, 1977–1978*. New York: Palgrave Macmillan.
Foucault, Michel (2012) 'The Mesh of Power', *Viewpoint Magazine*, available at: https://www.viewpointmag.com/2012/09/12/the-mesh-of-power/
Frase, Peter (2016) *Four Futures: Life after Capitalism*. London: Verso.
Frayne, David (2015) *The Refusal of Work: The Theory and Practice of Resistance to Work*. London: Zed Books.
Gibson-Graham, J.K. (2006) *A Postcapitalist Politics*. Minneapolis, MN: University of Minnesota Press.
Gorz, André (1968) 'Reform and Revolution', in Ralph Miliband and Ralph Saville (eds), *Socialist Register*. London: Merlin Press.
Hardt, Michael and Antonio Negri (2009) *Commonwealth*. Cambridge, MA: The Belknap Press of Harvard University Press.
Harvey, David (2017) *Seventeen Contradictions and the End of Capitalism*. Oxford: Oxford University Press.
Holland, Eugene (2011) *Nomad Citizenship*. Minneapolis, MN: University of Minnesota Press.
Hudis, Peter (2012) *Marx's Concept of the Alternative to Capitalism*. Chicago: Haymarket Books.
Huke, Nikolai, Monica Clua Losada and David Bailey (2015) 'Disrupting the European Crisis: A Critical Political Economy of Contestation, Subversion and Escape', *New Political Economy* 20(5): 725–751.
Jones, Sarah (2017) '"Antifa Isn't a Hobby or a Fad": A Q&A with Mark Bray', *The New Republic*, available at: https://newrepublic.com/article/144723/antifa-isnt-hobby-fad-qa-mark-bray
Kiersey, Nicholas and Wanda Vrasti (2016) 'A Convergent Genealogy? Space, Time and the Promise of Horizontal Politics Today', *Capital & Class* 40(1), 75–94, available at: https://doi.org/10.1177/0309816815627733
Konings, Martijn (2015) *The Emotional Logic of Capitalism*. Stanford, CA: Stanford University Press.
Lazzarato, Maurizio (2014) *Signs and Machines*. Los Angeles, CA: Semiotext(e).

Lilley, Sarah (2012) 'The Apocalyptic Politics of Collapse and Rebirth', in Sarah Lilley, David McNally, Eddie Yuen and James Davis (eds) *Catastrophism: The Apocalyptic Politics of Collapse and Rebirth*. Oakland, CA: PM Press.

Lilley, Sarah, David McNally, Eddie Yuen and James Davis (2012) *Catastrophism: The Apocalyptic Politics of Collapse and Rebirth*. Oakland, CA: PM Press.

Lordon, Frédéric (2014) *Willing Slaves of Capital*. London: Verso.

Lorey, Isabell (2015) *State of Insecurity: Government of the Precarious*. London: Verso.

Macherey, Pierre (2015) 'The Productive Subject', *Viewpoint Magazine*, available at: https://viewpointmag.com/2015/10/31/the-productive-subject/

Mason, Paul (2015) *PostCapitalism: A Guide to Our Future*. London: Allen Lane.

Mason, Sarah (2018) 'High Score, Low Pay: Why the Gig Economy Loves Gamification', *The Guardian*, available at: https://www.theguardian.com/business/2018/nov/20/high-score-low-pay-gamification-lyft-uber-drivers-ride-hailing-gig-economy

McNally, David (2010) *Global Slump: The Economics and Politics of Crisis and Resistance*. Oakland, CA: PM Press.

McNally, David and Susan Ferguson (2014) 'Precarious Migrants: Gender, Race and the Social Reproduction of the Global Working Class', *Socialist Register* 51: 1–23.

Mirowski, Philip (2013) *Never Let a Serious Crisis Go to Waste: How Neoliberalism Survived the Financial Meltdown*. London: Verso Books.

Moore, Jason (2015) *Capitalism in the Web of Life: Ecology and the Accumulation of Capital*. London: Verso.

Panitch, Leo (2015) 'On the Doorstep of Power', *Jacobin*, 25 January, available at: https://www.jacobinmag.com/2015/01/panitch-syriza-election-austerity-greece/

Pitts, Frederick Harry and Ana Dinerstein (2018) 'From Post-work to Post-capitalism? Discussing the Basic Income and Struggles for Alternative Forms of Social Reproduction', *Journal of Labor and Society* 21: 471–491.

Prichard, Alex and Owen Worth (2016) 'Left-wing Convergence: An Introduction', *Capital & Class* 40(1): 3–17, available at: https://doi.org/10.1177/0309816815624370

Read, Jason (2003) *The Micro-politics of Capital*. New York: SUNY Press.

Robinson, Kim Stanley (2018) 'Dystopias Now', *Commune Magazine*, available at: https://communemag.com/dystopias-now/
Slobodian, Quinn (2018) *Globalists: The End of Empire and the Birth of Neoliberalism*. Cambridge, MA: Harvard University Press.
Srnicek, Nick and Alex Williams (2015) *Inventing the Future: Postcapitalism and a World Without Work*. London: Verso.
Streeck, Wolfgang (2014) 'How Will Capitalism End?', *New Left Review* 87: 35–64.
Streeck, Wolfgang (2016) *How Will Capitalism End?* London: Verso.
Streeck, Wolfgang (2017) 'The Return of the Repressed', *New Left Review* 104: 1–18.
Terranova, Tiziana (2010) 'New Economy, Financialization and Social Production in the Web 2.0', in Andrea Fumagalli and Sandro Mezzadra (eds) *Crisis in the Global Economy*. Los Angeles, CA: Semiotext(e), pp. 166–170.
Tooze, Adam (2017) 'A General Logic of Crisis', *London Review of Books*, 5 January 2017, available at: https://www.lrb.co.uk/v39/n01/adam-tooze/a-general-logic-of-crisis
van der Linden, Marcel (2017) 'Is Capitalism Collapsing?', *Development and Change* 48(1): 180–188.
Wallerstein, Immanuel, Randall Collins, Michael Mann, Georgi Derluguian and Craig Calhoun (2013) *Does Capitalism Have a Future?* Oxford: Oxford University Press.

1
Critical IPE and the End of History

Owen Worth

The origins of what we understand to be critical International Political Economy (IPE) are contested. Increasingly, they appear to have contrasting points of departure and conjure up a contrasting collection of historical narratives that often are contained within disciplinary and generational boundaries. However, from the spirit of Kant and the various criticisms of political economy of Marx, the central objective of 'critique and transform' has been – at least tentatively – the primary objective of those who look to label themselves as working within 'critical IPE'. Commitments towards these twin notions of critique and emancipation, however, are also subjective. While it might be acknowledged that the concept of emancipation itself is subjective and is used for different purposes and towards different ends (Farrands 2002; Farrands and Worth 2005), the ontological reasoning that binds the different forms of critique are nevertheless methodologically geared towards transforming the present system towards their respective forms of enlightenment. This form of emancipation might be one that is geared towards ending or transforming capitalism in its various guises, yet it might also be used within the context of an academic exercise. It is one thus geared to academic emancipation through the pursuit of critical knowledge, as opposed to towards concrete visions of future utopias (Farrands 2002; Germain 2007).

Rather than debate what might or might not be understood as emancipation within forms of critical IPE, this chapter will suggest that a framework for emancipation needs to be more adequately spelt out in order to examine strategies to transform neoliberalism. To an extent, it looks to seek out how critical IPE might seek to reach its 'end of history'. While the term 'end of history' might be associated with Fukuyama's much maligned victory of liberalism at the end of the cold war, the term nevertheless provides a useful metaphor for reasoning within historical transformation (Fukuyama 1992). As critical IPE looks towards transforming neoliberalism, by its very essence its commitment towards emancipation must be one that contains within it a desire to inspire its own 'end of history' (in terms of an end to its historical struggle), no matter how subjective this might collectively appear. In this sense, an 'end of history' represents a metaphorical commitment towards an emancipatory strategy in a manner which, while it has not always been lacking, has certainly been inconsistent and ambiguous within IPE.

Notions of post-capitalism and the ability to utilise technological advancements in order to transcend capitalist models of production have in recent years provided us with useful models for further development (Srnicek and Williams 2015; Mason 2015). Yet, the era of neoliberalism has seen a lack of strategic ways of looking at methods by which such a transformation can be achieved. Indeed, it remains a symptom of the era of neoliberalism that, for all the material provided on critiquing its existence, little has been provided on how it can be challenged. The dearth of ideas has been prominent within traditional social democratic entities that have struggled to compete with the rise in forms of right-wing populism (Worth 2013). As a response, this chapter will suggest that by returning to the notions of Gramsci's 'war of position' and Luxemburg's understanding of 'dialectical materialism' – which, it will suggest, are not competing notions but are indeed compatible – we can provide strategic foundations that look to accompany such recent arguments and allow for their future understanding and development. Both Gramsci and Luxemburg are rightly heralded as stalwart pioneers of Western Marxism, yet it is their understandings of strategic transformation that I would like to develop here. In taking on the strategic mantle of the 'war of position', and of the logistics behind the method implicit within Luxemburg's framework of dialectical materialism, the chapter seeks to show how emancipation might be employed. By doing so, it suggests a route to strategising and imagining an emancipatory 'end of history', based upon a standard critical Marxist methodological framework of 'critique and transformation' that allows us to be much more explicit in outlining the transformative commitment that is central to any account that claims to be 'critical'.

CRITICAL IPE AND EMANCIPATION

The question of how we should understand critical IPE is one that is both much discussed and remains underdeveloped. The focal points of how it appeared and where it is drawn from is often dependent on the type of research undertaken and (often) the geographical areas where such work is being undertaken (Murphy and Tooze 1991; Murphy and Nelson 2001; Abbott and Worth 2002; Shields et al. 2010; Belfrage and Worth 2012; Cafruny et al. 2016). As the recent histories of Benjamin Cohen reveal, IPE was developed as a geographically specific discipline, with different parts of the world favouring different philosophies of study (Cohen 2008, 2014). In addition to this, as other studies have shown, IPE has had a tendency to create certain networks, and as a result has created different narratives and contrasting focal points of study (Shields and Nunn 2018; Seabrooke and Young 2017). This has also been the case with critical IPE. For, while critical IPE might have been united in its desire to locate and critique the development of neoliberal capitalism, its development has different starting points.

In the same way that IPE tended to emerge out of the British development of the subject, much current IPE scholarship can lay claim to the influence of Susan Strange and the emerge of the International Political Economic Group (IPEG) in the early 1970s. As a result 'new' IPE, the precursor of 'critical' IPE, emerged towards the end of the 1980s and in the early 1990s as the Thatcher–Reagan doctrine began to gain prominence and the collapse of the USSR and the Marxist-Leninist form of state socialism became imminent (Cohen 2008: 164–172). The term 'critical IPE' was developed and used throughout the 1990s in BISA (British International Studies Association) circles, with perhaps the most significant academic breakthrough being with a group of scholars based largely at Newcastle University and led by Barry Gills, who looked to form a collaborative project on the nature of contestation and resistance (Amoore 1997;

Gills 2000). Yet many of those involved were to move to other fields, such as Geography and Development Studies, where opportunities to contribute towards a more developed critical community are encouraged within the academy. Outside of the British dominated form of IPE that originated with BISA, 'Critical Political Economy' (CPE; as opposed to critical IPE) has perhaps managed to attract a wider multidisciplinary following. While initially taking its cue from the Amsterdam School project, it has produced a number of diverse projects that cut across the lines of the academy and activism. Those within the remit might situate CPE within a wider IPE framework (Jäger 2020; van Apeldoorn et al. 2010), it should nevertheless be stressed that it emerged from a different point of origin and largely from the remit of European Studies (that can include Comparative Political Economy, European Politics, European Sociology and European Political Economy).

While such academic differences often appear pedantic, especially when concerned with looking at the importance of emancipation within critical social science, the epistemological origins of narratives within critical IPE remain important when looking to understand the ways in which critical knowledge has been developed within IPE. For example, despite the minor differences in the origins and focus of study, many still see Robert Cox's distinctions between problem-solving and critical historicism as being the significant departure point in the emergence of *contemporary* critical IPE (Farrands and Worth 2005; Berry 2007; Germain 2007, 2016; Bruff and Tepe 2009). Robert Cox's now acclaimed piece from 1981 illustrated how logistical claims within the study of International Relations (IR) appeared from the point of view of the 'problem-solver' rather than from those who can see the faults of the workings of the order/system as a whole. The latter took on the form of the 'critical' as they looked to place IR within a wider lens in order to point out its inadequacies (Cox 1981). Part of this, as Randall Germain argues, was due to the historical framework in which Cox positioned himself. Despite Cox often being considered as the central figure in developing Gramsci's work for an IPE audience, his use of E.H. Carr and R.G. Collingwood was as important to his work as critical Marxists such as Gramsci (Germain 2016).

Others have tended to ignore the disciplinary developments of critical IPE/PE and looked to rely on more traditional inspirations. Alex Callinicos, for example, uses Marx as the ultimate source in order to understand both critique and emancipation. For him, the building of socialism through class struggle remains the main purpose for any form of critical application when looking at the international/global political economy (Callinicos 2009, 2016). Werner Bonefeld also sees Marx's 'critique of political economy' as the ultimate departure point but then looks to unravel the work of the Frankfurt School in order to provide a basis for ontological critique rooted within the conditions of contemporary open Marxism (Bonefeld 2014). The work of the Frankfurt School might have been absent in Cox, but it has been used within IPE as a means of strengthening his distinction between critical and problem-solving theory (Farrands and Worth 2005). Of particular interest here is Horkheimer's understanding of the differences between traditional theory and critical theory, with the latter having a central commitment towards emancipation (Shields 2011; Ryner 2015).

The separation of problem-solving or traditional theory and critical theory remains perhaps the fulcrum for critical IPE. The necessity for emancipation and for transformation that is enshrined within the critical method provides a methodological basis for ends of history to be imagined and understood. While the various forms of critical IPE have utilised different post-positivist forms of emancipatory strategies, like Bonefeld and Callinicos, I feel that the most effective form of understanding transformation is through the building of socialist transformation (Shields et al. 2011). Rather than extending this by building upon the critical ontology developed by the Frankfurt School, as others have done, I feel that the practical and strategic models provided by both Gramsci and Luxemburg appear more useful and less abstract in the contemporary era of neoliberalism. In addition, both look at ways of how to form such strategies which take their departure from capitalist crisis. As the wider purpose of this collection is to look at what alternatives might emerge from the contemporary crisis of neoliberalism, it is thus essential that critical IPE should seize this conjuncture in order to look at strategic ways to move beyond neoliberal capitalism.

WAR OF POSITION

Gramsci's entry to critical IPE has been central to its growth in its various guises. Cox's own constructions of critical theory placed Gramsci at its heart. Largely in reply to concepts that had been used in conventional IPE regarding the notion of hegemony and leadership, Cox substituted the notion of hegemonic stability theory, which understood leadership from economic and political data (indicators such as GDP and military capability), with Gramsci's idea of hegemony, which was geared around world orders being materially and ideologically forged over time (Cox 1983). Through this, the idea of countering the ideological composition of a hegemonic order by contesting its legitimacy emerged within the discipline. As such, the pursuit and study of forms of 'counter-hegemony' and of counter-hegemonic ideologies and discourse that look to construct ideological frameworks that oppose the prevailing order can be located (Chin and Mittelman 1997). Studies that look at the nature of resistance have thus been used to assess the strength of particular counter-hegemonic strategies in order to assess their potential for sustained opposition (Gill 2000; Gills 2000; Steger 2005; Worth 2013).

Yet 'counter-hegemony', as a concept, was not one that Gramsci himself used when referring to his own understanding of hegemony. His own understanding of challenging a hegemonic order was geared around the construction of an alternative socialist hegemony that could develop and sustain itself over time. While Lenin's understanding of hegemony was largely geared around how a state would build an order across society through a combination of the vanguard party, trade union activity and intellectual endeavour, Gramsci argued that it was through the mediums of popular culture, popular and traditional religion, national and local 'folklore' and the avenue of 'common-sense' that such hegemony was constructed (Williams 1980). Likewise, it is through the contestation of every facet within civil society that a hegemonic order must be challenged if there is a possibility for it to be defeated or transformed. From such assumptions, Gramsci developed his understanding of the war of movement and the war of position.

A war of movement or of manoeuvre represents a form of direct confrontation or insurgency against the state that not only includes revolt, a coup, the seizing of power but also general strike action and mass protests that affect the workings of the state (Gramsci 1971: 230–1). A war of movement can be thus understood as a frontal assault on the state and its institutions of power. Gramsci refers both to Trotsky's idea of 'total victory' of the revolutionary process within the Soviet Union and also to the process of the mass strike, suggested much earlier by Rosa Luxemburg (Gramsci 1971: 233–4 and 2007: 209). In contrast, a war of position refers to the battle of the 'hearts and minds' in society and where the key assumptions, principles and 'common-sense' of a particular order are contested, challenged and ultimately replaced (Gramsci 1971: 229–30). For Gramsci, the war of position was the more difficult to sustain as it required the building of a different form of hegemonic order so that a new set of values could be developed. The process is where the basis of an alternative hegemonic project is presented within civil and political society at large. As a result, a prolonged historical struggle can occur in order for norms and ideas to be built, challenged and debated. For Gramsci, the war of position was the real challenge in the building of socialism and one that both Bolshevik and other socialist leaders have often underestimated in their own perception of revolutionary strategy. Hence, any success of a socialist society depended upon the building of a hegemonic project that could win the 'hearts and minds' of the public at large through a prolonged war of position (Brodkin and Strathmann 2004).

For critical IPE, the notion of the war of position provides a mechanism where the contestation of neoliberalism can be both realised and also measured through academic enquiry. In this way, focal points of study are widened to include the political economy of every facet of hegemonic construction. Thus studies focusing upon culture, folklore and religion at the local, national and global level are necessary in order for a consistent framework of a war of position to be maintained. Critical IPE indeed has looked at many such studies and, by its very essence, is geared towards reaching out towards fresh dimensions (Belfrage and Worth 2012). Yet, more importantly, the notion of the war of position provides an ethical dimension. Gramsci placed considerable emphasis on the role of intellectuals when understanding how hegemony is maintained and contested. While part of this was to show how organic intellectuals – significant leaders within popular and/or local culture who were influential enough to reinforce certain ideas and norms – held a powerful position within civil society, he also placed a great deal of importance on the role of traditional intellectuals. Thus, for those in critical IPE, a commitment towards forming ideas and strategies that would contest the inadequacies of the prevailing order with a view towards transforming them, coupled with a firm commitment towards dissemination of critical knowledge, are essential parts of the construction of an emancipatory strategy. The war of position provides a framework and an understanding of the potential effects that such a role can provide.

In terms of constructing an 'end of history', the war of position provides a unique reference point for the process of emancipation that fuses the utopian dynamic of the 'possible' with a strategic model for such visions to be rationalised and realised. As stated earlier, one of the concerns during the neoliberal era has been the lack of viable alternatives put forward by progressive circles since the end of the cold war and the beginnings of the neoliberal order. Stuart Hall, for example, just before he died, cited the lack of imagination in leftist circles in recent years in looking at ways of mobilisation (Hall 2012). It is necessary to understand the dynamics involved within the war of position, then work out ways of utilising it as a method to understand, contest and transcend the fabric of the hegemonic order. In this sense, and as a focal point of study, critical IPE needs to consistently widen its area of study so that it looks at the different ways such a hegemonic order gains consent across different levels of (global) civil society. It also needs to continue to engage with such struggles – not just within the arena of activism but more prominently in the sphere of everyday life. Certainly within networks in critical political economy such as the CPERN (Critical Political Economy Research Network) group of the European Sociology Association, a great deal of time has been given to taking the issue of transformation and emancipation seriously through bringing together a wide range of multidisciplinary studies and making a commitment towards building networks across the various dimensions of civil society. The war of position provides a theoretical framework for such avenues to be assessed, measured and critically evaluated.

DIALECTICAL MATERIALISM

If the war of position provides a theoretical and mechanical framework for situated emancipatory goals and objectives, then what does it potentially lack in terms of its wider vision? One of the main criticisms of studies around Gramsci's ideas of hegemony is the question of who and what should characterise an alternative hegemonic system. Indeed, some of the most persuasive arguments from post-structuralism, post-colonialism and post-development studies have been those suggesting that any such alternative is characterised by a Western oriented meta-narrative (for example, as suggested by classics such as Said 1978; Scott 1990; Escobar 1995). Indeed, Laclau and Mouffe's basis for a 'post-hegemonic' society has led to the assumption that a diverse collection of subaltern movements can serve to de-legitimise hegemonic conditions, without needing to construct any centralised top-down replacement (Laclau and Mouffe 1985; Beasley-Murray 2010).

Yet, perhaps more significant has been the observation that such 'grand' projects merely become co-opted into the prevailing order and, as such, do not serve as an alternative. For example, the projects led by those influenced by Stuart Hall to contest Thatcherism in the late 1980s would be taken up by the New Labour/Third Way project that became associated with Tony Blair. In this instance, a body of intellectuals and policy advisers who were initially associated with the British Communist Party looked to inspire a new hegemonic project (called 'New Times'). Borrowing from the Euro-Communist movement of the 1970s, New Times quickly began to engage with the market logic of Thatcherism, which would see many involved embark upon constructing the foundations for the Blair project – a realisation that Hall himself found highly problematic (Hall 1997). In this case, the inability (consciously or sub-consciously) to contest an order with a fundamentally different set of principles resulted in the re-articulation of the same principles in a slightly different form.

With this in mind, the need to maintain a critical mind-set towards emancipation remains paramount and here Rosa Luxemburg's understanding of dialectical materialism provides a useful companion to the notion of the war of position. The first illustration of Luxemburg's unique approach to the social and material world was seen in her attack on Eduard Bernstein's concept of social democracy. She argued that Bernstein's understanding of the gradual reform of the capitalist system reflected a vulgar form of scientific determinism. The question of 'reform versus revolution' was to dominate socialist circles from the Second International at the end of the nineteenth century to the end of the twentieth century. Yet it is the ontological nature of the attack that gives us the more crucial point of reference. For Luxemburg, Bernstein's analysis was ahistorical and paid no attention to the forces of history. His assumptions were based upon the premise that processes were static and universal, and against this she argued that social relations should be considered and understood in relation to their specific historical conditioning (Luxemburg 1986). Rather than looking for a concrete and carefully conceived plan to build revolutionary change, Luxemburg's understanding of dialectics included a belief in thinking beyond what we see as the 'possible' in the present order.

This reading of dialectical materialism was also explicit within her understanding of trade union development and her notion of spontaneity. Rather than understanding the advancement of unionisation from within the bourgeois state, she favoured strategies where production could be socialised through specific actions that resulted from specific industrial disputes (Luxemburg 1980). It was from such victories that a new order would emerge, with a new set of principles which would move beyond bourgeois logic. The same criticisms that were made of the parliamentary reformers were extended to the Bolsheviks and to Lenin's understanding of the 'dictatorship of the proletariat'. For, in the same way that Kautsky and Bernstein pursued a bourgeois form of parliamentary socialism, Lenin's pursuit of dictatorship was based on the same bourgeois principles. As a result, while they appeared as two opposing poles of the political spectrum, they were in essence based upon the same bourgeois model (Luxemburg 1940). Luxemburg thus saw that the problem with the practical solutions of the time was that they were all drawn from within the prevailing political boundaries of the time. As a result, neither Bernstein and Kautsky, nor Lenin, could imagine an order where the configuration of social relations moved beyond this framework in line with a revolution in production.

Luxemburg's own model of spontaneity attracted the same sort of criticism within the Second International as John Holloway's accounts of the Zapatistas have in contemporary times (Davis 1976; Dinerstein 2005). As they lacked strategic objectives, they could not be regarded as providing anything more than empty actions that made no significant progress towards the building of a socialist alternative. Yet, Luxemburg's dialectical materialism provides us with a method, or even a mind-set, where critical knowledge can be utilised and developed, and where emancipation can be understood as a process that moves beyond the realms of empirical science (Worth 2012). Thus, 20 years before Max Horkheimer attacked the limits of traditional knowledge (Horkheimer 1937), Luxemburg was using the same ontological attacks on those involved in the different developments of political socialism in the first decades of the twentieth century. This critical spirit of Luxemburg, which was built upon by Adorno and Horkheimer (among others), remains central to understanding how we should perceive the idea of emancipation.

It can also be suggested here that there are several problems with twinning Luxemburg's understanding of the 'possible' with Gramsci's framework for the war of position. For a start, they appear at first glance to contradict each other in terms of strategy. To begin with, Luxemburg's notion of spontaneity appears to oppose the complex idea inherent within the war of position strategically. Luxemburg's spontaneity appears to lack any form of objective or end-game and is reliant upon a set of processes that cannot be adequately assessed or realised, while the war of position looks to consciously contest a specific order at its various levels and ultimately replace it. Yet, while these two theories might appear at odds in terms of how they relate to the tactics of change and transformation, they contain some striking ontological similarities. Both rely in different ways on the primacy of dialectics in their manner of thinking and critique the application of socialism on ontological grounds. For example, just as Lenin was guilty of underplaying the complexities inherent within a concept of hegemony, he was similarly guilty of underplaying the nature of social agency in revolutionary change. In this sense both Luxemburg and Gramsci rejected an appropriation of practical knowledge that would be implicit within the Frankfurt School as well as later in the assumptions of Robert Cox (Adorno and Horkheimer 1944; Cox 1981). In addition, as Mark Neufeld, one of the foremost scholars who developed critical theory within the wider discipline of IR points out, both Gramsci and Luxemburg situate these critiques in relation to the importance of human agency in the making of history (Neufeld 2002). In this sense, any form of emancipation must be understood as one that produces multiple meanings that reflect the complexities at the different levels of society as a whole, and cannot be reduced to a grand narrative.

Seen along these lines, Luxemburg's understanding of spontaneity can be read in a manner that places it within a critical context, rather than as a strategy, which has consistently been read as one that assumes the inevitability of class mobilisation and, as such, is guilty of reductionism (Levant 2012). More importantly for our purposes, it allows us to place instances of contemporary protests and campaigns that seek to disrupt the productive process within a wider context. For example, within contemporary IPE, recent accounts of anti-austerity protest movements have shown that, while they might lack a wider strategy of transforming neoliberal capitalism, they still perform a significant disruptive role (Bailey et al. 2016). By further understanding them within the dialectical materialist framework of spontaneity, we can place them within such a process of potential transformation and change. More importantly, for scholars and activists alike, it is the critical mind-set that I propose can benefit our understanding within critical IPE, particularly when looking for emancipation objectives.

IMAGINING AND CONSTRUCTING THE END OF HISTORY

The fusing of Luxemburg's mind-set of dialectical materialism alongside Gramsci's framework of the war of position might allow us to provide the content of how we might confront neoliberalism. Yet what about the form? If we are to take seriously the objective of transforming capitalism, then coherent strategic methods in order to do so must become central within critical IPE. In the political arena, left parties and organisation have lacked the same strategic visions as those within the academy. The diversity of criticism on the nature of neoliberal capitalism have not been matched with a flurry of transformative objectives to, as Marx famously put it, 'change the world'. The death of twentieth-century socialism, and the advance of the conditions of globalisation which has been the hallmark of the neoliberal hegemonic order, - meant that reliance on left-nationalism has become unworkable. The post-war appropriation of socialism, whether in its Soviet, post-colonial or parliamentary social democratic form, relied upon the nation-state in order to facilitate social change. In the contemporary neoliberal era, where borders have become less marked and where technological and knowledge-based industry has transformed the territorialisation of the economy, the retreat towards acting at the national level has become less and less relevant. Likewise, moves to extend the 'fortress' of the nation-state to the regional level have been equally problematic (Cafruny and Ryner 2003). Yet, at the same time, any attempt to construct bodies that attempt to confront the forces of neoliberal capital from a transnational perspective have – naturally – been thwarted due to persistence of the state system.

One response to this has been to argue that the nation-state remains the only plausible way of challenging neoliberal orthodoxy, and that movements and parties should rebuild at the national level, following the same mandate as they did in the post-war era. In this sense, as Samir Amin argued before his death, an international movement could be built based on the same rights to national sovereignty and self-determination as had been the case at the previous versions of the 'internationale' (Amin 2018). A new form of left-nationalism, centred on the principles of popular sovereignty, has been supported by some campaigns as a means to confront post-crisis austerity measures instigated by international organisations, and has also recently been popular among those putting forward left-wing arguments for Brexit. Yet these have drawn many criticisms and have generally been regarded as inadequate in the contemporary era (Worth 2013). In addition, when alternatives have been put forward they have also met with problems. For example, as already indicated, the attempt to re-situate social democracy by attempting to socialise the marketising frameworks inherent within neoliberalism quickly revealed its flaws (see Giddens 1998; Beck 1996). For while the Third Way attempted, in theory, to challenge neoliberal economics by working within its rhetoric to provide different outcomes, but ultimately (as illustrated by New Times and New Labour) became part of the same process. From a more radical position, the global justice movements reacted against this turn by socialist parties, leading to the construction of various Social Forums, where new global movements could be developed (such as the World Social Forum, European Social Forums and American Social Forums). However, despite the incentives within NGOs, little materialised with broad enough scope to provide an indication of a way forward in terms of what might develop.

However, as the spirit of Luxemburg's dialectical mind-set indicates, firm answers cannot merely be served up as simple solutions. Indeed, one of the prevailing characteristics of neoliberalism is its ability to allow capital to flourish in such a way that organised labour and regulated bodies do not have the means to confront it (Hughes 2005). Therefore firm solutions cannot merely be developed in a practical sense. Instead, it might be useful to look at how neoliberalism itself managed to gain its hegemonic ascendency in the first place. On the one hand, neoliberalism can be understood as capital being freed from its negotiated retreat through the partial advancements of labour. The stagnation of the post-war mixed economy, the increase in foreign direct investment and the demise of Soviet-style state socialism allowed a class-war conservatism to redress the balance and return to previous conditions (Miliband 2015). Yet there was also an intellectual drive that sought to contest Keynesian-inspired practical solutions for the economy that had gained prominence since the 1930s.

The intellectual development of the neoliberal project – from the inception of the Mont Pelerin Society through to the Chicago School, and from the role of the 'Chicago Boys' in Pinochet's Chile through to the economic advisers of Thatcher and Reagan – has always been one that was geared towards a long process and which did not produce the purity that its advocates wished it to (Peck 2010). As a result, the intellectual tradition found continuity in its consistent criticisms of the role of the state and/or regulation within the economy to the extent that new movements (such as the Tea Party) would emerge striving to reinforce the libertarian aspect of neoliberalism. For despite its ascent as a hegemonic process, those who adhere to its economic philosophy still strive for a process where the state plays an increasingly minimal role in the working of the market (Paul 2009). Just as von Mises argued against interference in the economy during times of apparent crisis, so his modern disciples maintain that the market has never managed to develop sufficient autonomy to reach its potential as a mechanism, because such interference has always occurred in some form. As such, the intellectual tradition inherent within neoliberalism is maintained through a desire to continuously seek market purity whenever a crisis appears in the system. What should be of interest to students of critical IPE is the manner in which the neoliberal project succeeded in gaining supremacy. Here I am not suggesting that neoliberal intellectuals provide us with a comparative methodological approach in terms of transcending capitalism – indeed their main purpose was to strengthen it – but they do provide an example of a different mode of inquiry that reached an outcome that was transformative.

From its first appearance as a marginal oppositional force during the rebuilding of the post-war economy, it began to wage a war of position on the dominant Keynesian approach to post-war reconstruction, which would gradually lead to fruition (Mirowski and Plehwe 2015; Stedman Jones 2014). By the time the Bretton Woods-inspired dollar system faltered and the international economy entered a phase of stagflation, the neoliberal doctrine has already managed to make significant advances. By the time the Soviet Union had collapsed, it had already mobilised to an extent that it had gained the ascendency as an economic model within Anglo-American states and was in a prime position to expand at a global scale (Harvey 2005). While the end of the cold war and the so-called 'victory of capitalism' might have been the main stimuli for the global spread of neoliberal hegemony, the battle for hearts and minds across corresponding national civil societies long pre-dated it and continued in different guises throughout the 1990s and beyond (Mirowski and Plehwe 2015). In this sense, the rise of neoliberalism provides us with an apt example of how a war of position can gain ascendency and develop across national and transnational arenas. The various forms of contestation and struggle that have occurred throughout this process also reveal the different ways in which the dominant classes respond to protect their interests within the prevailing order (Gills 2000).

A lot can thus be gained by studying how neoliberalism assumed ascendency. Two benefits in particular stand out. First, the fact that the intellectuals behind the neoliberal project saw themselves – in a rather perverse manner – as pursuers of critical knowledge. By looking to construct a system which they felt was emancipatory, they looked to transcend and transform the economic norms and assumptions of the era that they emerged from. The very fact that any problems that occur within the neoliberal system (such as the global financial crisis or the Covid-19 pandemic) are not attributed to the failings of these ideological roots but to the fact that they have not been implemented as vigorously as they should have been is a testament to such pursuit. Second, it is crucial to understand the ways in which the norms, assumptions and 'common-sense' of the neoliberal epoch have developed across all levels of politics in order to understand how to challenge it. For if any form of socialist alternative is to succeed, it needs to be able to expose and argue against these assumptions in order to replace them. Again, this is not to suggest that any practical positives can be taken from looking at the strategic development of the neoliberal project, but that it is useful to look at how neoliberalism has manifested itself culturally, nationally and globally through its different forms of articulation. It is through contesting this terrain that a war of position can be mobilised.

CONCLUSION: CRITICAL IPE AND THE END OF HISTORY

This chapter has suggested that for critical IPE to develop into a truly unique approach it needs to make its commitment towards emancipation far more explicit in its remit. While critical IPE has had a rather short history, it has developed in recent years – often alongside the more inclusive, more multidisciplinary and more historically defined tradition of CPE (as opposed to IPE) – to develop emancipatory objectives more seriously. In this way, critical IPE needs not only to study the composition of the neoliberal system but also to develop very real arguments over how it can be transcended. While I acknowledge that there are umpteen forms of emancipatory narratives, I have suggested that by twinning concepts from two classical, yet critical Marxists, we can develop a typology for both imagining and developing alternatives. Gramsci's idea of the war of position allows us to understand what is required in order for the neoliberal order to be contested, and it also provides us with a way of assessing how successful such resistance might be. Fused with the war of position, Luxemburg's understanding of dialectics allows us to think about emancipation in a manner that does not constrain us within certain boundaries or enclosures.

I also note that one of the ways we might understand how to adequately assemble a war of position is by learning from the neoliberal project itself. The emergence of traditional intellectuals such as Hayek and Freidman saw the construction of an oppositional form of political economy that would grow into a political and cultural project by the 1980s and reach global hegemonic proportions by the 1990s. Yet, while a lot can be learned by studying this trajectory, the neoliberal project also, and more crucially, was defined by class and by the re-mobilisation of capital against labour. Any attempt to mobilise an alternative against neoliberalism needs to be centred on the renewal of a class struggle against such developments of the past 40 years. It is here that any interest in the making of the present order meets its limitations, as social emancipation is not won through ideas alone but by material transformation. Indeed, it is from within these conditions that we can replace Fukuyama's false dichotomy and look towards an 'end of history'.

REFERENCES

Abbott, J. and O. Worth (eds) (2002) *Critical Perspectives on International Political Economy*. London: Palgrave.

Adorno, T. and M. Horkheimer (1944) *Dialectic of Enlightenment*. London: Verso.

Amin, S. (2018) 'It is Imperative to Reconstruct the Internationale of Workers and Peoples', available at: IDEAs http://www.networkideas.

org/featured-articles/2018/07/it-is-imperative-to-reconstruct-the-internationale-of-workers-and-peoples/ (accessed 8 October 2018).
Amoore, L., R. Dodgson, B. Gills, P. Langley, D. Marshall and I. Watson, I. (1997) 'Overturning "Globalisation": Resisting the Teleological, Reclaiming the "Political"', *New Political Economy* 2(1): 179–195.
Bailey, D., M. Clua-Losada, N. Huke, O. Ribera-Almandoz and K. Rogers (2016) 'Challenging the Age of Austerity: Disruptive Agency after the Global Economic Crisis', *Comparative European Politics* 16(1): 9–31.
Beasley-Murray, J. (2010) *Posthegemony: Political Theory and Latin America*. Minneapolis, MN: Minnesota University Press.
Beck, U. (1996) *The Reinvention of Politics: Rethinking Modernity in the Global Social Order*. Cambridge: Polity Press.
Belfrage, C. and O. Worth (2012) 'Critical International Political Economy: Renewing Critiques and Ontologies', *International Politics* 49(2): 131–135.
Berry, C. (2007) 'Rediscovering Robert Cox: Agency and Ideational in Critical IPE', *Political Perspectives* 1(1): 1–29.
Bonefeld, W. (2014) *Critical Theory and the Critique of Political Economy*. London: Bloomsbury.
Brodkin, K. and C. Strathmann (2004) 'The Struggle for Hearts and Minds: Organisation, Ideology and Emotion', *Labor Studies Journal* 29(3): 1–24.
Bruff, I. and D. Tepe (2009) 'What is Critical IPE?', *Journal of International Relations and Development* 14(3): 354–358.
Cafruny, A. and M. Ryner (2003) *A Ruined Fortress? Neoliberal Hegemony and Transformation in Europe*. London: Rowman and Littlefield.
Cafruny, A., L. Talani and G. Pozo Martin (2016) *The Palgrave Handbook of Critical International Political Economy*. London: Palgrave.
Callinicos, A. (2009) *Imperialism and Global Political Economy*. Cambridge: Polity.
Callinicos, A. (2016) 'Marxism: And the Very Idea of Critical Political Economy', in A. Cafruny, L. Talani and G. Pozo Martin (2016) *The Palgrave Handbook of Critical International Political Economy*. London: Palgrave.
Chin, C. and J. Mittelman (1997) 'Conceptualising Resistance to Globalisation', *New Political Economy* 2(1): 25–37.
Cohen, B. (2008) *International Political Economy: An Intellectual History*. Princeton, NJ: Princeton University Press.
Cohen, B. (2014) *Advanced Introduction to International Political Economy* (London: Edward Elgar).
Cox, R. (1981) 'Social Forces, States and World Order: Beyond International Relations Theory', *Millennium* 10(2): 126–155.

Cox, R. (1983) 'Gramsci, Hegemony and International Relations: An Essay in Method', *Millennium: Journal of International Studies* 12(2): 162–175.

Davis, H.B. (1976) 'The Right of National Self-determination in Marxist Theory – Luxemburg vs Lenin', in R. Luxemburg, *The National Question*, ed. H.B. Davis. New York: Monthly Review Press.

Dinerstein, A. (2005) 'On John Holloway's Change the World without Taking Power: The Meaning of Revolution Today – A Call for Emancipatory Reflection', *Capital and Class* 29(1): 13–17.

Escobar, P. (1995) *Encountering Development: The Making and the Unmaking of the Third World*. Princeton, NJ: Princeton University Press.

Farrands, C. (2002) 'Being Critical about Being Critical', in J. Abbott and O. Worth (eds) *Critical Perspectives on International Political Economy*. London: Palgrave.

Farrands, C. and O. Worth (2005) 'Critical Theory in Global Political Economy: Critique? Knowledge? Emancipation?', *Critical and Class* 29(1): 43–61.

Fukuyama, F. (1992) *The End of History and the Last Man*. London: Penguin.

Germain, R. (2007) 'Critical Political Economy, Historical Materialism and Adam Morton', *Politics* 27(2): 127–131.

Germain, R. (2016) 'Robert W. Cox and the Idea of History: Political Economy as Philosophy', *Globalizations* 13(5): 532–546.

Giddens, A. (1998) *The Third Way*. Cambridge: Polity.

Gill, S. (2000) 'Towards a Post-modern Prince? The Battle in Seattle as a Moment in the New Politics of Globalisation', *Millennium: Journal of International Studies* 29(1): 131–140.

Gills, B. (ed.) (2000) *Globalization and the Politics of Resistance* London: Palgrave.

Gramsci, A. (1971) *Selections from the Prison Notebooks*. London: Lawrence and Wishart.

Gramsci, A. (2007) *Antonio Gramsci – Prison Notebooks*, vol. 3. New York: Columbia University Press.

Hall, S. (1997) 'The Great Moving Nowhere Show', *Marxism Today* Nov./Dec.: 9–15.

Hall, S. (2012) 'The Saturday Interview' (with Z. Williams), *The Guardian* 11 February.

Harvey, D. (2005) *A Brief History of Neoliberalism*. Oxford: Oxford University Press.

Horkheimer, M. (1977 [1937]) 'Traditional and Critical Theory', in M. Horkheimer (ed.) *Critical Theory: Selected Essays*. London: Continuum.

Hughes, S. (2005) 'The International Labour Organisation', *New Political Economy* 10(3): 413–425.
Jäger, J. (2020) 'Marx to Critical International Political Economy', in E. Vivares (ed.) *The Routledge Handbook of International Political Economy*. London: Routledge.
Laclau, E. and Mouffe, C. (1985) *Hegemony and Socialist Strategy*. London: Verso.
Levant, A. (2012) 'Rethinking Spontaneity beyond Classical Marxism: Re-reading Luxemburg through Benjamin, Gramsci and Thompson', *Critique* 40(3): 367–387.
Luxemburg, R. (1940) *The Russian Revolution*. New York: Workers Age Publishers.
Luxemburg, R. (1980) *Theory and Practice*. Chicago, IL: News and Letters.
Luxemburg, R. (1986) *Reform or Revolution*. London: Militant Press.
Mason, P. (2015) *Postcapitalism: A Guide to Our Future*. London: Penguin.
Miliband, R. (2015) *Class War Conservatism and Other Essays*. London: Verso.
Mirowski, P. and D. Plehwe (eds) (2009) *The Road from Mont Pelerin: The Making of the Neoliberal Thought Collective*. Boston MA: Harvard University Press.
Murphy, C. and D. Nelson (2001) 'International Political Economy: A Tale of Two Heterodoxies', *British Journal of Politics and International Relations* 3(3): 393–412.
Murphy, C. and R. Tooze (eds) (1991) *The New International Political Economy*. London: Palgrave.
Neufeld, M. (2002) 'Democratic Socialism in a Global(izing) Context: Towards a Collective Research Program', *TIPEC Working Paper* 02/6.
Paul, R. (2009) *End the Fed*. New York: Grand Central Publishing.
Peck, J. (2010) *Constructions of Neoliberal Reason*. Oxford: Oxford University Press.
Ryner, M. (2015) 'Europe's Ordoliberal Iron Cage: Critical Political Economy, the Euro Area Crisis and its Management', *Journal of European Public Policy* 22(2): 275–294.
Said, E. (1978) *Orientalism*. New York: Pantheon.
Scott, J. (1990) *Domination and the Art of Resistance*. Yale: Yale University Press.
Seabrooke, L. and K. Young (2017) 'The Network of Niches of International Political Economy', *Review of International Political Economy* 24(1): 288–331.

Shields, S. (2011) 'Critical and International Political Economy', in S. Shields, I. Bruff and P. Macartney (eds) *Critical International Political Economy*. London: Palgrave.

Shields, S. and A. Nunn (2018) 'Exploring the UK International Political Economy Workforce', Paper presented at the International Studies Association Conference, San Francisco.

Shields, S., I. Bruff and H. Macartney (2011) (eds.) *Critical International Political Economy*. London: Palgrave.

Srnicek, N. and A. Williams (2015) *Inventing the Future: Postcapitalism and a World without Work*. London: Verso.

Stedman Jones, D. (2014) *Masters of the Universe: Hayek, Friedman and the Birth of Neoliberal Politics*. Princeton, NJ: Princeton University Press.

Steger, M. (2005) *Globalism: Market Ideology meet Terrorism*, Lanham, MD: Rowman and Littlefield.

van Apeldoorn, B., I. Bruff and M. Ryner (2010) 'The Richness and Diversity of Critical IPE Perspectives: Moving beyond the Debate on the "British School"', in N. Phillips and C. Weaver (eds) *Debating the Divide: Reflections on the Past, Present and Future of International Political Economy*. London: Routledge, pp. 215–222.

Williams, R. (1980) *Culture and Materialism*. London: Verso.

Worth, O. (2012) 'Articulating the Critical Spirit: Rosa Luxemburg and Critical IPE', *International Politics* 49(2): 136–153.

Worth, O. (2013) *Resistance and the Age of Austerity: Nationalism, the Failure of the Left and the Return of God*. London: Zed Books.

2
Dialectical Ends and Beginnings: Why Barbarism at the End of Capitalism Means Barbarism beyond Capitalism

Bryant William Sculos

Bourgeois society stands at the crossroads, either transition to Socialism or regression into Barbarism.
Rosa Luxemburg (1915)

You cannot build socialism – or a democratic, egalitarian, and ecological form of post-capitalism by any name – with capitalistic people, but capitalistic people are precisely the only ones who can. This is the dialectical paradox at the heart of this chapter. Taking the form of a speculative, exegetical – and at times polemical – essay, this chapter explores the various dimensions of this paradox through political exegeses of Luxemburg's 'socialism or barbarism' quote, Marx's claim that capitalism produces its own gravediggers, and, finally, by explicating Erich Fromm's possible social-psychological solution to this paradox.

While my attention has been focused on this paradox, articulated in various forms, for the better part of the past decade, this chapter in particular drew its specific inspiration from thinking through the argument made by Peter Frase (2016) in his *Four Futures: Life after Capitalism*. Frase's argument is that the post-capitalist future we end up with, or that our children or grandchildren end up with, will turn on the two axes of hierarchy/equality and scarcity/abundance. Prefiguring the argument I end with here, Frase argues that the character of the political struggles around distribution and production into the future will determine which of the four futures we end up with. It was in thinking through how we may end up with one of these futures or another that led me back to Luxemburg and then to Marx and Engels. However, it was the lack of emphasis on the psycho-social conditions of the transition from capitalism to post-capitalism that drove my eventual focus on Fromm's Critical Theory in this context.

In the revolutionary socialist tradition, from Marx and Engels, to Rosa Luxemburg, to Erich Fromm, to Peter Frase, and countless others in between, there has rarely, if ever, been a serious rejection of the foundational assumption that how capitalism ends will be mirrored in the post-capitalism that emerges. McKenzie Wark's (2019) contribution continues this radical trend. Wark presents a sophisticated but nonetheless controversial argument that we are no longer entirely within the capitalist mode of production, but what is most relevant in Wark's book to my exposition here is the enduring concern for the dialectical premise that what comes after capitalism will be determined precisely by the character of our exit from capitalism. And yet, the psycho-social conditions of that relationship – the various intersecting incentives, behaviours, norms, pathologies, beliefs, expectations and values that people are, differentially, conditioned with in a given society, in this case, capitalism – have been under-emphasised, particularly among contemporary critical Marxist theorists (though there are, of course, exceptions that are discussed later in this chapter).

THE MEANING OF 'SOCIALISM OR BARBARISM'

First, I want to unpack this quote a bit. 'Bourgeois society stands at a crossroads.' This is the least accurate point when read literally. First, not all bourgeois societies are at the exact same point in development. Second, partially though not exclusively based on the first point, a crossroads implies that there are two roads already built. In order for the metaphor to hold, we would need to have already built a road towards socialism with an already defined destination. While there is certainly a range of viable proposals that have been articulated for well over a century regarding both – from democratic centralist Marxists, horizontalist Marxists, evolutionary Marxists, and strands of anarchists – it is fair to say that many of the suggestions conflict with one another to varying degrees, but also that such disagreement is a healthy component of any substantively democratic process towards socialism. That there could be genuine political disagreement over the meaning of this part of the quote, by its very nature, shows that even if the destination were 'there' in some eventual historical future or 'there' in the sense that we have the basic principles that conceptually form the inspiration and constitutive guidance for a socialist society, the road, the path, is not already built.

Not only is the road towards socialism not already built, there are likely many ways to get to the same or proximal socialist destinations – and the same goes for barbarism, though our paths towards the many possible barbarisms of the future are surely further along in the construction process than the ones towards socialism. Lastly, the regression towards barbarism is a bit misleading. It implies that capitalism itself is not a systemic instantiation of various forms of barbarism, which leads to more individualised forms of barbarism. The barbarism of the future may well be worse, or at least different, but we are doing ourselves a disservice if we intentionally or incidentally suggest that the barbarism isn't already here – and it was 'here' when Luxemburg wrote her famous line.

I am most certainly reading the metaphor too literally, but I'm doing so to make a point – several points actually: (1) that the meaning of 'socialism or barbarism', if interpreted simplistically, effaces a lot of complexity about the similarity of a geographically diverse global capitalist system, (2) that what the socialist alternative to this world order will look like is unknown, and (3) most relevant to the argument of this chapter, that we must think more deeply about *how* to get to any just, democratic alternative to the more probable barbarisms of our possible futures.

It is worth emphasising one last point before I delve into the nature of the 'crossroads' we are at. We don't need to find the singularly right solution, right now. There are likely any number of possible paths towards socialism. The thing that we can be completely sure of (sorry epistemological sceptics ...) is that the path will not be linear, smooth, consistent or clean. It will be messy, and – because capitalism is so unbelievably bloody – sadly, our paths forward will all likely involve blood. Capitalism is a systemic bloodbath, and its defenders, much more so than its critics and opponents, are much more likely to resort to violence. While this is by no means 'necessary', it would be intellectually and politically dishonest to pretend it is not likely. However, as will be manifest later in this chapter, violence and force will not – cannot – be the primary mechanism of an egalitarian, democratic post-capitalist transition.

GRAVEDIGGERS AND THE EMERGENCE OF THE CEMETERY, OR, THE CEMETERY WITHOUT GRAVEDIGGERS

It is the barbarism of the present and near future that concerns me the most. This insane society, which Marx, and later Fromm more explicitly, forcefully described, makes up everyday life for most people in quite literally every part of the world. That global capitalism is a grotesque exploitative, oppressive and fundamentally violent system (including violence to the non-human world) will likely not be controversial or surprising to the readers of this collection, nor is it the primary focus of this particular chapter. What may be more surprising and controversial is how the barbarism of capitalism affects the possibilities for transition to socialism, which is the focus here. And, to develop the central paradox of this chapter – that while it will be alienated capitalistic people, those interpellated subjects of capitalism conditioned by and into a pervasively capitalistic mentality,[1] who will need to build the road(s) away from the barbarism of capitalism – it is useful to consider another poignant and oft-cited quote from the Marxist tradition, this one from Marx and Engels themselves, 'What the bourgeoisie, therefore, produces, above all, is its own grave-diggers' (Marx and Engels 1978a: 483).

Marx and Engels are neither completely clear nor absent-minded in their explanation for how capitalism does this. While there are certain interrelated structural and subjective contradictions that produce the revolutionary class of the proletariat, Marx and Engels didn't do enough to specify precisely how the structural and subjective dimensions relate. We are told, in the passage preceding this gravedigger line, that because of the inability or incompetence of the bourgeoisie, the working conditions of the proletariat will degrade, and they will, perhaps inevitably,[2] revolt against the capitalist class (the bourgeoisie).

Dialectical Ends and Beginnings

I want to home in on the crucial importance of the dialectical process here. While the systemic imperatives of the capitalist mode of production (re)produce certain contradictions, the one that is perhaps least automatic in the Marxian formulae is the emergence of a radical class consciousness that pushes capitalism to its final breaking point and produces a socialist – eventually communist – world. *How* precisely this is going to happen, beyond that it will, or must, is never explicitly stated. Regardless, though, the crux of the gravediggers line is not just that the institutional and technological seeds of socialism must emerge from within the deforming and alienating confines of the capitalist mode of production, but that the subjectivity of the post-capitalist world must find its origins in these conditions as well.

So, dialectically, capitalism creates its own gravediggers. While we can assume Marx and Engels meant something specific in this claim – that the proletariat created by the capitalist mode of production would, through the contradictions of capitalism, come together to overthrow capitalism and establish socialism and communism – there is something almost axiomatic about it. If capitalism has gravediggers, they will, by definition, have been created (even if just by the fact of birth by the people involved) by capitalism. If, by some chance, the modern capitalist state destroyed capitalism, it would be the gravedigger of capitalism created by capitalism. Similarly, if the contemporary bourgeoisie (the transnational capitalist class) were to destroy capitalism, they would be the gravediggers of capitalism created by capitalism.

Capitalism will not end because of the intentional efforts of either the state or the bourgeoisie – but why? For Marx and Engels, the answer is simple: to do so would be to cease to exist; they would cease not only to serve the historical role they are structurally positioned to carry out, but they would quite literally need to cease to be what they are. The modern capitalist state, as such, exists, as Marx and Engels claimed, to manage the common affairs of the bourgeoisie, to maintain the overall health of the core elements of the capitalist mode of production (Marx and Engels 1978a: 475). To act consciously (speaking of the agents of the state) against the system of capitalism would mean that the state is becoming something other than what it is.

The bourgeoisie, as a class, for related reasons are not going to consciously act against the system of capitalism. Similar to the mistakes that could occur through state action based on poor judgement or incorrect or incomplete information, firms within the capitalist system can, through their individual pursuit of profit and growth, do serious damage, unintentionally, to the capitalist system. For an individual capitalist firm or individual member of the bourgeoisie to act against the capitalist system would involve them in abdicating their ownership over the means of production they control, but even that act, however anti-capitalist it may be, could be an isolated act with little systemic impact. While there seems to be a tenuous justification for why a firm would ever do such a thing (since it would mean that the owners would lose enormous wealth and power), Marx and Engels did think it was possible at a certain point. They believed in the possibility that, at a certain stage in the development of revolutionary proletarian consciousness and action, a small number of the bourgeoisie would betray their class interests and align with the proletariat. In the *Manifesto*, Marx and Engels wrote:

> Finally, in times when the class struggle nears the decisive hour, the process of dissolution going on within the ruling class, in fact within the whole range of society assumes such a violent, glaring character, that a small section of the ruling class cuts itself adrift, and joins the revolutionary class, the class that holds the future in its hands. Just as, therefore, at an earlier period, a section of the nobility went over to the bourgeoisie, so now a portion of the bourgeoisie goes over to the proletariat ... (Marx and Engels 1978a: 481)

As temporally specific and contingent as that occurrence was hypothesised to be, what is far more difficult – perhaps impossible – to imagine is the whole, or even a majority or large minority, of the bourgeois class acting consciously against their own material interests, against the whole of the system of capitalism (Lukács 1972). With that said, if it is possible for individuals within the bourgeoisie to abdicate their class position, there is an implication that it is actually theoretically *possible* for that fundamental alteration of the limited consciousness of the members of the bourgeoisie to occur at a much wider scale.

'Life determines consciousness', yes, but this predicted abdication of class position reminds us that, although class is a crucial element of the *life that determines consciousness*, there are other dimensions of life within capitalism (Marx and Engels 1978b: 155). (And it is worth noting that this betrayal is itself not wholly dissimilar to when working-class people actively defend capitalism.) While this scenario whereby some element of the bourgeoisie abandon their class, as described by Marx and Engels, is speculatively rooted in the material deterioration of the lives of the bourgeoisie and proletariat within late-stage capitalism, it nonetheless suggests that class consciousness is not *always*, strictly speaking, *class* consciousness (or at least not inherently always articulated or enacted as such).

This leads us to an uncomfortable place for most Marxists, but it is a relevant detour in our exploration of the paradox of how capitalistic subjects become the harbingers of socialism, and this space is defined by the reality of the psycho-social and material conditioning of the bourgeoisie itself. Are the bourgeoisie not forced, by the systemic imperatives of capitalism, to become exploiters? Are they not deprived of their creative species-being potentials by the domineering logic of capitalism and its mindless pursuits of profit and growth? Are they not alienated (in mostly different ways – though not every way – than the ways that the proletariat is)? They own their labour in a way, but they are incentivised to not actually do genuinely creative labour. They own the means of production and end up with much greater access to the products of (others') labour, but do not generally 'work' under conditions of their own choosing (these are also largely determined by capitalism's market imperatives). While the elites in our societies are typically able to take more 'time off' for luxurious vacations and afford to pay workers to take care of their everyday chores (such as childcare, cooking, cleaning and so on), these superior material benefits are not necessarily inherently non-alienating, especially when we're referring to forms of alienation such as: alienation from others, alienation from species-being, and alienation from nature – all of which apply to both the proletariat and the bourgeoisie) (Marx and Engels 1978c; Fromm 1961). As Fromm (1961) argues convincingly, Marx is not best read as a believer in the idea that material gain is the fundamental drive of human beings, regardless of whether they are proletarian or bourgeois.

The mechanism by which the bourgeoisie 'know' that they are supposed to pursue profit and growth is the very same mechanism by which they are capable of being otherwise – and in the process cease to be bourgeois. Class position is not a static or stable identity, though it can certainly enduringly shape consciousness in ways that would remain salient even if one's class position were to change over the course of a lifetime – and certainly so if capitalism itself were to end. However, what is more generally true is that capitalism itself is the interpellating, conditioning structural force, regardless of class position (which, again is not to say there are not important differences based on class position). And, further, this is far from saying that capitalism is not a class system. It surely is, but where Marx and Engels were confident to suggest that class position (class-in-itself) would (necessarily) lead to class consciousness (class-for-itself), the mechanisms by which these conditions relate to and constitute one another is undeveloped in their respective oeuvres. To put this back into the language of Marx and Engels, precisely how capitalism creates its own gravediggers is not clear in practice – and it seems to me that this is the crucial question in relation to the paradox that is guiding the discussion in this chapter. How does the dialectical character of capitalism allow for, if not necessarily produce, the subjects that will not only vanquish capitalism but also produce its synthetic alternative, socialism?

The problem, then, for contemporary attempts to develop Marxian praxis in our world is that, despite the dialectical potential of the proletariat to assume its exclusive historical role as the revolutionary subject-object of history, Marx only ever elucidated clearly *why* this is the case – not *how* it becomes a historical reality, not, as Lenin asked, *what is to be done*.

Given the theoretical density of the preceding discussion, one could be forgiven for failing to appreciate the stakes here. Put simply, if capitalism ends before the gravediggers do their thing, or if capitalism were to end by some other way, the post-capitalist world we might find (if any humans are around to see it) would certainly not be a democratic, egalitarian, ecological post-capitalism; it would not be a socialist post-capitalist world. The endurance of the psycho-social conditions of capitalism – especially those that capitalism incentivises and rewards, elements always-already latent in the transhistorical psycho-biological potential of humanity – will ensure that whatever post-capitalism (or future mutation of capitalism) that emerges will be closer to the worlds of *The Road*, *Snowpiercer*, *Elysium* or *Mad Max* than anything worth calling socialism. Socialism must be built, as must be the road(s) to it.

ERICH FROMM ON PRODUCING THE ALTERNATIVE TO CAPITALISM FROM WITHIN CAPITALISM

To get at the question of *how* – this viable path forward from the contemporary conjuncture towards (hopefully) the development of socialist politics and the end of capitalism in the twenty-first century – I want to turn to a source that has been sadly under-appreciated, under-utilised and even often misunderstood by contemporary Marxists and socialists: namely, the work of twentieth-century Frankfurt School theorist Erich Fromm. Much of Fromm's diagnosis of historical and (still) contemporary capitalism overlaps with others' writing on similar questions, such as that of Herbert Marcuse, Fromm's former colleague in the Frankfurt School. Fromm's strength in relation to Marcuse and others is not so much in his unique diagnosis of capitalism as a psycho-social system that produces a pathologically normalised insanity, which masquerades as sanity and rationality, undermining the socialist project of emancipation. Fromm's strength is, in fact, in his efforts to articulate a more positive solution to the problems both he and Marcuse (among many others) diagnosed. Fromm's work, especially his later works, provide a strong groundwork for thinking and working for precisely that: building an alternative to capitalism, beyond capitalism, from within capitalism.

Fromm's diagnosis of liberal capitalism begins where its historical failure is most acute, specifically, the emergence of fascism in Europe in the 1920s and 1930s (though he also does the important historical-psychological work that builds to this moment). Fromm argues that liberal capitalism, insofar at it degraded the primary ties, or bonds, that pre-date the full formation of the historical individual we now rightly associate with the emergence of liberalism and capitalism, left people excessively unmoored from the community roots that would allow them to be both free and socially connected, free-thinking agents embedded in a social world that provided belonging and meaningfulness (or at least a strong possibility for belonging and meaning), that people would be forced to choose between conformity or destructiveness, between the destruction of the self or the destruction of others. These choices are what Fromm refers to as the 'escape from freedom' (Fromm 1994). And it is a particularly liberal-capitalist notion of freedom, a negative freedom that provides for total destruction of primary ties, but does not offer clear pathways to regain a sense of meaning or belonging. This becomes the choice between the heinously unmeritorious marketplace whereby people are treated as commodities and their value determined by generic bosses and faceless capitalists – or authoritarianism. Authoritarianism, primarily in the form of fascism, provides the feeling of meaning and belonging that liberal capitalism denies to most people. In its own perverse ways, fascism provides the alienated, isolated liberal-capitalist subject with the promise, and at least somewhat substantially realised, of regaining primary ties, though these primary ties are premised on the exclusion of others. This is not wholly dissimilar to the conditions that have led to the resurgent attractiveness of right-wing populism in the current period.

The pull of the impulse to escape freedom is not limited just to these options: throwing oneself on the whims of the market or throwing away one's individuality to the cause of authoritarianism. If we consider both the 'escape from freedom' options under the label 'barbarism', Fromm (1994) argues there is a second set of options. We either escape from freedom through conformity to the demands of the market or fascism, or we remake ourselves and our world in a way that democratically and lovingly eliminates the alienating, isolating, dehumanising individualism of liberal capitalism; that is, we build some kind of a socialist world. Our options are, as ever, socialism or barbarism – socialisms or barbarisms.

While Fromm is certainly concerned about redeveloping primary ties through a democratic socialist transformation, he never fetishises the hierarchical, typically patriarchal, oppressive and violent social foundations that maintained the specific primary ties that pre-date capitalism. He is interested, more so, in the social grounding they provide for the psyche of people, that was, due to the aforementioned context of the primary bonds, responsible for the underdevelopment of the individual prior to the emergence of liberal capitalism. That liberal capitalism would develop and largely supersede the pre-capitalist modes of production is consistent with Fromm's broader social-psychological argument that societies, modes of production and indeed modes of existence, which fail to meet the psycho-social-biological needs of humanity cannot and will not endure (Fromm 1955). This is not to suggest that human beings are not extremely adaptable; they surely are, which is why social orders that are inadequate to the genuine needs of humanity, endure for so long (Fromm 1955). Ideological justifications about one's place in the world or individual responsibility for failures are important components – components that have achieved their full false expression within late capitalism – that contribute to the zombie-like existence of social systems that are so widely recognised as failures.

Actual physical force, and/or the threat of physical force is also part of the dynamic of endurance for inadequate systems, but it turns out that ideological rationalisations can work to reproduce these systems as well or better than force. People, if they are not provided with an ideological justification for systemic inadequacies that they are conditioned to internalise, that mitigate their emergent neuroses, will have little problem risking physical harm to change their world. Thus, we have the bourgeois revolutions of the eighteenth and nineteenth centuries (and eventually the anti-colonial revolutions of the twentieth century) (Fromm 1955).

Feudalism was increasingly seen for the restrictive mode of production that it was, hindering the development of the kind of individualism better suited to the emergent liberal-capitalist technologies and relations of production that were developing. Feudalism was, over time, superseded through the political and economic developments of the Industrial Revolution. Over time, the dominant social character of feudalism that lingered through the early years of capitalism (the hoarding social character), gave way to the predominance of the marketing character orientation (Fromm 1955, 1990). It is the marketing social character (the character orientation becomes a social character when it is totally rooted in the generalised mode of production and consumption in a given society or world order) that we experience today. People are, and see themselves as, commodities to be bought and sold on a market, whether a literal job market or metaphorically within other marketised aspects of our society, such as the dating market.

This is the social character that will live on beyond capitalism's lifespan – that is, unless we consciously develop our societies toward a productive character orientation, a productive social character. It is precisely the overcompensation of liberal capitalism with respect to individuality/individualism – this corrosion of primary ties that provided belonging and meaningfulness, denying the full development of creative, cooperative social individuality – which provides the opportunity and impetus for progressive action towards a democratic, egalitarian, and ecological post-capitalism, which Fromm refers to variously as 'communitarian socialism', 'democratic socialism' – or simply just 'socialism'.

While there have been plenty of coarse individualistic and outright inhumane responses as well, we can see positive examples of the alternative Fromm points toward in particular events of 2020, namely the solidaristic community responses to Covid-19 and the police murders of George Floyd and Breonna Taylor in the US. For-profit health care and the racist, capitalistic function of police are increasingly being called into question and struggled against – through collective organisation and action that is multi-racial, multi-gender, and cross-class. These moments, these periods, of defiance and dissensus are possible seeds.

This is where the ultimate value of Fromm's psycho-social critical-political theory shines brightest: it provides a cogent and coherent path (if still slightly underspecified, to leave room for genuine creativity and democracy) beyond simply 'socialism or barbarism'. As I argued earlier in my negative-dialectical reading[3] of this Luxemburgian quip, there is no road to socialism that we can simply travel down. The road has yet to be built. The trees haven't been cleared (metaphorically, of course; literally, far too many trees have been cleared in the service of extractive capitalist profiteering). Fromm isn't our surveyor or civil engineer of the landscapes of our movements and the movements yet to rise. He is merely a teacher of those leaders and activists who will give rise to the transitional movements, should they emerge at all. Before moving to the conclusion, where we will justifiably return to the hopeful pessimism that inspired the title of this chapter, let us travel a bit further with Fromm, towards his conception of the productive social character that should define a socialist world.

Leaving metaphor behind again, Fromm, extending Marx's 1844 conceptualisation of alienation within capitalism, theorises a sane society beyond the insanity of capitalism, a sane society that is coterminous with the productive social character.[4] The productive social character includes dispositions towards cooperation, love (of life, others, and even objects with lived histories – as opposed to the fetishising of the new, characteristic of the marketing character orientation), compassion, creativity, imagination, and spontaneity (though not in a way that is incompatible with genuinely rational organising or planning, as determined by an inclusive participatory politics).

It is noteworthy that many contemporary critical Marxist theorists have developed arguments that are very much prefigured in Fromm's extensive explication of the psycho-social conditions of the capitalist mode of production that interfere with the emergence of a revolutionary movement aimed at a humane post-capitalist world. Whether we look at the work of Franco 'Bifo' Berardi or Mark Fisher, we are reminded that capitalism is a psychologically disfiguring mode of production that severely inhibits the development of the kind of people best suited for the struggle necessary to achieve a post-capitalism that would alleviate the diverse harms of capitalism (Fisher 2009, 2018; Berardi 2009a, 2009b). By reading the arguments of these contemporary thinkers alongside Fromm's, we can fully appreciate how it is that through the survival- and fulfilment-driven adaptive impulses of the human being – whether it is the pressure to be 'successful' or to merely continue existing day-to-day, month-to-month, year-to-year – capitalism puts perverse demands on the human psyche to disfigure itself. While this disfigurement results in a wide range of pathologies and neuroses of varying degrees of severity and disruption, this can be, as another of Fromm's early Frankfurt

School colleague's Theodor Adorno posited, the splinter in the eye that becomes a magnifying glass, opening up the opportunity for a reactive desire for a different world, more amenable to healthy and fulfilling human life, broadly conceived (Adorno 2002: 55). This is not to imply any automatic (that is, simplistic accelerationist) process whereby the harms of capitalism produce genuinely revolutionary energies aimed at the radical transformation of society – only the possibility for such a result to occur. Sadly, more often than not, those people who are most severely and debilitatingly victimised by capitalism are, in practice, simply unable to see the true systemic origins of their condition, or, even if they are able to appreciate the systemic origins of their condition, remain unable to garner the requisite psycho-social resources to consistently participate in the enormous efforts needed to achieve an organised opposition to capitalism.

While it would be easy to overstate the implications of this, it is not irrelevant that some of the great Marxist thinkers over the past twenty-five plus years have committed suicide (including Fisher himself). Awareness is not enough. It is important, but therapeutic mechanisms must be an explicit dimension of any organised struggle against and beyond capitalism. It will be up to those engaged in struggle, while they engage in struggle, to determine what the best ways are to address the very real mental health effects of capitalism, especially because socially rooted mental illnesses, whether they culminate in the extreme outcome of suicide or not, offer serious interference in the achievement of a democratic egalitarian post-capitalist world.

Returning to Fromm, a key practical element of the path towards the socialist post-capitalism he sketches, one consistent with those posited by Fisher and Berardi (even if conceptualised somewhat differently), is the role of mass participation. Participation, especially participation in de-alienating organisations and movements, has a truly transformative potential. If one of the worst elements of liberal capitalism is its alienating effects, participation (and relatedly, cooperation) is the antithesis of liberal capitalism. In many ways, prefiguring much of the debate about deliberative democracy that emerged in the mid- to late twentieth century, Fromm offers a sophisticated case for something close to direct democracy at the local levels, which would then be carried through to the variously federated levels of representation beyond the local – with decision making and decision makers always accountable to the people. The same model must be applied in the workplace as well. Fromm's pathway towards achieving and maintaining a society rooted in the productive social character must have workplace democracy, or what he calls (citing G.D.H. Cole), 'self-government in industry'.

Fromm doesn't leave these spheres separate though. Workplace democracies must also be represented at the various levels of government as well, fully integrating conventional political decision making with economic planning conducted democratically. Fromm's proposed alternative to liberal capitalism also includes another contemporarily familiar policy, universal basic income (UBI), or what he calls a 'universal subsistence guarantee' to ensure that all people, regardless of their capacity or ability to work or otherwise contribute to society, should have all of their basic needs met (Fromm 1955: 335). By ensuring that all people have their basic needs met, the opportunity to choose how one labours and under what conditions is greatly enhanced, and it is this shift that moves us from capitalism to socialism – by enlarging the opportunity for humanity's productive character traits to assert their superiority and predominate. If deprivation and exclusion (and the attendant feelings of the same) are significant components of the alienation produced by and through capitalism, our struggles must challenge these forces, both in the process of struggle and as transitional policy demands that our struggles aim to fulfil. This is one of the most vital lessons of Fromm's approach to the achievement of post-capitalism.

The question of how we get to the point where we need to be, both in regard to the preconditions for effective struggle and eventual successful struggle and building of post-capitalism, is perhaps the simplest and most difficult question of all. It is in the gap, the gap between humanity's genuine psycho-social needs (to say nothing of material needs) and capitalism's increasing inability to satisfy them, that the power of participatory, democratic struggle emerges as our answer. Because Fromm has provided us with some guidance for what kinds of character traits are important to develop to challenge capitalism, once we have the awareness of the roots of our alienation and suffering in the capitalist mode of production and consumption (and its marketing social character), we can begin to develop ways of being otherwise and fighting together to organise our homes, our workplaces, our towns, our cities, our states, our countries, and our world differently.[5] Oh, is that all? It is simply put to be sure, but it is far from simplistic, nor simple to accomplish – but it is worth re-emphasising that it is through the process of developing inclusive and participatory organisations and movements, directed towards this conception of socialism, that the initial psycho-social changes begin to take hold.

In a telling, but technically inaccurate, critique of Marx, Fromm expresses the importance of a multidimensional process to emancipation (ending economic exploitation being a necessary but insufficient condition): 'Just as Freud believed that freeing man [sic] from unnatural and overstrict sexual taboos would lead to mental health, Marx believed that the emancipation from exploitation would *automatically* produce free and cooperative beings' (Fromm 1955: 265, emphasis added). Fromm is suggesting, again incorrectly, that Marx was both hyper-focused on the endpoint of struggle and limited that struggle exclusively to the economic realm. While the economic realm was certainly the central focus for Marx, still probably more so than Fromm would have thought was appropriate, Marx did not limit his own conception of struggle to that realm, nor did he eschew the vital transformative function of struggle itself. While one can quibble over any particular interpretation of Marx or Fromm here, the key point is that there is no reason to limit struggle to the economic realm (though certainly without struggle and transformation in this realm, other struggles will fail or only ever achieve limited, fleeting success). We cannot dismiss the transformative power of struggle. This is the *how*. As Marx wrote, 'we say to the workers: "You will have to go through 15, 20, 50 years of civil wars and national struggles not only to bring about a change in society but also to change yourselves, and prepare yourselves for the exercise of political power"...' (Marx 1853).

Dialectical Ends and Beginnings

THE END (OF CAPITALISM)

Again, to suggest what I've just described, by way of Fromm's critical-political theory, is simple, easy, or likely – to say nothing of whether it is definitively possible – would be cruel overstatements. All of what has been presented here is exceptionally complex, immensely difficult, and therefore unlikely – perhaps even impossible. The goal however is to show what is necessary. While some specific parts may develop differently, some elements may be less crucial than claimed here, and other facets may end up being more important (perhaps even some that have been left out), in general, this is how change can, and hopefully will, happen. But within this hope, this dialectically salvaged pessimistic hope,[6] we must grapple intensely with our current trajectory, our past and ongoing failure. What might happen if we do not build viable roads to socialist sanity? For Fromm, as for Luxemburg and Marx, we have two general paths ahead of us, socialism or barbarism.[7] What the future barbarism(s) may look like is probably best captured by science fiction. We can imagine any number of terrible futures such as the worst of those imagined in *Black Mirror, Altered Carbon, The Expanse, The Road, I Am Legend*, any number of Ursula K. Le Guin and Kim Stanley Robinson novels, or perhaps our future will resemble the dystopia that produced the Bell Riots imagined in *Star Trek: Deep Space Nine*. Sadly, any of these speculative extrapolations from our present are more likely futures than the one imagined by Fromm or Marx or Luxemburg. They are not our only futures though. Fromm's work provides us with a strong basis to predict that the exploitative, or at least oppressive, class lines, however they may evolve specifically, will be maintained into the future, within and beyond capitalism, absent a productive democratic socialist transition. The possessive, destructive, and indeed 'necrophilic'[8] tendencies of the marketing social character and its attendant pathologies will endure for some time beyond whatever death the capitalist mode of production experiences, assuming (and this is a huge assumption!) it is not the death of most of our species or the planet itself (or some other regressive systemic transformation). The psycho-social instantiation of capitalism will live on – so long as there are people left (though given the rapid ecocidal progression of climate change, this is a big 'if').

Beyond the often horrible worlds the aforementioned works of fiction imagine, they all, in their own ways, depict resistance. Things do not have to turn out how we or they or their characters imagine, in either positive or negative visions. The path we are on may not be fully determined, at least not yet. Resistance may indeed be futile; it also may be the only solution, but let's find out for sure. And the only way to do that is to starting building the road(s) to socialism and away from barbarism now, to become not just the gravediggers of capitalism – but the road-builders towards a democratic, egalitarian, and ecological post-capitalism, which must be born in the tired ruins of our still decaying capitalist planet.

NOTES

1. For more detailed discussion of the capitalistic mentality, see Sculos (2018).
2. The next sentence after gravediggers is, 'Its [capitalism's/the bourgeoisie's] fall and the victory of the proletariat are equally inevitable' (Marx and Engels 1978a: 483).
3. On negative dialectics as a mode of interpretation, see Sculos (2017).
4. The productive social character, despite Kathi Weeks's (2011) claims otherwise, is not productivist in the classical sense. Fromm's understanding of 'productivity' is not necessarily cognate to conventional notions of productivity. Creative activity, such as painting or writing poems in one's mind (absent capitalist economic 'value'), would be perfectly compatible with Fromm's concept of productive social character – and as such is entirely inconsistent with productivism writ large.
5. For more on Fromm's theory of socialist democracy (and progress towards it), see Wilde (2004: chs 7–8).
6. For more on this concept, see the early issues of *Salvage Quarterly*. Most essays are available online at https://salvage.zone/.
7. Fromm distinguishes between what he calls old and new barbarisms (Fromm 1955: 265). For him, new barbarisms were the evils produced by the Nazis, Stalinism and super-capitalism (what we might call neoliberal capitalism). For us today, these are also old barbarisms. However, Fromm's distinction should serve as a caution; we haven't seen all the evil the world could throw our way. New barbarisms are typically predictable

(usually in hindsight) and unpredicted (beforehand), but nonetheless develop of out the social-systemic ills that precede their emergence (Fromm 1955).

8. For Fromm's non-normative usage of this term (which has nothing necessarily to do with a sexual attraction to corpses), see Fromm (1964).

REFERENCES

All URLS were last checked on 28 November 2020.

Adorno, Theodor (2002) *Minima Moralia: Reflections from Damaged Life*. New York: Verso.

Berardi, Franco (2009a) *The Soul at Work: From Alienation to Autonomy*. South Pasadena, CA: Semiotext(e).

Berardi, Franco (2009b) 'Communism is Back But We Should Call It the Therapy of Singularisation', *generation online*, available at: http://www.generation-online.org/p/fp_bifo6.htm

Fisher, Mark (2009) *Capitalist Realism: Is There No Alternative?* Ropley: Zero Books.

Fisher, Mark (2018) *K-Punk: The Collected and Unpublished Writings of Mark Fisher (2004–2016*. London: Repeater Books.

Frase, Peter (2016) *Four Futures: Life after Capitalism*. New York: Jacobin/Verso.

Fromm, Erich (1955) *The Sane Society*. New York: Holt.

Fromm, Erich (1961) *Marx's Concept of Man*, available at: https://www.marxists.org/archive/fromm/works/1961/man/index.htm

Fromm, Erich (1964) *The Heart of Man: Its Genius for Good and Evil*. New York: Harper & Row.

Fromm, Erich (1990 [1947]) *Man for Himself: An Inquiry into the Psychology of Ethics*. New York: Holt.

Fromm, Erich (1994 [1941]) *Escape from Freedom*. New York: Holt.

Lukács, Georg (1972) *History and Class Consciousness*. Cambridge, MA: MIT Press.

Luxemburg, Rosa (1915) 'The Janius Pamphlet', available at: https://www.marxists.org/archive/luxemburg/1915/junius/

Marx, Karl (1853) 'Revelations Concerning the Communist Trial in Cologne', available at: https://www.marxists.org/archive/marx/works/1853/revelations/ch01.htm

Marx, Karl and Friedrich Engels (1978a) 'The Manifesto of the Communist Party', in Robert C. Tucker (ed.) *The Marx–Engels Reader*, 2nd edn. New York: W.W. Norton.

Marx, Karl and Friedrich Engels (1978b) 'The German Ideology', in Robert C. Tucker (ed.) *The Marx–Engels Reader*, 2nd edn. New York: W.W. Norton.

Marx, Karl and Friedrich Engels (1978c) 'Economic and Philosophic Manuscripts of 1844', in Robert C. Tucker (ed.) *The Marx–Engels Reader*, 2nd edn. New York: W.W. Norton.

Sculos, Bryant William (2017) 'Negative Dialectical Interpretation: Contradiction and Critique', in Sean Noah Walsh and Clement Fatovic (eds) *Interpretation in Political Theory*. New York: Routledge, pp. 158–181.

Sculos, Bryant William (2018) 'Demystifying the Capitalistic Mentality: Reconciling Adorno and Fromm on the Psycho-social Reproduction of Capitalism', *Constellations* 25(2): 272–286.

Wark, McKenzie (2019) *Capital is Dead: Is this Something Worse?* New York: Verso.

Weeks, Kathi (2011) *The Problem with Work: Feminism, Marxism, and Anti-work Politics*. Durham, NC: Duke University Press.

Wilde, Lawrence (2004) *Erich Fromm and the Quest for Solidarity*. New York: Palgrave.

3
A New Wheel to Keep Capitalism Moving? The Artificial Womb in Feminist Futures and the Capitalist Present

Catia Gregoratti and Laura Horn

CA/JV 4 was a woolly long-term survivor with normal brain magnetic resonance imaging at one year old. Unlike any of the other lambs that came into the world that year, however, CA/JV 4 was not born of a ewe. Rather, it was incubated in a 'biobag', an extra-uterine system that supported it from premature fetal stage to full gestation (Partridge et al. 2017). In other words, CA/JV 4 came out of an artificial uterus.[1] Pictures of the lamb made headlines across the world in 2017. While technological developments around the artificial uterus had been generating discussions around reproductive possibilities for many decades, the experiment with an extreme premature lamb fetus, and its successful gestation into a healthy animal that survived into adulthood came at a time when the future of biological and social reproduction had become more malleable, more open to technological and social change than ever.

Meanwhile, the crisis dynamics of capitalism have become more and more pronounced especially in the realm of social reproduction (e.g. Fraser 2016; Hester and Srnicek 2018). The deeply precarious and gendered nature of everyday life has given rise to renewed debates about feminist post-capitalist imaginaries and strategies (Vrasti 2016; Arruza et al. 2019). Thinking about the future through the prism of actually existing processes such as the developments in reproductive and non-reproductive technologies has been part of feminist analyses for a long time (see for example Mies 1987; Hester 2017). Most notably, the artificial womb features as part of Shulamith Firestone's post-revolutionary society. It has also been captured in emancipatory imaginaries in feminist science fiction, such as the brooder in Marge Piercy's utopia *Woman on the Edge of Time* (1976). In contemporary debates, the artificial womb resonates with fundamental questions raised about its potential to level inequalities in biological and social reproduction (Cavaliere 2020).

In this chapter, we engage with the utopian dimensions of freedom that have been read into reproductive technologies, and hold them against the light of concrete social relations of (re)production in contemporary capitalism. As Fishwick and Kiersey write in the introduction to this volume, 'drawing out the specificities of the current intersecting crises of global capitalism enables us to envision the complex dynamics of class, gender and race through which it plays out'. And, in turn, this provides for thinking about post-capitalism as embedded in and overwritten by these distinctive logics as intrinsically contestable crises. To facilitate such a discussion on post-capitalism and social reproduction, we traverse some of the main discussions about technological change and the transformation of sex and gender. Here, we draw on the work by Shulamith Firestone and other radical feminists of the 1970s, and subsequent discussions and imaginaries of the artificial womb, many of which seem to be predominantly occupied with ethical issues of ectogenesis.

We then focus on two recent and exciting feminist perspectives – xenofeminism (Laboria Cuboniks 2015; Hester 2018) and Sophie Lewis's feminist manifesto for full surrogacy now (Lewis 2019a, 2019b). Xenofeminism constitutes the central manifestation of a feminist accelerationist perspective heralding the liberatory potential of technology in relation to sex and gender. Full surrogacy now, on the other hand is a revolutionary programme gesturing towards the dissolution of distinctions between reproducers and non-reproducers through the contradictions shored up by contemporary commercialised surrogacy – Surrogacy™. Our combined engagement with xenofeminism and 'full surrogacy now' is one of much interest, but ultimately one that allows for further scaffolding. While both xenofeminism and Lewis's work can be seen as revolutionary projects that give hope – hope in our ability to seize the technological means of reproduction, and hope in a future 'gestational commune' – despite all their anti-capitalism they hardly grapple with the techno-capitalist conditions and developments around ectogenesis. Xenofeminism evades the question altogether, gazing on self-reproducing groups and movements that develop and repurpose technologies 'against the production of the social as it stands' (Hester 2018: 64). Lewis, on the other hand, repudiates the 'biobag' in the capitalist present but speculates about its enabling functions for gestators in a future queer commune (Lewis 2019a).

Advances in the development of the artificial womb, we argue, warrant renewed, critical attention, not least because the public discourse around it is replete with normative promises of equality and freedom (Cavaliere, 2020; Horn and Romanis 2020). If, as the Wages for Housework campaign maintained, 'our uterus is the wheel that keeps capitalism moving' (cited in Lewis 2019b: 46), then does the artificial womb hint at a feminist revolution in the making or can it be accommodated perfectly well in the capitalist order? And/or how will it shape relations of reproduction and production? In the remainder of the chapter, we formulate an exploratory Marxist feminist perspective that helps us take these questions seriously; navigating between a historical materialist ambivalence about technology and a fundamental commitment to emancipation and social change.

THE SPECTRE OF THE WOMB: ADVANCES IN REPRODUCTIVE TECHNOLOGIES

It seems pertinent to provide a contextualisation of the social reproductive technology that is at the centre of breathless techno-optimist imaginaries of the eventual possibilities for ectogenesis. The development of an artificial placenta, and concomitantly an artificial uterus, has been the subject of investigation in advanced medical science for many decades, though initially only with limited success. The first successful results in Japan in 1997 saw a goat fetus survive for three weeks. In related research areas, significant developments in neonatology, for example, womb lining and ventilation with amniotic fluid have been made; all with the core objective to increase the chances of survival for extremely premature fetuses (for an overview, see Partridge et al. 2017; Usuda et al. 2019). At the same time, advances in reproductive technologies such as in vitro fertilisation (IVF) and assisted reproductive technology (ART) engendered major bioethical discussions about philosophical, normative and legal boundaries of these technologies (Greely 2016). Human gestation in the form of the artificial uterus, and by extension ectogenesis, has become an extreme case for these discussions (for an overview see, for example, Singer and Wells 2006; Romanis 2018). The development of ectogenesis has even been formulated as an ethical imperative by a prominent advocate, arguing that: 'there is a fundamental and inexorable conflict between the demands of gestation and childbirth, and the social values we share as human beings: independence, equality of opportunity, autonomy, education, and career and relationship fulfilment' (Smajdor 2012: 101). In this vein, it is often suggested that the artificial womb could act as 'biological and social equaliser', which also could potentially put an end to transnational surrogacy (Sandiu 2017; for a critique see Cavaliere 2020).

In 2017, the widely published results of a team of researchers in Philadelphia highlighted the technological advances in the field of artificial gestation. While there are multiple research facilities working on artificial womb technology around the world, the 2017 study was a catalyst for an unprecedented surge in interest in the medical and, more importantly, social implications of this technology. The visual material of the lamb fetus, visibly moving in its biobag, rendered the technological progress tangible for a broader public; the lamb fetus that was used was at the biological equivalent of the 22–24-week gestation stage of the premature human infant. As the researchers themselves noted, their system offers:

> an intriguing experimental model for addressing fundamental questions regarding the role of the mother and placenta in fetal development. Long-term physiologic maintenance of a fetus amputated from the maternal–placental axis has now been achieved, making it possible to study the relative contribution of this organ to fetal maturation. (Partridge et al. 2017: 11)

While it should be highlighted that, given the current state of technological development, the application of an artificial uterus, let alone full ectogenesis, still remains a distant possibility due to formidable technological challenges, the artificial uterus has become a point of contention in many contemporary public debates. Reactions to the possibility of ectogenetic reproduction, essentially the question 'How would making babies without requiring women to be pregnant change the world?' (Greely 2016: 189), range between techno-optimism, with the artificial womb as a modernist inevitability, and a conservative defence of a (heteronormative) biologically determinist division of labour. A certain level of sensationalism permeates these discussions; at the same time many crucial questions about motherhood, parenting and the role of technology in mediating social power relations have been raised also in mainstream debates (see for example Bhatia and Kendal 2019; Kleeman 2020). What is often absent from these discussions, though, is a fundamental understanding of how the discussion of technological possibilities and their societal consequences needs to be seen against broader, and historically specific social power relations – in particular a capitalist system where the social reproduction of bodies has become subordinate to capital accumulation, among other forms of oppression (Federici 2020).

We contend that it is only through a Marxist feminist perspective that we can grasp the consequences of technological change, not for some distant future, but the lived reality and possibility for emancipatory alternatives of living labour in contemporary capitalism. To do so, we need to transcend academic discussions to also include art, more specifically feminist science fiction that raises the spectre of (social) reproductive change.

ECTOGENESIS IN SPECULATIVE FEMINISM

Ectogenesis has long been a theme in science, and science fiction (cf. Haldane 1924), but mostly without questioning its potential for social emancipation for women (e.g. *Brave New World*, *The Matrix*). With the emergence of feminist science fiction, the exploration of technological and social change through developments in biological and social reproduction took on a new meaning. As Ursula Le Guin noted, 'one need not smash one's typewriter and go bomb the laundromat, after all, because one has lost faith in the continuous advance of technology as the way towards utopia. Technology remains, in itself, an endless creative source' (Le Guin 2017 [1982]: 94). New imaginaries rendered it possible to think through the possibilities and contradictions of reproductive technologies. While Shulamith Firestone, at the time of publication of *The Dialectic of Sex*, lamented that 'we haven't even a literary image of this future society; there is not even a utopian feminist literature yet in existence' (Firestone 1970: 211),[2] subsequent feminist authors, in art as well as academic debates, have provided crucial contributions for making sense of the discussion about the artificial womb. Most prominently there has been Haraway's work, based on the premise that science fact and (speculative) feminism need each other, but always in an awareness that it is necessary to foreground the present (Haraway 2016: 3). Contemporary feminist science fiction, such as Anne Charnock's Dreams *Before the Start of Time* (2017), here offers important glimpses into the interlinkages between the commodification of social reproduction inherent in this technology, and the ambivalent emancipation from patriarchal and heteronormative structures that it promises.

In feminist thought Shulamith Firestone's work is often considered a precursor of cyberfeminism. In the *Dialectic of Sex*, Firestone maintains that is *nature* that produced the fundamental inequality between sex classes: women, or rather beings with reproductive organs gestate and give birth, not men. Menstruation, pregnancy, painful birth, responsibilities for child-bearing and caring 'cost women dearly' (Firestone 1970: 215), limiting women's lives and creating hierarchical dependencies. This harsh materiality is not inevitable and, in Firestone's anti-naturalist view, it can and must be changed by harnessing technological developments. As she argues, 'the reproduction of the species by one sex for the benefit of both would be replaced by (at least the option of) artificial reproduction: children would born to both sexes equally, or independently' (1970: 11). The *Dialectic* urges women to seize the means of reproduction from the patriarchal scientific establishment that excluded them and continued to control them. It is important to stress that 'seizing' is the fundamental political message of the *Dialectic*, as Firestone is well aware that 'in the hand of our current society and under the direction of current scientists (few of them are female or even feminists), any attempt to use technology to free anybody is suspect' (Firestone 1970: 193). More daringly, she proposes a 'dangerous utopia' – a feminist post-revolutionary world in which the sex and class distinctions are abolished. In this utopia, reproduction would be replaced by (optional) artificial reproduction, the nuclear family would be disbanded in favour of collective forms of child-raising, differences in physical strength would no longer matter, while the division of labour would be eliminated altogether through cybernation (Firestone 1970: 11).

Marge Piercy's utopian protagonist manifests this by arguing that reproductive technology in form of ectogenesis has been 'part of women's long revolution [...] as a sacrifice of women's one great power in return for no more power for anyone' (Piercy 1979: 105). At the same time, Piercy acknowledged the contradictions of this technology seen against the real existing power relations of her contemporary protagonist, Connie:

> She felt angry. [...] These women thought they had won, but they had abandoned to men the last refuge of women. What was special about being a woman here? They had given it all up, they had let men steal from them the last remnants of ancient power, those sealed in blood and milk. (Piercy 1979: 134)

Just as Piercy's novel does not offer an easy utopian solution, many contemporary observers highlight the intensifying contradictions of technological change. Feminist dystopias dealing with reproductive crises caused by industrial pollution or the overextension of the working day abound. For example, we can think of the rediscovery of Margaret Atwood's *The Handmaid's Tale* (1985) or the acclaim of Johanne Ramos' first novel *The Farm* (2019). Notwithstanding important differences, in both Atwood's and Ramos's fictional worlds, heavily surveilled and 'assisted' by latest reproductive technologies, women are turned into birthing machines for the ruling elites.

THE HOPE OF XENOFEMINISM: HARNESSING TECHNOLOGY FOR EMANCIPATION

Repudiated for its techno-determinism and its tendency to side with patriarchal science, *The Dialectic of Sex* has not had an easy afterlife

(Merck and Sandford 2010). Firestone is being rediscovered today when social reproduction is in crisis, inequalities are widening and reproductive freedoms are under assault. As Piercy (2016) suggests: 'when our political energy goes into defending rights, and projects we won and created are now under attack there is far less energy for imagining fully drawn future societies we might wish to live in'.

Firestone has gained renewed visibility and popularity through xenofeminism, a new feminist movement heralding the liberatory potential of technology. Helen Hester's *Xenofeminism* (2018) is explicit in its acknowledgement of Firestone and extends its intellectual debts to cyberfeminism, post-humanism, accelerationism, material feminism and neo-rationalism. Xenofeminism is 'technomaterialist, anti-naturalism and gender abolitionist form of feminism'. Its tripartite structure maintains that technology is part of life and instead of rejecting it should become the focus of activism. In contrast to early strands of ecofeminism – embodied in the figure of Maria Mies – it holds that nature should neither be romanticised nor thought of as an enclosed category but as a 'technologized space of conflict' (Hester 2018: 13). If nature is unjust, the *Xenofeminist Manifesto* argues, the political project should be to change nature (Laboria Cuboniks 2015). This manifests in an imperative to harness technological possibilities, as Hester insists. Biology, she argues, 'can be technologically transformed, and *should* be transformed in the pursuit of reproductive justice and the progressive transformation of gender' (Hester 2018: 22, original emphasis). It is a feminism that wants to fully accommodate a full spectrum of embodied differences, in other words, all differences that harbour injustices should be abolished. Above all, its post-capitalist wager lies in its investment in the construction of 'an alien [xenos] future', beyond the household, the family and the child, or a 'social reproduction against the production of the social as it stands' (Hester 2018: 64).

Margree (2019) suggests that xenofeminism not only intersects with Firestone's feminism but also modifies it and expands it in significant ways. With sensitivity to the intersectional histories and entanglements of various technologies, Helen Hester shows what a xenofeminist technology, but above all, politics, could look like in the present. Her examples – Del-Em, Testogel, the 3D specula, Open

Source Gender Codes – revolve around self-help groups/cyborgian witches that appropriate, repurpose and freely circulate technologies for gender-progressive ends while circumnavigating medical gatekeepers and the capitalist pharmaceutical establishment.

This very much resonates with the broader accelerationist perspective. For accelerationists, notions of the future remain stuck between an unenticing 'folk politics' of local actions and horizontalism, and dystopias projecting ecological catastrophes, corporate-led takeovers of the world and the dismantling of the welfare state (Srnicek and Williams 2015: 70). Technological imaginaries are key to supercharge political processes heralding post-capitalism. As Srnicek and Williams famously call for towards the end of their 2015 book:

> rather than settling for marginal improvements in battery life and computing power, the left should mobilise dreams of decarbonising the economy, space travel, robot economies – all the traditional touchstones of science fiction – in order to prepare for a day beyond capitalism.

For xenofeminists, this engagement with technology is inexorably linked with a post-human alienation that embodies liberation from oppressive social relations, most crucially gender. 'Make kin, not babies', Donna Haraway insists in her forceful engagement with the Anthropocene and its technological entanglements (Haraway 2016). The xenofeminist call for alienation as liberation here brings together the post-human with the post-capitalist perspective. As Annie Goh argues convincingly, though, this call for, essentially, *more* alienation, glosses over the existing forms of alienation that bodies can already be struggling with, and hence lacks an account of the uneven stakes of humanness and subjecthood (Goh 2019). It also raises fundamental questions of the politics of agency, which we will take up again towards the end of the chapter.

TRANSCENDING THE FAMILY, AND THE UTERUS?

One of the most interesting discussions relevant to the technological development of ectogenetic possibilities is certainly Sophie Lewis's call for the abolition of the (nuclear) family through full surrogacy (Lewis 2019b). Gestational labour is just that – labour, Lewis argues; as such, it is subjected to exploitation and appropriation like any other form of labour. Her work thus offers an important and powerful critique of the biological determinism and idealisation of motherhood and parenting. While feminist perspectives have long highlighted the uncompensated reproductive labour of women, recent contributions have shown the contradictions between giving birth and the social reproduction of a capitalist system that at the same time commercialises, exploits and fetishises this very process. The social struggles around reproduction are discussed forcefully in Brown's work *Birth Strike*: 'Just as workers have found that bargaining power comes from uniting and refusing to work – striking – women's bargaining power has increased when we have refused to produce children at desired rates' (Brown 2019: 1). Lewis, however, develops a much more radical notion of social change for gestational justice. Drawing on Firestone, among others, she puts forward the case for a 'gestational communism' that allows for non-proprietary and collaborative forms of bearing and raising children that do away with the family.

In the context of this chapter, the clear link between the call for full surrogacy, and the possibilities a technology for an artificial uterus would offer is highly relevant. Lewis (2019a) here offers a nuanced discussion of the case of the artificial uterus, also pointing to the possibility that artificial womb technology would essentially serve as an instrument to *cement* rather than change existing power relations. Not only would any doubts over biogenetic paternity and the 'human gestator' as a possible intervening variable be removed from the process, the anti-abortion position would also be significantly strengthened. Against this scenario, she develops her position in arguing that 'researching alternatives that would enable people not to gestate if they don't want to – while still making babies together, perhaps in non-dyadic ways – is not only justified, but highly ethical', in particular when considering the risks associated with pregnancies; not just medical/biological ones, but also especially for black and working-class gestators (Lewis 2019a). There is a clear understanding of the state of contemporary reproductive technology, in that its current trajectory, focusing on artificial womb devices to extend survival for premature fetuses, 'has nothing whatsoever to do with reproductive justice struggle'. Nonetheless, in her post-capitalist vision, this technology could indeed be the means to 'help denaturalize motherhood and liberate those with uteruses from the imperative to gestate' (Lewis 2019a), which has a clear resonance with the feminist utopias of Firestone and Piercy.

Nina Power's (2010) critique of Firestone's take on scientific progress remains relevant here. Will technologies be the catalyst for social change, as accelerationists posit, or will there first have to be cultural shifts to facilitate the progressive implementation of these technologies? As Power argues, the first position is 'open to accusations of technological determinism; the second, to free-floating utopianism' (Power 2015). Rather, as we argue in the next section, it is only with a materialist understanding of the social and economic power structures of a system that subordinates the health and autonomy of gestators, and the relationships with their children, to the imperatives of capital accumulation and oppressive forms of social power, that we can grasp the complex politics of reproductive technologies. As Power reminds us, 'politics mediates nature and technology, and has to if progressive or revolutionary projects are to be advanced' (Power 2015).

BEYOND SHINY NEW THINGS, TOWARDS REPRODUCTIVE JUSTICE

It is not that the post-human perspective does not acknowledge at all the context in which technological change renders possible the emergence of a social reproduction constituted along an anti-naturalist, cyborgian bent. As Braidotti argues:

> The posthuman feminist knowing subject is a complex assemblage of human and nonhuman, planetary and cosmic, given and manufactured, which requires major readjustments in our ways of thinking. But she remains committed to social justice and, while acknowledging the fatal attraction of global mediation, is not likely to forget that one-third of the world population has no access to electricity. (Braidotti 2017: 29)

And yet, lurking behind the shiny abode of technological progress, the question of social power relations lies, relentless and with all the contradictions inherent in how capitalism intersects with racism, colonialism, imperialism and other forms of social oppression. It is to these power relations that we turn now, drawing on some of the key issues and questions that Marxist feminist scholars commonly ask in relation to reproductive technologies. This also means that our ontological starting point is living labour, rather than the machine.

As Mies argued at a point when reproductive technologies emerged as a new medical paradigm, 'reproductive technologies have been developed not because women need them, but because capital and science need women for the continuation of their model of growth and progress' (1987: 324). Echoing Mies, Silvia Federici questions the possibilities for empowerment and social liberation of reproductive technologies that are not controlled from below. Throughout the history of capitalism women have been unevenly subject to the discipline of work – paid and unpaid – while their bodies have been turned into sex objects and 'breeding machines' (Federici 2004, 2020). Capitalism needs to tightly control – through population policies or welfare (dis)incentives – women's reproduction because human labour constitutes its very condition of possibility. Without workers, soldiers and consumers, capitalism would not exist.

Emplaced in a complex matrix of relations of exploitation and oppression, the full or partial externalisation of reproduction to *another* machine is likely to amplify rather than act as a leveller of gender, class and racial divisions in biological reproduction. Developments around the artificial womb, as Cavaliere suggests (2020), are likely to offer reproductive choices and prospects for career advancement to privileged cis white women, while leaving unattended the economic insecurity and forms of control that are exercised on bodies deemed unfit to procreate, often the bodies of black, migrant, indigenous and disabled women. The promise of a choice to gestate otherwise or the choice to interrupt a pregnancy without terminating a fetus operates, as Dorothy Roberts argues (1999: 289): 'like blinkers that obscure issues of social power that determine the significance of reproductive freedom and control ... not by ignoring them altogether, but by claiming to achieve individual freedom without the need to rectify social inequalities'. Furthermore, as Horn and Romanis highlight (2020: 235), the biomedical development of ectogenetic technology poses severe ethical and legal challenges, as the only way this could take place is through testing on humans. Given the historical context of medical trials on reproductive health products that have been conducted on marginalised social groups, sometimes without their consent, even the development stage of these technologies would have to put human beings at risk. But beyond the ethical discussion, there are crucial political economy dimensions that require attention.

Uncoupling gestation from the body is also unlikely to redress the inequalities of other forms of socially reproductive labour, such as care work and productive labour. By itself, ectogenesis is unlikely to either shift the norms that define women in their reproductive capacities or alter the precarious and gendered nature of labour markets. As Cavaliere poignantly remarks: 'the way technologies go about shaping extant arrangements and norms seems to depend more on how these technologies are designed, implemented and regulated, and to serve whose interests, than on the technologies themselves' (Cavaliere 2020: 79). The question of how technologies may reconstitute relations of social reproduction and production can also be stretched further afield, in abodes even more hidden, so as to consider more fully who and what it takes to produce 'shiny new things'. Both Federici (in Elliot and Franklin 2018; see also Federici 2020) and Lewis (2019b), for example, stress that the production of new technologies is made possible by the immense amount of physical labour and extraction of rare minerals in the 'Third World'.

To consider reproductive technologies in the capitalist present also requires a critical perspective on the institutional and financial conditions of their emergence and development. It is a question of who owns reproductive technological developments, in terms of patents and trademarks, but also broader financial structures of pharmaceutical companies. Who funds research and development? What is the role of the state and state institutions in regulating and monitoring these developments? As Federici highlights (in Elliot and Franklin 2018: 173), already now 'processes of procreation [have] become a goldmine'. There is no reason to expect that the development and governance of advanced social reproductive technologies such as ectogenesis would follow a different logic. Cavaliere discusses arguments that advocates of ectogenesis bring to debates, namely the role of the state in financing the development of, and regulating access to ectogenetic technologies (Cavaliere 2020: 78). And yet, as she convincingly argues, even where access to reproductive technologies such as IVF are mediated through institutional structures such as the National Health Service (NHS) in the UK, it is unlikely that there would be equal access to ectogenesis.

More importantly still, the question is very much about how the condensed, institutionalised system of social power relations that govern social reproduction can be seen as social terrains for political struggle towards reproductive justice. If, as Mies argues (1987: 335), the artificial womb can function as the 'final rationalisation of reproductive behaviour' in the capitalist present, then the (hegemonic) struggle against this rationalisation also needs to focus on contesting existing institutional and ideological structures. With regard to the possibilities and boundaries of technological development, a Marxist feminist position would thus advocate for and support social struggle articulating a reproductive justice perspective to enhance the autonomy of bodies of living labour against the uneven development of capitalism. Coined in 1994 at a US caucus of black feminists, reproductive justice is a mobilising frame that revolves around two axioms: a woman's right *not to* have a child, and the right to have children and to raise them in a safe and supportive environment (Lewis 2019b: 11). Today, demands for true reproductive freedom such as 'the right to abortion, a living wage, universal health care, and the abolition of prisons' (Roberts 2015) are echoed and extended in solidarity in all the place-based and transnational struggles subsumed under the banner of a feminism for the 99 per cent (Arruzza et al. 2019).

CONCLUDING REFLECTIONS

For the current discussions about the ending(s) of capitalism and the emergence of post-capitalism, we read xenofeminism, and techno-optimistic queer visions such as Lewis' call for full surrogacy (or gestational communism), as invitations to think critically about existing contemporary power relations – not to engage in techno-utopian fantasies, but to consider where the real terrain for social change and transformation lies. At the same time, we insist that there is a need to retain and engage with radical imaginaries, to think beyond crisis and hope in post-capitalist futures. In this vein, the imaginary that perhaps best captures the counterpoint to the bright and lineal techno-optimist futures of ectogenesis is Le Guin's description of a 'yin utopia' – 'it would be dark, wet, obscure, weak, yielding, passive, participatory, circular, cyclical, peaceful, nurturant, retreating, contracting, and cold' (Le Guin 1982: 89).

There is no technological resolution to the liberation of women from specific biological and social imperatives, and the economic system that drives and constructs and them. There can only ever be political negotiation and reconciliation of the individual as autonomous, social being – with its contending and contradictory objectives, desires and subjectivities embodied in living labour – with these technologies and the structures from which they emerge. In this context, Federici reminds us, maternity should be understood as 'a political, value-positing decision' (2020: 19). Control over reproductive processes in post-capitalism rely on generative power and agency that defy a universal, singular trajectory. Rather than intensifying and accelerating alienation, it is only through harnessing and mobilising political power that social change can be made possible. Marxist feminist analyses here show the potential and contradictions of these actual political struggles over social reproduction (Fakier et al. 2020; Battacharya 2017).

NOTES

1. We refer to the artificial womb or uterus throughout this chapter, as this is the term most commonly used in popular discussions. This term covers the possibility for *partial* ectogenesis, that is extra-uterine gestation of a fetus that has been removed from a human womb, as well as *full* ectogenesis, that is gestation of a fetus from the initial zygote stage to maturation.
2. Though it is important to note that some examples did exist, among the most widely known are Charlotte Perkins Gilman's *Herland* (1915) and William Marston's *Wonder Woman* comics (1940s), which featured the all-female community of Themyscira, or Paradise Island.

REFERENCES

All URLS were last checked on 21 November 2020.

Arruzza, Cinzia, Tithi Bhattacharya and Nancy Fraser (2019) *Feminism for the 99%*. New York: Verso.

Atwood, Margaret (1985) *The Handmaid's Tale*. Toronto: McClelland and Stewart.

Battacharya, Tithi (ed.) (2017) *Social Reproduction Theory: Remapping Class, Recentering Oppression*. London: Pluto Press.

Bhatia, Neera and Evie Kendal (2019) 'We May One Day Grow Babies Outside the Womb, but There Are Many Things to Consider First', *The Conversation*, available at: https://theconversation.com/we-may-one-day-grow-babies-outside-the-womb-but-there-are-many-things-to-consider-first-125709

Braidotti, Rosi (2017) 'Four Theses on Posthuman Feminism', in Richard Grusin (ed.) *Anthropocene Feminism*. Minneapolis, MN: University of Minnesota Press, pp. 21–48.

Brown, Jenny (2019) *Birth Strike: The Hidden Fight over Women's Work*. San Francisco: PM Press.

Cavaliere, Giulia (2020) 'Gestation, Equality and Freedom: Ectogenesis as a Political Perspective', *Journal of Medical Ethics* 46: 76–82.

Charnock, Anne (2017) *Dreams Before the Start of Time*. London: 47th North.

Elliot, Jane and Seb Franklin (2018) '"The Synthesis Is in the Machine": An Interview with Silvia Federici', *Australian Feminist Studies* 33(96): 172–177.

Fakier, Khayatt, Diana Mulinari and Nora Räthzel (eds) (2020) *Marxist-Feminist Theories and Struggles Today*. London: Zed.

Federici, Silvia (2004) *Caliban and the Witch: Women, The Body and Primitive Accumulation*. Brooklyn: Automedia.

Federici, Silvia (2020) *Beyond the Periphery of the Skin: Rethinking, Remaking and Reclaiming the Body in Contemporary Capitalism*. Oakland, CA: PM Press.

Firestone, Shulamith (1970) *The Dialectic of Sex: The Case for Feminist Revolution*. New York: Bantam Books.

Fraser, Nancy (2016) 'Contradictions of Capital and Care', *New Left Review* 100: 99–118.

Goh, Annie (2019) 'Appropriating the Alien: A Critique of Xenofeminism', *Mute*, available at: https://www.metamute.org/editorial/articles/appropriating-alien-critique-xenofeminism

Greely, Henry T. (2016) *The End of Sex and the Future of Human Reproduction*. Cambridge, MA: Harvard University Press.

Haldane, John B.S. (1924) *Daedalus, or Science and the Future: A Paper Read to the Heretics, Cambridge on February 4th, 1923*. London: Kegan Paul, Trench, Trubner & Co.

Haraway, Donna (2016) *Staying with the Trouble: Making Kin in the Chthulucene*. Durham, NC: Duke University Press.

Hester, Helen (2017) 'Promethean Labours and Domestic Realism', *e-flux architecture*, available at: https://www.e-flux.com/architecture/artificial-labor/140680/promethean-labors-and-domestic-realism/

Hester, Helen (2018) *Xenofeminism*. Cambridge: Polity.

Hester, Helen and Nick Srnicek (2018) 'The Crisis of Social Reproduction and the End of Work', *OpenMind*, available at: https://www.bbvaopenmind.com/wp-content/uploads/2018/03/BBVA-OpenMind-Helen-Hester-Nick-Srnicek-The-Crisis-of-Social-Reproduction-and-the-End-of-Work.pdf

Horn, Claire and Elizabeth Chloe Romanis (2020) 'Establishing Boundaries for Speculation About Artificial Wombs, Ectogenesis, Gender, and the Gestating Body', in Chris Dietz, Mitchell Travis and Michael Thompson (eds) *A Jurisprudence of the Body*. Cham: Palgrave Macmillan.

Kleeman, Jenny (2020) '"Parents Can Look at Their Foetus in Real Time": Are Artificial Wombs the Future?', *The Guardian*, available at: https://www.theguardian.com/lifeandstyle/2020/jun/27/parents-can-look-foetus-real-time-artificial-wombs-future

Laboria Cuboniks (2015) 'Xenofeminism: A Politics for Alienation', available at https://laboriacuboniks.net/manifesto/

Le Guin, Ursula (2017 [1982]) 'A Non-Euclidean View of California as a Cold Place to Be', in Ursula Le Guin, *Dancing at the Edge of the World*. Newburyport, MA: Grove Atlantic.

Lewis, Sophie (2019a) 'Do Electric Sheep Dream of Water Babies?', *Logic Magazine*, issue 8. available at: https://logicmag.io/bodies/do-electric-sheep-dream-of-water-babies/

Lewis, Sophie (2019b) *Full Surrogacy Now: Feminism against Family*. London: Verso.

Margree, Victoria (2019) 'Shulamit Firestone: Xenofeminist Before Her Time?', *The Mantle*, available at: https://www.themantle.com/philosophy/shulamith-firestone-xenofeminist-her-time#footnote3_cqlb2y7

Merck, Mandy and Stella Sandford (2010) *Further Adventures of the Dialectic of Sex*. New York: Palgrave Macmillan.

Mies, Maria (1987) 'Sexist and Racist Implications of New Reproductive Technologies', *Alternatives* 12: 323–342.

Partridge, Emily, Marcus Davey, Matthew Hornick et al. (2017) 'An Extra-uterine System to Physiologically Support the Extreme Premature Lamb', *Nature Communications* 8, article 15112, available at: https://www.nature.com/articles/ncomms15112

Perkins Gilman, Charlotte (1915) *Herland*. New York: The Forerunner Magazine.

Piercy, Marge (1976) *Woman on the Edge of Time*. London: Women's Press.

Piercy, Marge (2016) 'Woman on the Edge of Time, 40 Years On: Hope is the Engine for Imagining Utopias', *The Guardian*, available at: https://www.theguardian.com/books/2016/nov/29/woman-on-the-edge-of-time-40-years-on-hope-imagining-utopia-marge-piercy

Power, Nina (2010) 'Toward Cybernetic Communism: The Technology of the Anti-Family', in Mandy Merck and Stella Sandford (eds) *Further Adventures of the Dialectic of Sex*. New York: Palgrave Macmillan.

Power, Nina (2015) 'Decapitalism, Left Scarcity, and the State', *Fillip* 20(Fall), available at: https://fillip.ca/content/decapitalism-left-scarcity-and-the-state

Ramos, Joanne (2019) *The Farm*. New York: Random House.

Roberts, Dorothy E. (1999) *Killing the Black Body: Race, Reproduction and the Meaning of Liberty*. New York: Vintage Books.

Roberts, Dorothy (2015) 'Reproductive Justice, Not Just Rights', *Dissent Magazine*, fall, available at: https://www.dissentmagazine.org/article/reproductive-justice-not-just-rights

Romanis, Elizabeth C. (2018) 'Artificial Womb Technology and the Frontiers of Human Reproduction: Conceptual Differences and Potential Implications', *Journal of Medical Ethics* 44: 751–755.

Sandiu, Ana (2017) 'Artificial Womb Technology: Who Will Benefit?', *Big Think*, available at: https://bigthink.com/artificial-womb-technology-who-benefits

Singer, Peter and Deane Wells (2006) 'Ectogenesis', in John R. Shook (ed.) *Ectogenesis: Artificial Womb Technology and the Future of Human Reproduction*. New York: Rodopi, pp. 9–25.

Smajdor, Anna (2012) 'In Defense of Ectogenesis', *Cambridge Quarterly of Healthcare Ethics* 21: 90–103.

Srnicek, Nick and Alex Williams (2015) *Inventing the Future: Postcapitalism and a World without Work*. London: Verso.

Usuda, Haruo, Shimpei Watanabe, Masatoshi Saito et al. (2019) 'Successful Use of an Artificial Placenta to Support Extremely Preterm Ovine Fetuses at the Border of Viability', *American Journal of Obstetrics and Gynecology* 22(1): 69.e1–17.

Vrasti, Wanda (2016) 'Self-reproducing Movements and the Enduring Challenge of Materialist Feminism', in Aida A. Hozic and Jacquie True (eds) *Scandalous Economics*. Oxford: Oxford University Press.

4
Development Alternatives: Old Challenges and New Hybridities in China and Latin America

Paul Bowles and Henry Veltmeyer

'Development', according to its institutional advocates and practitioners in the mainstream of international development studies, makes at least one major emanicipatory claim – emanicipation from poverty for the more than 1 billion people (exactly how many depends on how poverty is defined and counted) that pursue their daily lives in conditions of poverty (understood as the inability of people to meet their basic human needs) in a world which has never been richer in material terms. The World Bank, for example, on its masthead describes its goals as being to 'end extreme poverty within a generation and boost shared prosperity'.[1] The latter is understood to mean increasing the income of the bottom 40 per cent of the population in each country; hence the Bank's interest in 'pro-poor' and 'inclusive' growth / development. The UNDP (United Nations Development Programme), for its part, in its conception of Human Development and its Sustainable Development Goals, and in its 'universal call to action to end poverty, protect the planet and ensure that all people enjoy peace and prosperity',[2] defines development more broadly but poverty reduction remains as a core strategy.

Critical Development Studies (CDS) is a branch of development studies that seeks to examine why, despite more than five decades of concerted efforts and dedicated resources, the bold emancipatory claims made for development have not been realised and how alternatives to the mainstream model need to be found. In this regard CDS is based on a number of key understandings. The first is that it is essential to examine closely and theorise the development dynamics of the underlying operating system – capitalism. In the mainstream of development studies, the taken-for-granted assumption that capitalism provides the best, if not the only, system for achieving development's fundamental emancipatory aim has led to the virtual disappearance of any mention, let alone theorisation, of capitalism as a system. However, the production of poverty is associated with and a direct outcome of a multiplicity of forces such as colonialism, imperialism, war, racism, patriarchy and ecological destruction that cannot be fully understood or overcome without a clear understanding of the dynamics and fundamental contradictions of capitalism. Accordingly, CDS is concerned with and offers much more than just emancipation from poverty – namely, emancipation from capitalism. While there have been previous instances of 'crises in development' or 'impasses in development', the current conjuncture leads us to argue that, from a CDS perspective, the crisis of development cannot be separated from the propensity of capitalism towards crisis. This is especially the case for the current conjuncture, characterised as it is by the periodic outbreaks of at least five crises – (1) the crisis of neoliberal globalisation, which has exposed fundamental fissures and what some see as the central contradiction of the system, namely, the inequalities derived from the capital–labour and the centre–periphery relation; (2) a global financial crisis which can traced back to the dramatic advance and speculative ventures of finance capital over the past three decades and an associated disjunction between the money economy based on the transactions of largely fictitous capital, and the real economy based on the accumulation of productive capital and the advance of industrial capital; (3) a global food crisis which periodically threatens many on the periphery of the world system; (4) an ecological and climatic crisis associated with the emission of greenhouse gases and global warming; and now (5) the global pandemic crisis, which has exposed the linkages between the global circuits of capital, ecological destruction and public health (see Wallace et al. 2020).

Second, 'development' viewed through critical lens – Critical Development Studies – provides a rich terrain and useful tools for examining how states, societies and communities have sought to build better lives for their members while challenging prevailing orthodox models, and drawing lessons from these experiences. In these experiences, we can better see the potential and pitfalls of different pathways and ways of moving beyond capitalism. This historical analysis also enables us to move beyond the often eurocentric focus of much of the post-capitalism debate and of authoritarian neoliberalism which, in fact, was tested on the periphery, for example in Chile in the 1970s, before its current populist manifestation in parts of the core.

Third, CDS takes as axiomatic that the resistance to the advance of capital in the development process, and the search for alternatives to capitalism, are capable of being articulated, advanced and implemented on the periphery of the world capitalist system. For much of the 20th century this was the case as state socialist revolutions, starting in Russia in 1917, spread through the periphery of the system from China, to Cuba, to Vietnam and to Angola for example. In fact, resistance to capital was prevalent in much of the periphery, although its mixing with anti-colonial and anti-imperialist struggles meant that it took different forms in different places. At any rate, the periphery is no stranger to searches for alternatives to capitalism; in fact, quite the opposite.

Fourth, the development of the productive forces and associated social conditions of people in countries and macro-regions across the world system are very uneven, allowing us to conceive of underdevelopment or peripheral capitalist development in some instances and post-capitalism or post-development in others. This concept of uneven capitalist development is central to Marxism. What CDS adds is a fundamental concern with conditions that are specific to capitalism on the periphery of what has emerged as a world system. For example, Marxists have long theorised that the capitalist development of industry is based on the capitalist development of agriculture and an associated process of proletarianisation – the transformation of a peasantry of small-scale agricultural producers into an industrial proletariat and the creation of an industrial reserve army of surplus labour. However, they have failed to understand what this has meant for capitalism on the periphery of the system, namely, the formation of a semi-proletariat of impoverished rural landless workers that in the 1990s would constitute the primary social base of the resistance to capitalism in the form of neoliberal globalisation (Petras and

Veltmeyer, 2013). Another failure of traditional Marxism, focused as it was on the construction of a theory of the fundamental laws of capitalist development, was an inability to appreciate the magnitude and significance of the advance of resource-seeking 'extractive capitalism' on the Latin American periphery of the system (Veltmeyer and Petras, 2014). Analysts operating within a CDS framework, which combines political economy with social ecology, have determined that the contradictions of extractive capital, combined with the contradictions and forces of change generated by the capital–labour relation and the centre–periphery relation – arguably the major contradictions of capitalism – underlie and help explain the emergence of the fundamental and most powerful forces of capitalist development and the organised resistance to capitalism today. This allows us not only to theorise the fundamental dynamics of capitalist development – the current form taken by capitalism as a world system – but also to identify the most powerful forces of resistance, which in the Latin Americam context are pointing towards various models and pathways of alternative development.

Fifth, mainstream economic development theory, the parameters of which are institutionally exemplified by the World Bank, the UNDP and ECLAC (the UN Economic Commission for Latin America and the Caribbean), have for some six decades pursued diverse strategies designed to bring about transformative social change and development (improvement in the social condition of targeted populations) based on the assumption of the need for institutional and policy reform. None of these strategies have worked because the various theories and policy prescriptions advanced by these institutions fail to grasp, or ignore, the underlying systemic dynamics of capitalist development. At the same time, while some Marxist political economists (Foster 2002; Foster et al. 2010) have identified the roots of the fundamental crisis that has beset the capitalist system – and that, according to some, will eventually lead to its collapse or overthrow – and elucidated the system-wide form taken by the forces of capitalist development, they have singularly failed to identify the anti-systemic forces that are leading to, or have the potential for transforming or moving us beyond capitalism. Neither development economics or Marxist political economy have served to identify the forces that have the potential for systemic change. For this, it is argued, we might well turn towards CDS.

MOVING BEYOND CAPITALISM: FORCES OF PROGRESSIVE CHANGE AND ALTERNATIVE DEVELOPMENT

Capitalism is a system in crisis – a multifaceted and multidimensional crisis with deep roots in the normal functioning of the capitalist system. Experience over the past three decades within the institutional and policy framework of what, in the 1980s, was described as 'the new world order' – a system designed to liberate the 'forces of economic freedom' (the market, private enterprise, capital) from the regulatory constraints of the interventionist state – has made this fact patently clear. The CDS paradigm in this context has emerged as a heterogeneous field of emancipatory studies, a diverse set of ideas of alternative development and alternatives to development in response to changing conditions of capitalist development and as an intellectual challenge to the ideology of neoliberal globalisation and mainstream approaches to 'development'. The range of contributions to CDS are extensive and have been reviewed elsewhere (see Veltmeyer and Bowles 2018; Veltmeyer and Delgado Wise 2018). In this chapter, we complement this work by focusing on the experience of capitalist development in two macro-regions (one of them a country, and the other some 30 countries), to analyse the implications for and the possibilities and pathways for moving beyond capitalism. We focus on these two cases of capitalist development not because of their putative 'successes' or cause for 'hope' for a better future but because of their importance. In both, we find the ongoing challenges of who 'development' should be for and what constitutes 'development', of what the role of the state could and should be, of what non/post-capitalist property relations might be possible, of identifying the forces of resistance and of those blocking social transformation.

China, as the world's second largest economy, has witnessed decades of sustained rapid economic growth and has an increasingly important global role and influence over development thinking elsewhere in the periphery. As only the second non-Western country to challenge Western dominance of the global system since the

Industrial Revolution, and as the only one that is not part of the Western security alliance, it holds a unique place in potentially challenging dominant models and practice. For example, its exercise of 'soft power' and its financial clout, as evidenced in the Belt and Road Initiative, mean that its influence in shaping 21st-century development in the periphery cannot be ignored. Latin America, on the other hand, historically a region of rich contributions to alternative development thinking, from dependency theory onwards (Kay 2018), in recent years has served as a virtual laboratory of experiments with alternative development models – alternatives to the advance of capital in the development process, and alternatives to the powerful forces of capitalist development. These include a decade-long 'pink tide' of progressive regimes as multiple governments in South America sought to advance a more inclusive form of (capitalist) development or to move beyond capitalism, promoting new ways of thinking such as those encapsulated by the notion of *Buen Vivir/ Vivir Bien* (to 'live well' in social solidarity and in harmony with nature), a notion institutionalised in the constitutions (if not political practice) of both Bolivia and Ecuador (Acosta, 2012; Gudynas 2011). And the search for alternative forms and models of development also included the construction of a 'social and solidarity economy' based on cooperativism, workers' self-management and local development, as well as the attempt to build a 'socialism of the 21st Century' in Venezuela (Azzellini 2017). In this connection, we analyse how the experiences of China and Latin America are shaping thinking as to what options for transformatory change in peripheral areas in the future might be possible or feasible.

In keeping with the the approach of this volume, we focus not on the possibilities for sudden revolutionary transformational change – the overnight collapse of capitalism and its replacement with a detailed blueprint for an alternative – but on the prospects for change which do not rely on what the editors have termed 'catastrophism' as their starting point. Rather, we focus on pathways and the existence of hybridities as transitional institutional forms. As we will argue, hybridities are emerging which blur and break down the boundaries between capitalism and post-capitalism.

We conclude that many of these hybridities may not be desirable from an emancipatory perspective and contain problematic contradictions. While there may be islands of hope in the capitalist ocean, the general lesson drawn from our case studies is that the prospects for a transition to an emancipatory form of development in the periphery in present conditions are low. Even so, the widespread and diverse forms and forces of resistance that are emerging or that have emerged in the current conjuncture of the capitalist development process provide a measure of hope for the emergence of a potential alternative to capitalism. In Latin America, for example, people and communities with a legitimate claim to territory have engaged – in the words of David Barkin (2019: 2) – 'in concerted processes to consolidate a different constellation of societies on the margins of the global capitalist system'. In the words of the Introduction to this volume, we do find some instances of 'islands of non-capitalist life'.

CHINA'S HYBRIDITIES

China may at first sight be an odd place to look for alternatives to capitalism or post-capitalism as it has been widely described as shifting inexorably towards, and integrating with global capitalism over the past three decades. This turn to capitalism has generated its forces of resistance from workers, including migrant workers and a rural proletariat as well as the peasantry (Fan 2018; Bieler and Lee 2019; Zhang 2015). That China represents a form of capitalism is clear. But there remain two reasons why China raises interesting and awkward questions for a consideration of post-capitalism/alternatives. The first concerns the possibilities for economic 'catch-up', the second the nature and implications of property relations. Both have been challenges for the periphery: how can countries close the gap with the levels of material well-being found in the industrialised countries and what forms of (non-capitalist) property relations might be consistent with this? These were, of course, central concerns of the twentieth-century 'state socialist' countries but their demise does not make the challenges any less relevant for the future.

With respect to the first question, despite its many failings capitalism has proven itself as a dynamic system capable of raising living standards for a minority of the world's population. One central question in CDS is how such living standards might be achievable more broadly. In addressing this, the role of the state, and more specifically the uses of state power, has been seen as essential. This has crystallised around the idea of a developmental state, a state capable of grappling with the task of undertaking the multiple transformations necessary to rapidly and decisively raise mass living standards. In the Soviet case, this was encapsulated by the phrase 'Soviet power plus electrification'. This model did not succeed, but then few have. The central problem of how to achieve industrial country living standards through the exercise of state power has been addressed by many countries but answered successfully by only a small number. There are those, of course, who would argue that it is the wrong objective. The global ecological crisis, the privileged over-consumption of the global minority, and the drudgery of industrialisation are all reasons why other countries should not seek to emulate the path of the capitalist core, even if they seek to do so by more humane means. A different future should be imagined in which the crises of capitalist modernity are replaced with new forms of solidarity and human dignity; indeed this is the premise of some of the visions discussed in the next section.

But one strand of CDS thinking is not so quick to abandon the role of the state. The nagging issue of global inequality won't go away and utopian post-capitalist globalist visions confront the historic fact that no more than a handful of countries have successfully transitioned to the living standards of the capitalist core, and none have done so without the state being the central institutional vehicle for its achievement. Starting from the recognition of an unequal world, the potential of the state remains a key concern for CDS. As Katz (2018: 446) writes, a major lesson that can be drawn from political developments in the twentieth century is that both capitalism and socialism require the agency of the nation-state. In the absence of global redistribution on a scale hitherto unimaginable, the state is likely to remain central to efforts to close the gaps in living standards between the privileged Global North and the majority of the world's population in the Global South.

In accepting this starting point, CDS is then faced with the uncomfortable fact that the handful of successful (East Asian) developmental states have been neither democratic nor non-capitalist. The success of the East Asian model is well known but in many accounts the role of the state is seen primarily as that of an effective economic manager, an institution with the organisational capacity to effectively 'get prices wrong', in Amsden's (1992) famous phrase. The reorganisation of global capital into global value chains/global production networks has cast doubt on whether nation-states can pursue this path any longer, but this is again a question of how to manage insertion into global capitalism. CDS accepts the role of the state as manager but places this within the context of the state as a locus of power. That is, state power is exercised for a purpose and with class and gender consequences; the exclusion and suppression of organised labour in the successful capitalist developmental states, together with their inclusion of exploited low-waged, typically female, labour means that their path is seen as neither desirable nor as an alternative to anything but a neoliberal capitalist path. It is for this reason, that the search for a democratic developmental state model in both theory (White 1998) and in practice (see, for example, contemporary debates in South Africa) continues.

Within this strand of CDS, China is but the latest in the line of East Asian developmental states (such as Japan, South Korea and Taiwan) with China's 'rise', although still at modest levels of per capita GDP and a long way from those of the core capitalist countries, sharing many of the characteristics of its East Asian capitalist developmental state forerunners: suppressed labour, gendered employment, and authoritarian politics, along with the application of a fairly typical set of strategic economic policies (its openness to foreign investment being a notable exception to the 'standard package'). In many ways, therefore, China leads us to confront the old challenge of how to raise living standards in the periphery in ways which do not rely on the brutality of the capitalist developmental state, the only institutional configuration that has proven historically capable of the task thus far. CDS therefore contains a strand which views state agency as central for economic and social transformation. What CDS has not resolved though, is how the state can be captured and/or reconfigured to facilitate a progressive path to economic 'catch-up'. In this, China offers little hope and is beset with its own forms of economic, social, political and ecological crises.

Within the Chinese experience, however, we can also find some new hybridities when it comes to another central question, that of property rights. While for many, China is on a clear transition to capitalism, albeit with debates over what variety of capitalism (see, for example, Naughton and Tsai 2015; McNally 2012; Zhang and Peck 2016), it is also possible to see China's political economy as a hybrid form not (yet) entirely conforming to the dictates and logics of capitalism. In part, this is the result of path dependency and the residual elements of the Maoist model which continue to exist. Any alternative or post-capitalist society needs to find ways to move beyond private property. In China's rural sector the process of removing the peasantry from the land to form a proletariat remains to some degree incomplete. Arrighi (2009) identified this aspect of hybridity – the continued collective ownership of land – as a reason to argue that 'in spite of the spread of market exchanges in the pursuit of profit … the nature of development in China is not necessarily capitalist' (2009: 24).

What elements of 'not necessarily capitalist' property relations might be found in China which could inform future transitions? Ireland and Meng (2017) have argued that the rural sector displays a hybrid form of property rights that is consistent with Marx's delineations for post-capitalist property relations (see also Meng 2019). They argue that for Marx, post-capitalist societies would abolish capitalist private property but that other (non-capitalist) individual private property could coexist with collective forms and also '*within* property rights structures through a fragmentation of the property rights *bundle*' (2017: 372, emphasis in original). This, they argue, is exactly what is found in China's rural Household Responsibility System (HRS), where some parts of the property rights bundle (such as decisions as to what to grow, what inputs to use, and income streams derived from land use) are held privately, whereas others (such as the right to reallocate assets) are held collectively. Furthermore, they argue that the HRS, with its hybrid property rights system, was responsible for dramatic increases in agricultural productivity and incomes 'as well as the enhancement of individual autonomy and dignity' (Ireland and Meng, 2017: 21). For Ireland and Meng, therefore, at the theoretical level the HRS points to the possibilities for malleable property rights in post-capitalist societies which are not based on either full private or state ownership. Of course, in practice rural China has also experienced forced expropriations and illegal rural land use, as the authors acknowledge, to which we can add gender biases (Hare et al. 2007). Even in the case of land expropriation, however, it has not all been a process of 'accumulation by dispossession'.

In this connection Zhan (2019) has argued that at least a part of the expropriation has taken place without dispossession. As an example of one of a number of forms which this has taken, consider the case of the land expropriated for use by townships for the creation of rural industries in the 1980s. Here Zhan argues that, in return for giving up their land use rights, peasants were provided with secure jobs in the newly created rural industries, jobs which they typically preferred. Compensatory mechanisms such as these were substantially weakened in the 1990s, although returned to some extent as a result of peasant protests in the 2000s (Zhan 2019). The point again is to show that multiple pathways to industrialisation are possible with the right to land, a legacy of the socialist collective period, important in determining outcomes for peasants. The question of property rights is central to rural populations everywhere, with the benefits of 'group property' being analysed in India by Agarwal (2018), for example, and where Latin American experiences, discussed in the next section, are also instructive.

Of course, ownership per se is not the critical variable, but if it changes the system dynamics then we might argue that capitalism has been, if not replaced, then at least transformed into something else. In this respect, Ireland and Meng (2017) argue that the diffused bundle of property rights under the HRS has acted as a brake on the emergence of a 'fully capitalist dynamic', an outcome which they view as desirable.

A quite different conclusion about the benefits of China's property rights hybridities, however, is reached by Smith (2017) in his analysis of whether China can solve its (and our) ecological collapse. In providing his answer, he argues that the state-owned industrial sector is freed from the normal self-regulating constraints of capitalism, and that the absence of a capitalist dynamic leads to even less desirable outcomes. Smith argues that:

> in capitalism there is a one [sic] built-in, if temporary, limit to growth: profits. If companies cannot make a profit, they will cease production and lay off workers, sometimes masses of workers. Now and again, economic recession or collapse brings growth to a halt, at least temporarily, until sufficient value has been destroyed such that the cycle can begin all over again on an enlarged scale. Hence the business cycle. Further, in capitalist democracies, there is still some freedom to organise, so environmental organisations have been able to impose some restraint on pollution – gains which, as we know, are now under unprecedented assault. (2017: 5)

But, Smith adds, most of this does not apply to China's state-sector economy because China's rulers are not private capitalists but 'are bureaucratic collectivists who run a hybrid bureaucratic-collectivist capitalist economy, a system largely – although, of course, not entirely – exempted from the laws of capitalism' (2017: 6). So, here we have a form of capitalism – 'hybrid bureaucratic-collectivist' capitalism – that is 'largely exempted' from the 'laws of capitalism'. The reason is that, according to Smith, China's economy is not driven by profit maximisation but by the aim of 'maximising the security, power, and wealth of the Chinese Communist Party (CCP) bureaucracy' (2017: 6). This driver, Smith notes, is not automatic like the motor of competition in capitalism. In China's state-owned economy, growth is driven by the conscious decisions of party authorities. 'If the leaders choose to develop (or not develop) an industry, it will be developed (or not). Central planning replaces market competition to shape economic development' (2017: 6). This proposition that the economy is not subject to the profit constraints applied under capitalism in fact harks back to Kornai's (1992) analysis of state socialist societies as operating with 'soft budget constraints'. In Smith's hands, soft budget constraints lead not simply to Kornai's charge of economic inefficiency but to ecological destruction.

China's development experience therefore raises important questions. One is that tackling global inequalities between countries remains a central and inescapable concern, but the capitalist developmental states which have had some success in meeting this (limited) goal have not been progressive in the sense that they promoted democracy, equity or liberty, and China is no exception. Second, hybrid property forms which represent a movement away from capitalist property relations are possible, but they are capable of intensifying crises as well as spurring hope. There is no simple ending, but an ongoing struggle in China as elsewhere on the role of the state, forms of property relations, and class formation and resistance.

LATIN AMERICA'S HYBRIDITIES

It is a fundamental principle of Marxist political economy, that is, Historical Materialism, that progress in the development of the forces of production, and each advance in the march of capital, brings about a corresponding change in the relations of production as well as the forces of resistance and the class struggle associated with these forces. This principle is clearly illustrated in the cycles of development and resistance that have unfolded on the periphery of the world system in the post-Second World War period of capitalist development. In this period it is possible to trace out the contours of three such cycles, the first associated with the era of the developmental state (the 1950s–70s); the second relates to the neoliberal era associated with the installation of the new world order in the 1980s and 1990s; the third cycle is associated with the expansion of resource-seeking 'extractive' capital (invested in the extraction of natural resource wealth and its exportation in primary commodity form) in the 2000s and the reconfiguration of world economic power associated with the rise of China and the other BRICs.

Latin America is an important and particularly useful analytical laboratory for studying the dynamics of these three development-resistance cycles, and this is primarily because in no other region has the neoliberal policy agenda – a driving force in the current capitalist development process – been implemented so fully and with such a

Development Alternatives

devastating impact on the existing forces of production in both agriculture and industry; and in no other macro-region have the forces of resistance been so effective, generating not only powerful social movements to mobilise the forces of resistance, but also a number of theoretically defined and politically constructed alternatives – alternative (post-neoliberal) forms of development and alternative to (capitalist) development (Munck and Delgado Wise 2018).

These proposals for alternative models of development, alternative to both neoliberalism and to capitalism, were elaborated in the context of the 'progressive cycle' in Latin American politics (2002–15) associated with the turn of governments in South America – including Argentina, Brazil, Bolivia, Ecuador and Venezuela – towards 'inclusionary state activism', 'neodevelopmentalism' and 'neoextractivism' (using resource rents and the proceeds of primary commodity exports to finance poverty reduction programmes). On the economic and political dynamics of this progressive cycle or 'pink tide' see, among others, Veltmeyer and Petras (2014).

In this context, alternative proposals 'from below' (within the communities negatively impacted by the advance of extractive capital and the social movements formed to mobilise the forces of resistance) took three basic forms: that of (1) a post-development model (*Vivir Bien*, or *Buen Vivir*) elaborated on the basis of an Indigenous cosmovision as to how people can 'live well' in social solidarity and harmony with nature (Acosta 2012); (2) a model of community-based local development based on cooperativism and workers' self-management, as well as a culture of social solidarity. This model has taken the predominant form of experiments with constructing a 'social and solidarity economy' (SSE); and (3) a third model designed to find a pathway towards the 'socialism of the 21st century' as advanced in Venezuela (Katz 2018).

Buen Vivir as post-development

The concept of *Buen Vivir* or *Vivir Bien* is embedded in an Indigenous culture of solidarity and a conception of humans as part of nature and as guardians of a healthy environment and the rights of nature (Acosta 2012). The latter have been enshrined in new political constitutions of a plurinational / multi-ethnnic state enacted in both Bolivia and Ecuador by 'progressive' regimes with their social base in the country's Indigenous communities and nationalities (Acosta 2012).

As for the model of post-development so conceived, given the unsettled debate regarding the neoextractivist strategy of national development adopted by both regimes – a strategy that has come under heavy criticism from the Indigenous communities and the intelligentsia/leftist economists – it has yet to take a definitive form. These continue to debate the contradictory features of a strategy and policies that rely on the agency of extractive capital – direct foreign investment in the large-scale acquisiton of land and the extraction of natural resources that are exported in a form and under conditions that entail superprofits for global capital, exceedingly high socio-environmental costs borne by the communities most directly affected by the destructive operations of extractive capital, and the violation of the territorial rights of these community members as well as the rights of nature (Gudynas 2013; Veltmeyer and Petras 2014).

As Barkin (2019) has argued, the struggle of the Indigeneous communities on the frontier of extractive capital should be understood not as a class struggle for land and labour but as a territorial struggle[3] – a struggle of these communities to reclaim their territorial rights and the rights of nature – a struggle fundamentally informed by an Indigenous conception of an alternative universe, an alternative reality or uchronia, which Barkin views as embedded in the notion *Buen Vivir*. In terms of this ucronia, Indigenous and peasant communities throughout the Americas are self-consciously restructuring their organisations and governance structures, taking control of territories they have claimed for generations. As documented by Barkin, in addition to mobilising their forces of resistance against the operations of extractive capitalism these communities, which Barkin conceives of as a 'collective revolutionary subject', are also 'reorganizing production [so as] to generate a surplus, assembling their members to take advantage of underutilized resources and peoples' energies for improving their ability to raise living standards and assure environmental conservation and restoration' (2019: 1).

These communities do not operate in isolation. They coordinate activities, share information, and build alliances (Abya Yala 2009). Indeed, Barkin (2019) argues that hundreds of millions of people are participating in this growing movement; furthermore, there is great potential for others to join them, expanding from the substantial areas where they are already operational, and forming alliances and regional and global social networks to ensure that this dynamic of social change might grow.

Constructing a social and solidarity economy

As Barkin and Sánchez (2017) have noted, across Latin America today people are organising alternative ways of securing their livelihoods and communities based on local development, social exchange and cooperativism – local development, or ecological economics, either constructed 'from below' (that is, from within the community) or in pursuit of a strategy designed by agents of international cooperation (agencies of development, such as the World Bank) as a way of relieving pressures on a saturated or dysfunctional urban labour market, or governments seeking to manage the demands and needs of a burgeoning surplus urban population.

In these diverse collective actions and experiments, there are two fundamentally different conceptions of a social and solidarity economy: one advanced as part of a strategy to manage the complex dynamics of urban and rural development, the other as part of a grassroots and social movement strategy for confronting what the Zapatistas term the 'capitalist hydra' (EZLN Sexta Comisión 2015) and finding alternatives that offer more opportunities and a better quality of life than that offered by today's capitalist economy. The idea here is that the various strategies devised by the international organisations and forces involved in the project of international cooperation and development, including a strategy of community-based local development based on the empowerment of the poor (mobilising their social capital for self-development, to have them 'own' their own development), are designed as mechanisms of adjustment that are functional for the continuation of capitalism. From a leftist perspective this strategy can well be seen as a neoliberal ploy to defend the system from the forces of resistance, a bastardised hybrid form of 'local development'.

In contrast, in the Latin American context, the construction of a social economy has been closely associated with diverse experiments with the cooperative movement and diverse experiences with worker self-management and worker-managed factories based on workers' councils and factory assemblies that emerged in the broader context of what might be described as a class struggle (Azzellini 2017). This is evident in all three phases of post-war capitalist development.

For example, in Chile under the socialist regime of Salvador Allende (1970–73), over 125 factories came under some system of worker self-management. About half of these factories were controlled by public officials or functionaries, representing a parliamentary form of government with its left–centre–right political split; the other half was run by factory-level commissions of workers organised along the lines of workers' councils or soviets, much like the Paris Commune of mid-nineteenth-century France. And then we have Argentina in the context of the 2001–2 crisis, when workers occupied and took over more than 200 factories, defending them from closure, protecting workers' employment and vastly improving the social conditions of work – and, most importantly, raising workers' political consciousness. Most of these factories – ERTs as some have termed them (Enterprises Recovered by their Workers) – were organised as worker self-managed cooperatives or worker collectives (Azzellini 2017). We can also cite the experience of Bolivia in the wake of the 1952 Revolution, and Peru in 1967, when a group of progressive nationalist military officers led by General Velasco Alvarez took power and expropriated a large number of mines/factories/plantations, establishing a system of industrial cooperatives (and communities) based on joint decision making by management and workers.

The case of Brazil is very important, although rarely discussed in the literature. Currently more than 200 companies have been 'recovered' by workers, with the first experience being at the shoe factory Makerli in 1991. ANTEAG (the National Association of Workers in Self-Managed Companies) was established in 1994 with the aim of coordinating the various projects that materialised in conditions of crisis and near collapse of industry. It has offices in six states in charge of accompanying self-management projects, seeking integration with non-governmental organisations, state and municipal governments. ANTEAG views self-management as an organisational model that combines collective ownership of the means of production with autonomy of enterprise decision making and active participation in democratic management.

The important point about these and other such experiments with cooperativism and unionism, and the construction of a social and solidarity economy based on community-based local development, is that they need to be understood in the broader context of capitalist development, the history of capitalism in the region.

CONCLUSIONS

For countries on the periphery of the global capitalist system, the challenges of the future include some familiar ones, namely, how to close the gap in living standards with the industrialised countries, and how to share the world's resources and income more equitably within and between countries. To these familiar challenges may be added the new one of ecological destruction. CDS argues that such challenges cannot be understood without analysing the systemic dynamics and fundamental contradictions of capitalism, and that alternatives to capitalism are likely to be found on the periphery rather than at the centre of the world system.

In surveying the recent experiences and development dynamics of China and Latin America we have highlighted a number of hybridities which may inform how alternatives to capitalism may evolve. For example, the hybrid ownership forms in rural China offer some evidence of how capitalist property relations might be transformed; the Latin American experiments in constructing a social and solidarity economy also show how post-capitalist property relations and participatory development (truly democratic decision making) might be constituted; the powerful forces of resistance to the advance of capital on the extractive frontier that have emerged in Latin America have paved various ways of moving beyond capitalism in the twenty-first century.

One way has been pioneered by the Indigenous communities on the extractive frontier engaged in a territorial struggle to reclaim their access to the global commons of land, water, and their territorial rights. The key to this struggle is an Indigenous conception of how to live well in social solidarity and harmony with nature. The problem with this approach, however, is how to scale up the process of productive and social transformation to the level of national development. Two governments in Latin America (Ecuador and Bolivia) have taken up the challenge, but in the context of a world system dominated by capital, and the pressures on them to integrate into this system via a globalisation process, both governments were constrained to develop a hybrid form of post-development, combining an Indigenous conception of *living well* (*Buen Vivir*) with *neodevelopmentalism* (the search for a more inclusive form of development) and *neoextractivism* (using the proceeds of community exports to finance a process of poverty reduction). However, it seems that this hybrid model, dependent as it was on a cycle of high prices for commodity exports, has failed, foundering on the reef of capitalist development.

Another pathway of alternative development and transformative change has been pioneered in Venezuela: 'the socialism of the twenty-first century', advanced with the agency not only of the state but grassroots organisation in the communities. However, this hybrid form of socialism cum capitalism has also fallen victim not only to the forces of US imperialism but also to various problems and contradictions of extractive capitalism (such as an over-reliance on natural resource extraction).

At best, the diverse Latin American experiments and experiences with 'socialism' and alternative forms of 'post-development' offer glimpses of what might be possible. And in times of multiple and profound capitalist crises glimpses of alternatives are important.

NOTES

1. See: https://www.worldbank.org/en/about
2. See: https://www.undp.org/content/undp/en/home/sustainable-development-goals.html

3. In discussing the 'global commons' a distinction needs to be made between 'land', which, according to Walter Barraza, a representative member of the Tonokote people – the *camache* (chief) of the Tonokote people of the Santiago del Estero province, Argentina – 'relates to private property' as a 'capitalist concept', whereas 'territory includes ... people who live in that place ... [with an] obligation to take care of its nature'. He adds that 'we native peoples live in harmony with our animal brothers, plants, water. We are part of the territory, which provides us with everything we need. Cutting forests down is like cutting a limb. They are coming for natural resources, while we live in harmony with those resources' (Pedrosa 2017).

REFERENCES

Abya Yala – Movimientos Indígenas, Campesinos y Sociales (2009) 'Diálogo de Alternativas y Alianzas', Minga Informativa de Movimientos Sociales. La Paz, 26 de Febrero.

Acosta, A. (2012) *Buen Vivir. Sumak kawsay. Una oportunidad para imaginar otros mundos*. Quito: Abya Yala.

Agarwal, B. (2018) 'Can Group Farms Outperform Individual Family Farms? Empirical Insights from India', *World Development* 108: 57–73.

Amsden, A. (1992) *Asia's Next Giant: South Korea and Late Industrialization*. Oxford: Oxford University Press.

Arrighi, G. (2009) *Adam Smith in Beijing: Lineages of the 21st Century*. London: Verso.

Azzellini, D. (2017) *Communes and Workers' Control in Venezuela: Building 21st Century Socialism from Below*. Leiden: Brill.

Barkin, D. (2019) 'The Communitarian Revolutionary Subject: New Forms of Social Transformation', *Third World Quarterly* June.

Barkin, D. and A. Sánchez (2017) 'The Collective Revolutionary Subject: New forms of Social Transformation', unedited paper for 'Revolutions: A Conference', Winnipeg, September.

Bieler, A. and C.-Y. Lee (2019) *Chinese Labour in the Global Economy: Capitalist Exploitation and Strategies of Resistance*. London: Routledge.

EZLN, Sexta Comisión (2015) *El pensamiento crítico frente a la hidra capitalista*, vol. 1. http://enlacezapatista.ezln.org.mx/2015/07/13/indice-volumen-uno-participaciones-de-la-comision-sexta-del-ezln-en-el-seminario-el-pensamiento-critico-frente-a-la-hidra-capitalista (accessed 9 November 2020).

Fan, S. (2018) *Striking to Survive: Workers' Resistance to Factory Relocations in China*. Chicago: Haymarket Books.

Foster, J.B. (2002) 'Capitalism and Ecology: The Nature of the Contradiction', *Monthly Review* 54(04): 6–16.

Foster, J.B., B. Clark and R. York (2010) *The Ecological Rift: Capitalism's War on the Earth*. New York: Monthly Review Press.

Gudynas, E. (2011) 'Buen Vivir: Today's Tomorrow', *Development* 54(4): 441–447.

Gudynas, E. (2013) 'Debates on Development and its Alternatives in Latin America: A Brief Heterodox Guide', in M. Lang, L. Fernando and N. Buxton (eds) *Beyond Development: Alternative Visions from Latin America*. Amsterdam: Transnational Institute.

Hare, D., L. Yang and D. Englander (2007) 'Land Management in Rural China and its Gender Implications', *Feminist Economics* 13(3–4): 35–61.

Ireland, P. and G. Meng (2017) 'Post-capitalist Property', *Economy and Society* 46(3): 369–397.

Katz, C. (2018) 'Socialism and Development: A Latin American Perspective', in H. Veltmeyer, and P. Bowles (eds) *The Essential Guide to Critical Development Studies*. London: Routledge, pp. 435–450.

Kay, C. (2018) 'Development Theory: The Latin American Pivot', in H. Veltmeyer and P. Bowles (eds) *The Essential Guide to Critical Development Studies*, London: Routledge, pp. 73–83.

Kornai, J. (1992) *The Socialist System: The Political Economy of Communism*. Princeton, NJ: Princeton University Press.

McNally, C. (2012) 'Sino-capitalism: China's Reemergence and the International Political Economy', *World Politics* 64(4): 741–776.

Meng, G. (2019) 'The Household Responsibility System, Karl Marx's Theory of Property and Antony M. Honoré's Concept of Ownership', *Science & Society* 83(3): 300–326.

Munck, R. and R. Delgado Wise (2018) *Rethinking Latin American Development*. London: Routledge.

Naughton, B. and K. Tsai (2015) *State Capitalism, Institutional Adaptation and the Chinese Miracle*. Cambridge: Cambridge University Press.

Pedrosa, M. (2017) 'Argentina: Native Communities Face Eviction, Death if Protective Law is not Renewed by Congress', *Tiempo Argentino / Resumen Latinoamericano* 8 September.

Petras, J. and H. Veltmeyer (2013) *Imperialism and Capitalism in the Twenty-first Century: A System in Crisis*. Farnham: Ashgate.

Petras, J. and H. Veltmeyer (2019) *Latin America in the Vortex of Social Change*. London: Routledge.

Smith, R. (2017) 'China's Drivers and Planetary Ecological Collapse', *Real-World Economics Review* 82.
Veltmeyer, H. and P. Bowles (2018) *The Essential Guide to Critical Development Studies*. London: Routledge.
Veltmeyer, H. and R. Delgado Wise (2018) *Critical Development Studies: An Introduction*. Halifax: Fernwood Publications.
Veltmeyer, H. and J. Petras (2014) *The New Extractivism: A Model for Latin America?* London: Zed Books.
Wallace, R., A. Leibman, L. Chaves and R. Wallace (2020) 'COVID-19 and Circuits of Capital', *Monthly Review* 72: 1.
White, G. (1998) 'Building a Democratic Developmental State: Social Democracy in the Developing World', *Democratization* 5(3).
Zhan, S. (2019) 'Accumulation by and without Dispossession: Rural Land Use, Land Expropriation, and Livelihood Implications in China', *Journal of Agrarian Change* 19: 447–464.
Zhang, J. and J. Peck (2016) 'Variegated Capitalism, Chinese Style: Regional Models, Multi-scalar Constructions', *Regional Studies* 50(1): 52–78.
Zhang, W. (2015) 'Leadership, Organization and Moral Authority: Explaining Peasant Militancy in Contemporary China', *The China Journal* 73: 59–83.

5
'Property Belongs to Allah, Capital, Get Out!' Turkey's Anti-capitalist Muslims and the Concept of Alternatives to Capitalism

Gorkem Altinors

This chapter[1] analyses the emergence of Turkey's Anti-capitalist Muslims as a non-Eurocentric example of the struggle against capitalist modernity and it discusses their understanding of anti-capitalist visions vis-à-vis the endings of capitalism. The Anti-capitalist Muslims is a socio-political movement, made famous by their participation in the 2013 Gezi Park protests and their stance against the rise of Islamic capitalism. In 2013, the insistence of Erdoğan and his party, the AKP (Justice and Development Party), on demolishing Gezi Park in Taksim Square, Istanbul, to replace it with a shopping centre, caused a popular outcry nationwide demanding that the government resign. Although the Anti-capitalist Muslims' ideological foundation is based in Islam, in 2013 their fellow Muslim co-religionists in power did not share the same understanding as far as the commodification of the public sphere is concerned. The group's participation in and support for the protests was crucial in terms of demonstrating that the uproar was not necessarily aimed against Islamic values by secular fractions of society, it was rather against the commodification of public goods and increasing authoritarianism. For example, İhsan Eliaçık, a critical theologian and one of the prominent names among the Anti-capitalist Muslims, 'addressed a huge crowd, linking Prophet Mohammed's struggle for social justice with the Gezi Park uprising against the "Muslim elites and bourgeoisie"' (Uestebay 2019). The emergence of Anti-capitalist Muslims not only challenges the notorious 'secularists versus Islamists' dichotomy in Turkey, it also opens a new window in terms of the imagining of an anti-capitalist society.

What would an anti-capitalist society look like, or, given the variegated nature of capitalism (Peck and Theodore 2007) and the multiplicity of alternatives to capitalism, will there be variegated or multiple anti-capitalist alternatives at the end of capitalism? Perhaps the question of alternatives to capitalism will remain a nebulous subject because the question itself has different answers for different people. Like all socially constructed concepts, alternatives to capitalism and visions of anti-capitalism also differ according to geographical and cultural variations. This not only means there is a variety of understandings among different people within individual societies and different social contexts, it also means something different to individuals in the West and people in the East. This spatio-cultural division brings us to another question: Does religion have an impact on the perception of the alternative to capitalism? If so, what would an anti-capitalist society look like within Islam? If there is an Islamic capitalism, will there be an Islamic alternative to anti-capitalism too? By taking a look at the Islamic alternatives to capitalism and incorporating Islamic alter-globalisation movements within the discussion, the purpose of this chapter is to provide a non-Eurocentric vision of an anti-capitalist future. Islam's relationship with capitalism has always been considered controversial and notoriously antagonistic (Weber 1965 [1922]; Turner 2010). Islam and the capitalist mode of production have long been considered incompatible, and it has been assumed that the lack of liberal principles in the Islamic world derives from Islam's own disharmony with capitalism (Huntington 1996). The pre-capitalist mode of production in the non-West has been explained through an understanding based on 'patrimonialism', that is, a non-feudal Asiatic type of production. Patrimonialism takes for granted the historical difference between the Western and the Eastern world and constructs the development of capitalism on these differences. However, today, this representation has changed. Although there are several (perhaps overlapping and contradictory) explanations attempting to provide a sensible theory of how Islam integrated into capitalism, there is no doubt that the Islamic world is undeniably articulated with the capitalist mode of production. Capitalist development in Turkey, Egypt, Iran, Saudi Arabia and Tunisia in the twentieth century could be given as examples, though each represents a unique case and is distinct from the others. There is recent progress in the research agenda that focuses on the symbiotic relationship between (political) Islam and capitalism (Rodinson 1974; Banaji 2007; Tuğal 2009; Atasoy 2008). However, it is equally imperative that this research programme should also focus on anti-capitalist movements in the Islamic world and study how the anti-capitalist future is perceived within Islamic capitalism and its discontents. If the development of capitalist modernity has taken a diverse path in the Middle East and North Africa, would there be divergence in forms of resistance to this development too?

In this contribution, I aim to provide answers to these three questions: (1) Are there any Islamic alternatives to global capitalism or is it simply Islam's articulation into capitalism (i.e. Islamic capitalism)? (2) If there is an Islamic capitalism, will there be an Islamic alternative to anti-capitalism too? (3) What are the possibilities of progressive and radical alter-movements against capitalism within Islamic social movements? The aim of this chapter is to provide answers to the questions of what the possibilities of progressive and radical alter-movements against Islamic capitalism and the alternatives to global capitalism are. This chapter will focus in particular on Islamic capitalism in Turkey, and will analyse what the anti-capitalist Islamic movements in Turkey are offering to the anti-capitalist future. In Turkey, there will be a specific focus on the Anti-capitalist Muslims, a resistance group that emerged as a grassroots movement and gained popularity during the Gezi Park protests. I conducted a semi- structured interview with a prominent founding member of this group.

BACKGROUND

In this section, three arguments are elaborated. First, it is argued that our understanding of capitalism in the 'East' is Eurocentric; second, the analytical tools we have used to interpret it are, therefore, also Eurocentric; and, third, a critical International Political Economy

(IPE) perspective can overcome Eurocentrism. To start with, it is important to elucidate why/how our understanding of capitalism in the 'East' and the analytical tools to unravel it are Eurocentric. The pre-capitalist mode of production in the non-West is explained through an understanding based on patrimonialism. This Weberian term indicates the dominance of the head of state over civil society in the pre-capitalist era. The emergence of patrimonialism could be dated back to the Roman Empire. As opposed to the Ancient Greek *polis* and the short-lived Macedonian Empire, politics in the Roman Empire was based on private property and its social relations. For instance, according to the famous Roman statesman, Cicero, the purpose of the state is to protect private property (Wood N. 1983). This understanding manifested itself under the separation of the public and private spheres, or in other words the *imperium* and the *dominium*. The first term defines the right of the head of state as the sovereign to rule, the latter rather describes the right of the owner on their property. This separation later articulated in Christianity, and led to the famous separation of Church and state – render unto Caesar the things that are Caesar's, and unto God the things that are God's (Wood E.M. 2008). Following the collapse of the Western Roman Empire in 476, civil society groups in Europe gained autonomy from this separation and the lords, who started to confiscate the agrarian surplus from the peasants who lived on their land, formed the aristocracy against the kingdom/state throughout the medieval ages amidst the lack of a strong empire.

Feudalism emerged in Europe on the ruins of the Roman Empire and manifested itself as what Perry Anderson (1974) calls the 'parcellisation of sovereignty'. Lords started to overstep on *imperium* and used the right of the head of state as sovereign on the peasants who lived on the lord's land. This could be seen as the fragmentation of law in one state as there were four different authorities at times who claimed to be the holder of *imperium* over peasants: the lords, the king, the emperor, and the Pope. With one exception (England), this was pretty much the case in continental Europe until the early modern ages, when secular authorities started to gain power as the understanding of 'absolute and inseparable sovereignty' became the dominant regime. In England, even under agrarian feudalism, the state was centralised and law was unified. According to this understanding, a secular authority (king, queen, prince, etc.) is the absolute sovereign, as neither lords nor the Pope can legitimately claim sovereignty because neither of them is given the authority to rule by the people. This strengthened the separation of Church and state as the source of political legitimacy had moved from God to the people. Following the Reformation, the Renaissance and the Enlightenment, European states became more and more centralised in terms of sovereignty within the separation of Church and state. Capitalism arguably was born in England, initially as agrarian capitalism in the aftermath of the enclosure movement, partly because of its exceptional conditions under feudalism. The convergence of capitalism with secularism in the West derived from the political legacy of the Western Roman Empire and its private property regime.

On the other hand, the Eastern side of the Roman Empire, which split away to form the Byzantine Empire, did not have the same separation as such. The head of the state was also the head of Church and also the owner of the most significant amount of land in the state. Therefore, the emperor was the main extractor of the agrarian surplus and, at the same time, was the holder of both what is Caesar's and God's. This situation was more or less the same under the Arab/Islamic Empire and the successor of the Byzantine Empire, the Ottomans. This absolutist regime created almost no room for civil society to flourish and led to the unification of Church and the state under one ruler, until the contemporary age. According to notions of patrimonialism, feudalism did not develop in the East as the state never allowed any lords to extract a substantive agrarian surplus and thus become competitors to the emperor. Ultimately, this led to an underdevelopment in the East and thus capitalism never became part of the Islamic world. Even Gramsci subscribed to this division of the West and the East in his formulation of 'the integral state', stating that: '[i]n the East, the state was everything, civil society was primordial and gelatinous; in the West, there was a proper relation between state and civil society, and when the state tottered, a sturdy structure of civil society was immediately revealed' (Gramsci 2007: 169). Patrimonialism's attempt to conceptualise capitalism and Islam in a mutually exclusive way is rooted in this historical narrative.

I identify three main problems with understandings based on the notion of patrimonialism. The main problem with patrimonialism derives from the way it is used to compare the West and the East. The lack of institutions such as feudal lords, serfs, vassals and so on in the East is interpreted as the lack of feudalism. However, if feudalism is defined as an agrarian regime in which the peasantry used the land as a means of production to feed themselves and their family but then the rest of this production was confiscated by somebody else (the head of state or landlords) all pre-industrial societies can be given as examples. This approach is clearly Eurocentric as it relies on empirical evidence from Europe or the West to make a comparison with the East (Dinler 2003). The second problem with patrimonialism is that the state and civil society are considered as ontologically autonomous and antagonistic entities. The dualist understanding of state–society relations does not consider the split between those concepts methodologically but ontologically. Those two spheres appear as two independent entities without a symbiotic relationship or with very limited interconnectedness. This understanding, based on a non-symbiotic relationship, is called 'ontological exteriority' (Morton 2013). This feature is problematic because it obstructs the ability of the analysis to comprehend the internal dynamic between the state and civil society, as it neglects their interdependent relationship or downgrades their relationship into one of limited dependence. Third, as a result of the state–society dualism, the economic and the political (in other words, the market, and the state) are considered separately and antagonistically. The pitfalls of 'ontological exteriority', such as the neglect of interdependence and interconnectedness between spheres, apply in these dualisms too. Similar to the first problem, this feature causes an a-historical understanding of the relationship of those spheres and prevents us understanding the internal relations between them.

Given the shortcomings of patrimonialism, Eurocentrism, and ontological exteriority, the relationship between Islam and capitalism has always been conceptualised externally by Weberian accounts. I argue that a critical IPE perspective can overcome these shortcomings; thus this contribution will adopt a critical IPE approach to the historical sociology of Islam and capitalism. The crises of contemporary capitalism reflect its variegated nature, and the conceptualisation of anti-capitalism is variegated too. Today, the development of capitalism in the Islamic world is historically distinct from its counterpart in Europe. Thus, it is safe to argue that resistance against capitalism and the imaginaries of anti-capitalism are characteristic of this distinctive capitalism too. To avoid the pitfalls of patrimonialism in conceptualising Islamic capitalism, it is imperative to move beyond methodological nationalism and internationalism, as these are embedded in the patrimonial understanding. 'Methodological nationalism' is one of the crucial understandings that mainstream IPE inherited from sociology. Societies are assumed to be separate from each other and they are immune to 'the international'. Social change and domestic politics in one individual state are determined by only its own 'isolated' dynamics. The borders between states not only separate the sovereigns but also societies from one another. History, as well, is based on this same 'state-centrism', and its 'methodological internationalism' assumes that individual states are isolated from each other and also from their own civil societies, while nation-states, oriented towards their own self-interest, are believed to be the main actors in the making of the inter-state system. Also, a nation-state's domestic and international affairs are assumed to be mutually exclusive, as each individual state's external relations with its own civil society is limited to a certain territory. The role of 'the international' and civil society is almost entirely neglected. Mainstream IPE adopts this externally constructed and yet symbiotic relationship between history and sociology, and ultimately this makes mainstream International Relations (IR) a Eurocentric discipline because assumptions based on an understanding that derives from spatially and historically constructed state–society and inter-state relations are considered as universally acknowledged. Hence (mainstream) 'International Political Economy' is based on state-centric methodological nationalism/internationalism. Today, a non-Eurocentric IR that goes beyond the limits of methodological nationalism/internationalism is needed.

This chapter argues that, alone, neither history nor sociology nor mainstream IPE can challenge Eurocentrism in IR/IPE theory and elucidate the origins and emergence of capitalism holistically.

However, critical IPE can. Ironically, the legacy of sociology and history makes mainstream IPE an a-historical discipline that ignores the social. Critical IPE's dialectical unity transcends the pitfalls of ontological exteriority in methodological nationalism/internationalism, and incorporates history and sociology integrally within the international. Critical IPE, on the one hand, does not consider state–civil society relations as external to each other, nor does it consider them within a territorially limited context; on the other hand, it amalgamates state–civil society relations with history. In other words, critical IPE first considers state–civil society relations as a symbiosis, as it does not separate them ontologically, it then provides to state–civil society relations (1) a historical depth as the vertical axis and (2) an international context as the horizontal axis and, finally, puts state–civil society relations at the centre. Therefore, it is safe to argue that it not only challenges the *a-historical*, *a-sociological* and *positivist* features, and thus the Eurocentric nature of mainstream IPE by bringing in a historical, sociological and post-positivist perspective, it also reveals the limits of the neo-Weberian criticism of Eurocentrism by its understanding of state–civil society relations. Critical IPE will not only provide a path that leads to a holistic understanding of the development of capitalist modernity across the globe by challenging Weberian patrimonialism, it will also help us to comprehend the variegated nature of capitalism, in which contemporary neoliberalism is incorporated with authoritarianism (Bruff 2014; Bruff and Tansel 2018; Tansel 2017, 2018) under austerity to move towards emancipatory anti-capitalism(s).

THE ANTI-CAPITALIST MUSLIMS IN TURKEY

The relationship between Islam and capitalism in Turkey has always been a unique case (Altinors 2019), like its forms of anti-capitalist resistance. To identify and capture these, I undertook interviews with some activists who joined the Gezi Park protests in 2013. The Gezi Park protests in 2013 were perhaps the greatest challenge to the rule of the AKP up to that point. The AKP's 'Turkish Model' has long been considered as a challenge to the orthodox claim that Islam and Western values – such as liberalism, capitalism, modernity, and democracy – cannot coexist as they are ontologically incompatible. The electoral success of the pro-Islamic AKP in 2002 was welcomed as an example of this. The AKP was rooted in political Islamic mobilisation on the one hand, and yet its political discourse was articulated around liberal democracy and a free-market economy on the other. The AKP's pro-Islamic, but still liberal, democratic and pro-EU governance has been taken as evidence that the orthodox claim is flawed. However, this did not last forever and, after eleven years, things had changed. Most of the analysts specialising in the politics of Turkey and MENA (the Middle East and North Africa) saw the Gezi uprising in 2013 as a breakdown in Turkish politics in terms of the AKP's transition from a democratic-liberal government to a heavy-handed and authoritarian power cluster. Despite the problematic nature of the chrono-dualism and a clear-cut temporal dissociation (Tansel 2018) in this reading, it is safe to argue that the Gezi Park protests have changed politics in Turkey.

The emergence of Anti-capitalist Muslims reflects the crisis of Islamic capitalism in Turkey. The crisis of Turkey's Islamic capitalism in 2013 involves not only resistance against the authoritarian neoliberal assault on people's right to their city (Kuymulu 2013) but also contained a challenge to the top-down Islamicisation of society. The Anti-capitalist Muslims had gained nationwide popularity during the Gezi Park protests. Their background as devout Muslims and pious members of society, combined with their political standpoint against the AKP's neoliberal globalisation, was a big challenge to the orthodox claim that the main struggle in Turkey is between secularists and Islamists. The portrayal of the Gezi uprising in the mainstream media and academia was based on this narrative: neglecting working-class agency in the protests and labelling the uprising as secularist civil society opposing the Islamist government. First of all, ignoring the class character in these protests is problematic. For example, Cihan Tuğal claims that 'only the middle class participated with a discernible *class belonging* in the protests, while 'working-class *unions were near-absent* and *professional associations weighed in heavily*'. 'What is as important is that proletarian and subproletarian participation was heaviest in Alevi regions' (Tuğal 2016: 259, original emphasis).

However, it is evident that both the KESK (Confederation of Public Workers' Unions – around 250,000 members) and DİSK (Confederation of Revolutionary Trade Unions of Turkey – around 120,000 members) called for a general strike during the uprising. The success or failure of a call for a general strike cannot simply be reduced to the lack of working-class participation, it rather lies with neoliberal governance. Second, it is very problematic to neglect the proletarian class character of professional associations in Turkey, which played a key and pivotal role during the Gezi revolt. Third, reducing Alevi identity to proletarian characteristics is also problematic in terms of ignoring the intersectionality of class relations. Finally, reducing class-belonging to consumption habits and education levels, and defining wage labour as middle class demonstrate a misreading of the Gramscian term, hegemony (Altinors 2017). Furthermore, research on the protesters indicates that 67.1 per cent of protesters were aged 30 and below and, given Turkey's youth unemployment rate of 20.1 per cent in 2013, one of the highest among the OECD (Organisation for Economic Co-operation and Development) countries, and the precarious work conditions that employed youngsters are compelled to accept, it is safe to argue that there was a very strong working-class agency in these protests.

Labelling the entire body of demonstrators 'secular' is also an over-generalisation. The movement was initially organised by Taksim Solidarity, which consisted of 118 constituent groups from different backgrounds. Apart from Taksim Solidarity, the profile of individual protesters was quite heterogeneous and included Kurds, Alevis, LGBT communities, feminists, nationalists, liberals, socialists, anarchists, communists, social democrats, ultras of football clubs, students, Kemalists and Muslims (Kuymulu 2018). Muslims' involvement in the movement cannot be ignored. In particular, Anti-capitalist Muslims, Revolutionary Muslims, and Mazlumder were the main Muslim communities involved in the protests. For instance, the spokesman of Anti-capitalist Muslims, İhsan Eliaçık, led the Friday prayer twice, on 7 and 14 July, in front of the tent mosque in Gezi Park, and participation levels were high. Those who were not praying at that moment formed a human chain to protect praying protesters. The *iftars* on İstiklal Avenue organised by Anti-capitalist Muslims were much more popular than the official *iftars* organised by Istanbul's AKP municipality in the square. One of the Anti-capitalist Muslims' slogans was self-explanatory in understanding their presence there: 'Property is Allah's; capital, get out of Taksim!' A Revolutionary Muslims' banner was more detailed: 'Trees worship Allah, the AKP worships capital'. Ozgur Kazim Kivanc, one of the founding members of Anti-capitalist Muslims, who define themselves as 'anti-capitalist Muslim workers', clarified their participation in Gezi as follows: 'Urbanisation is a class project where only one certain class benefits from the blessings of the city whereas the poor are being imprisoned in ghettos, I know because I live in a ghetto' (personal interview, 14 February 2015).

Anti-capitalist Muslims are the members of the Foundation to Fight Against Capitalism. The name of this foundation refers back to one of the Islamist-conservative organisations from the 1970s, the Foundation to Fight Against Communism. It was founded in 2012 and has been very active since then. The members adopted an Islamic discourse to combine it with anti-capitalism. For example, one of the historical slogans of labour movements in Turkey, 'work, bread, freedom' was changed by them to 'Allah, bread, freedom'. They also refer to Islam's doctrine and terminology to indicate the contemporary class struggle: 'There is no way that we are in the same line during the prayer, but in different lines in terms of *rızık* [an Islamic term to define livelihood]'. They use Quranic verses to justify their cause as well: 'And we wanted to confer favour upon those who were oppressed in the land and make them leaders and make them inheritors' (Al-Qasas 25:5).

In his interview, Ozgur Kazim Kivanc explained the Anti-capitalist Muslims' view on capitalism in urban space as follows:

> The emergence of cities and classes are parallel and the dominant class imposes its lifestyle on us. This is like production of consent. The project [demolition of park and establishment of shopping centre in the Gezi Park] will help the dominant classes make the masses in metropolitan cities serve them. Because shopping centres means hotels, it means fast food, so it leads to consumption. However, a park is public; nobody needs to pay to go there. That's why we said 'Property belongs to Allah, capital get out' on

our banner. I think it was the most meaningful banner in Gezi.... Also, we were representing the closest group [ideologically] to the AKP. That's why it is very crucial in terms of class. For instance, some groups made a security chain while we were praying, and they offered to celebrate *kandil* [Islamic holy nights] at Gezi, and we forgot it was *kandil*. This convergence of different ideological groups was really important in class terms ... such as LGBT communities that built the mosque there for us, actually it wasn't us.... Because it was so crucial to be there to resist against someone monopolising the means of production and Allah's blessings of the earth such as land, water, and air. (personal interview, 14 February 2015)

It is important to highlight the usage of Islamic and Marxist terminology in the same sentence. Notwithstanding that, Mücella Yapıcı, a socialist feminist who is the former general secretary of the Chamber of Architects and the Secretary of Taksim Solidarity, who comes from a secular background, shares the same understanding:

The public sphere should be understood as a 'World's property', I mean 'property belongs to Allah'. We have to say that these properties like water, air, land, and the planet are everyone's property; no state, no person should claim any of them exclusively. (personal interview, 26 November 2015)

Also, some prominent Muslim authors and scholars penned a declaration under the name of the Labour and Justice Coalition. They point out how capitalism is not in accordance with Islam and how neoliberalism has damaged Islamic society. As noted in the following statement, this group has also highlighted that the current government's rise to power was marked by a struggle against a heavy-handed Kemalism, but eventually they ended up replacing their former foes' practice:

In every location undergoing gentrification, attempts are being made to clear the path for a new and elite style of life – partly modern and partly conservative.... People who fought for trees harbouring the poor and homeless were faced with the harshest form of the State's hubris for protesting the top-down decision to transfer this park into capital.... Our neighbourhood is dying out. We almost turned into a society whose poor and rich are praying in different mosques. Don't you want our kids to neighbour the poor, and befriend them? A consumption culture that finds its expression in malls is leading us all into a future from which we cannot return. (Labour and Justice Coalition's website)

These quotations demonstrate that, as opposed to the orthodox claim of patrimonialism, neither capitalism nor anti-capitalism is mutually exclusive in relation to Islam or Islamic movements. As social constructs, Islam and Islamic movements could be articulated with both capitalism and anti-capitalism. Therefore, reflecting on the variegated nature of capitalism, anti-capitalism could be also shared in the Islamic movements. For example, Ozgur Kazim Kivanc elaborated that in the name 'Anti-capitalist Muslims', the 'Muslim' is a permanent identity, whereas, 'Anti-capitalist' is temporary because it is only a historical phase. They argue that they exist not simply to oppose neoliberal Islamism or Islamic Calvinism as it exists in Turkey, they are actually against neoliberalism, capitalism and Calvinism in general. They are against secularist capitalism as well. In fact, they define secularism as inherent in capitalism historically.

'We refused "Islamism" or "political Islam", and became Muslims again because being a Muslim means you are pro-justice, -equality and -freedom automatically.' This quotation from the interview with Ozgur Kazim Kivanc indicates that, according to Anti-capitalist Muslims, justice, equality, and freedom are embedded in Islam, whereas secularism is identified as an inheritance of capitalist development. For example, Kivanc highlighted that Mohammad was in favour of 'nationalisation of private property' and he made a 'social contract' between equals that was based on multiculturalism, multi-legalism and that ultimately means 'property and political power belongs to Allah'. It is also argued that democracy is very much compatible with the Anti-capitalist Muslims' version of Islam, based on five principles in the Qur'an: justice, custody, qualification, consultation, and public good (Goksel 2017).

The anti-capitalist visions of Anti-capitalist Muslims represented by their political stance almost indicate a form of anarcho-communism. No political power, no government, and no property belonging to private individuals. It is almost as if they were against the historical development in the West that led to the emergence of capitalism, whereas the East was exposed to capitalist development through modernisation, colonialism, and post-colonialism. The East did not have the historical background for the emergence of such modes of production.

Anti-capitalist Muslims' vision of capitalism and anti-capitalism has a clear inspiration in Ali Shariati's Third Worldism and 'authentic intellectual' profile. Unlike Fanon, Shariati did not believe that it is necessary to put religion away when fighting against imperialism. Shariati's version of anti-imperialism indicated a radical left Islamism, as his stance was a combination of revolutionary Islamism and nationalism. As well as Liberation Theology, Latin American left-nationalism and Qutb's Islamic Socialism are often compared with Shariati's ideas. For example, Qutb was a follower of the Muslim Brotherhood founded by Hassan al-Banna, who imagined a supra-nationalist Islamic society. Matin (2016) argues that the 'essentialist conceptions of "political Islam" as the ideology of an internally generated rejection of modernity' is challenged by 'Ali Shariati's idea of "revolutionary Islam" as an internationally constituted mediation of modernity' (Matin 2016: 1). It is equally safe to argue that the Anti-capitalist Muslims' version of Islam has a similar internationalist perception.

CONCLUSION

At the beginning of this chapter, three questions were asked, aimed at making sense of Islam's relations with capitalism. In this concluding section, these questions will be answered by the information discussed in the previous sections.

Are there any Islamic alternatives to global capitalism or is the only possibility Islam's articulation into capitalism (i.e. Islamic capitalism)? According to the narrative of Anti-capitalist Muslims, capitalism is a Western phenomenon that was articulated into Muslim society. They believe that capitalism was born in the West and embodies the historical features of the West. This is perhaps a similar vision to that of the political Marxist tradition (social property relations approach) rather than the theory of uneven and combined development of capitalism. Islamic capitalism is an articulation that transformed Muslim societies and the overall Islamic perception of property and relations of production. Therefore, it is safe to argue that, according to the Anti-capitalist Muslims, Islamic capitalism is not an alternative to global capitalism; on the contrary, it is a part of it.

If there is an Islamic capitalism, will there be an Islamic alternative to anti-capitalism too? Islamic capitalism in Turkey made the Islamic anti-capitalist movements more visible. The Anti-capitalist Muslims argue that they are neither against simply the AKP's version of Islamic capitalism nor fighting against the Islamic part of capitalism. Their standpoint against capitalism makes them 'real' Muslims again. Therefore, they are attributing an anti-capitalist notion to Islam's own ontology. Although capitalism and Islam are historically distinctive, currently they are mutually inclusive. Thus, today, it is possible to see anti-capitalist visions within Islamic societies. These visions are generally, but not necessarily, tied up with the Islamic ideas or traditions from pre-capitalist times.

What are the possibilities of progressive and radical alter-movements against capitalism within Islamic social movements? The struggle against imperialism within the Islamic social movements can be dated back to the beginning of the twentieth century. However, these movements were generally mobilised against the imperialist West's capitalist systems. It is possible to see a Leninist tradition in these movements. On the other hand, today's anti-capitalist movements with Islamic characteristics are mostly originated in capitalist societies within the Muslim world. Specifically, for the case of anti-capitalist Muslims in Turkey, their anti-capitalism, alter-globalisation and anti-capitalist vision are not necessarily 'Islamic', in fact, anti-capitalism and alter-globalisation are inherent in 'true' Islam itself. Therefore, a progressive anti-capitalist future will embody Islam's true nature anyway.

What would an anti-capitalist society look like? Will there be variegated or multiple anti-capitalist alternatives at the end of capitalism? These questions were raised at the start of this chapter to address the main problems that this volume engages with. Clearly, given the multi-coloured nature and the multiplicity of capitalism itself, anti-capitalist society will reflect this too. Alternatives to capitalism will not be tailor-made for future societies, but will stem from capitalism's historically specific and variegated contradictions. The formation of the modern state and the development of capitalist modernity in the Middle East did not follow the same path as in its Western counterparts. This peripheral capitalism, blended with ideological support of nationalism and Islamism, was born in the wake of colonialism. Particularly in Turkey, the transition from import-substitution industrialisation to free-market neoliberalism brought not only the rise of Islamism as a political project but also the convergence of Islamism with neoliberal capitalism. Reflectively, anti-capitalist resistance did not necessarily stem from secularism but was also rooted within Islamism. These particular constellations of anti-capitalist thinking and practices therefore gave rise to not just the secularist opposition but also the Anti-capitalist Muslims. The Gezi Park uprising was a specific moment for these social movements to finally find each other and learn from one another. The crystallisation of anti-capitalist Muslim movements in Turkey represents the first substantial non-secular and class-based opposition to the AKP's decade-long rule. The heterogeneity of protesters in Gezi Park did not necessarily advance an Islamic critique of capitalist modernity and its authoritarian neoliberal state formation, rather it developed an anti-neoliberal and class-based opposition to the AKP's Islamic capitalism in the historical materialist sense.

NOTE

1. An earlier version of this chapter was presented at 'Critical International Political Economy at the End(ings) of Capitalism: The End of Capitalism Beyond Critical IPE', the BISA (British International Studies Association) Research Workshop in International Studies on 12 June 2018, in Bath, UK.

REFERENCES

Altinors, G. (2017) 'Book Review: The Fall of the Turkish Model: How the Arab Uprising Brought Down Islamic Liberalism by Cihan Tuğal', *Capital & Class* 41: 183–185.

Altinors, G. (2019) 'The State and Society in Contemporary Turkey', *Political Reflection Magazine* 5(2): 17-21.

Anderson, P. (1974) *Passages from Antiquity to Feudalism*. London: New Left Books.

Atasoy, Y. (2008) 'The Islamic Ethic and the Spirit of Turkish Capitalism Today', pp. 121-140 in *Global Flashpoints: Reactions to Imperialism and Neoliberalism. Socialist Register 2008*, available at: https://socialistregister.com/index.php/srv/article/view/5878 (accessed 9 November 2020).

Banaji, J. (2007) 'Islam, the Mediterranean and the Rise of Capitalism', *Historical Materialism* 15(1): 47-74.

Bruff, I. (2014) 'The Rise of Authoritarian Neoliberalism', *Rethinking Marxism* 26: 113-129.

Bruff, I. and C.B. Tansel (2018) 'Authoritarian Neoliberalism: Trajectories of Knowledge Production and Praxis', *Globalizations* 16: 233-244.

Dinler, D. (2003) 'Türkiye'de Güçlü Devlet Geleneği Tezinin Eleştirisi', *Praksis* 1(9): 17- 54.

Goksel, O. (2017) 'Revolutionary and Libertarian Islam: A Divergent Islamic Perspective on Modernity', *ASOS Journal* 48: 144-162.

Gramsci, A. (2007) *Prison Notebooks*, vol. 3. New York: Columbia University Press.

Huntington, S.P. (1996) *The Clash of Civilizations and the Remaking of World Order*. New York: Simon and Schuster.

Kuymulu, M.B. (2013) 'Reclaiming the Right to the City: Reflections on the Urban Uprisings in Turkey', *City* 17(3): 274-278.

Kuymulu, M.B. (2018) 'Confronting "Aggressive Urbanism": Frictional Heterogeneity in the "Gezi Protests" of Turkey', in D. Kalb and M. Mollona (eds) *Worldwide Mobilizations: Class Struggles and Urban Commoning*. New York: Berghahn Books.

Matin, K. (2016) 'The Alchemist of Revolution: Ali Shariati's Political Thought in International Context', *Spectrum Journal of Global Studies* 6(1).

Morton, A.D. (2013) 'The Limits of Sociological Marxism?', *Historical Materialism* 21(1): 129-158.

Peck, J. and N. Theodore (2007) 'Variegated Capitalism', *Progress in Human Geography* 31(6): 731-772.

Rodinson, M. (1974) *Islam and Capitalism*. New York: Pantheon Books.

Tansel, C.B. (2017) *States of Discipline: Authoritarian Neoliberalism and the Contested Reproduction of Capitalist Order*. London: Rowman and Littlefield International.

Tansel, C.B. (2018) 'Authoritarian Neoliberalism and Democratic Backsliding in Turkey: Beyond the Narratives of Progress', *South European Society and Politics* 23(2): 197–217.

Tuğal, C. (2009) *Passive Revolution: Absorbing the Islamic Challenge to Capitalism*. Stanford, CA: Stanford University Press.

Tuğal, C. (2016) *The Fall of the Turkish Model: How the Arab Uprisings Brought Down Islamic Liberalism*. London: Verso.

Turner, B.S. (2010) 'Islam, Capitalism and the Weber Theses', *British Journal of Sociology* 61(6): 147–160.

Uestebay, L. (2019) 'Between "Tradition" and Movement: The Emergence of Turkey's Anti- capitalist Muslims in the Age of Protest', *Globalizations* 16(4): 472–488.

Weber, M. (1965 [1922]) *The Sociology of Religion*. London: Methuen.

Wood, E.M. (2008) *Citizens to Lords: A Social History of Western Political Thought from Antiquity to the Middle Ages*. London: Verso.

Wood, N. (1983) 'The Economic Dimension of Cicero's Political Thought: Property and State', *Canadian Journal of Political Science / Revue Canadienne De Science Politique* 16(4): 739–756.

6
Socialist Governmentality and the Problem of the Capital Strike, or, a Defence of Fully Automated Luxury Communism

Nicholas Kiersey

INTRODUCTION: THE CAPITAL STRIKE AS STRATEGIC PROBLEM

While the left is crossed by numerous internal divisions, there would appear nevertheless to be a degree of consensus that the functional limit of socialist strategy is the possibility of the capital strike. The existence of this consensus can be observed in a number of contemporary debates, at a variety of sites and scales. Some debates focus on it in a more theoretical sense, drawing on the economist Kalecki's (2018) discussion of it in a famous 1943 essay, as a limit to the demands of the Keynesian welfare state (see also Frase 2017). Others address it more concretely, as a variable explaining for example the failure of Swedish social democracy in the 1970s (Benanav 2019a), or the ultimate decision of Greece not to exit the European Union (EU) in 2015 (Ginden and Panitch 2015). More recently, we see discussion of so-called platform corporations, like Uber, leveraging the capital strike directly to challenge legislation passed by the state government of California (Shure 2020). In each case, it is clear that the capital strike is understood as a hard limit, defining the very horizon of possibility of socialist transformation.

That said, if the achievement of some kind of 'escape velocity' from the gravitational field of the threat of the capital strike really is an essential precondition for the creation of a viable socialism, it is not clear the left today is fully cognizant of this fact. While organised labour has lately presented the imperatives of capital with little by way of any kind of meaningful impediment, leftist intellectuals appear nevertheless to be in the embrace of a relatively voluntarist outlook (Srnicek and Williams 2015; Frost 2017). True, the 2008 crisis bequeathed us the Occupy Wall Street movement, and generated a wave of militant subjectivities. True again, the relative success of recent electoral campaigns, such as those of Bernie Sanders, Jeremy Corbyn, and others, bespeak a surprisingly widespread continued belief in the possibility of 'democratic socialist' revolution. Nevertheless, the contemporary left has as yet failed to present any kind of real challenge to what appears to be a newly emerging mode of capital, where the activity of the financial realm is 'decoupling' from the realm of real productive activity (Varoufakis 2020). This decoupling will be a serious problem for the left, should it succeed, because it will dissolve the very basis of labour's ability to maintain the accountability of capital to basic democratic norms.

The coronavirus pandemic has added a degree of urgency to this question of the power of contemporary capital. As Yanis Varoufakis put it in a recent interview, the issue is not so much that Covid-19 has created a brand new crisis of capitalism but that it has intensified an essential dynamic of the post-2008 financial world (Varoufakis and McWilliams 2020). The decision of economic elites to pursue Quantitative Easing (QE) in response to the 2008 crisis marked the moment where the rules of capitalism were effectively suspended, at least for the rich, and a more arbitrary regime of political economy was inaugurated. QE was introduced supposedly as a means to offset weak demand by encouraging borrowing; however, it has not only failed to stimulate demand, it has also fuelled an unprecedented stock market bubble. Thus, in August 2020, as coronavirus shut down the global economy, with unprecedented numbers of Americans registering for unemployment, and with the short-term emergency unemployment benefits put in place by Congress reaching their expiration, we witnessed the turbulent spectacle of the Apple computer corporation becoming the first ever company to reach $2 trillion in market value, having been worth only $1 trillion in March. In September 2020, Apple would then record the greatest ever stock value drop in history (Rossignol 2020).

There is no doubt, therefore, that the left has long been conscious of the strategic priority of warding off the capital strike, a goal which must be accomplished before humanity can move beyond capitalism. Equally, there is no doubt about the fact that capitalists themselves are lately meeting with no small success in the project of creating their own unaccountable version of post-capitalism. We might add, of course, that the left has also long understood the central stake of its struggle to be 'socialism or barbarism' (see Le Blanc and Scott 2015). Yet, with multiple crises of historic magnitude popping up all around us, from financial collapse, to climate catastrophe, to coronavirus, this choice has arguably only rarely been presented so starkly as it is today. A critical question of our moment, therefore, pertains to the adequacy of socialist strategy in relation to these two poles: a *bad* post-capitalist future that we must avoid at all costs, but which appears nevertheless to be in the process of arriving, and a wholly different and *better future* that we must struggle to achieve, if the possibility of the former is ever to be properly vanquished.

In this chapter, I want to leverage this strategic polarity in the debate about post-capitalism as an occasion for the evaluation of a relatively recent arrival on the left theoretical scene. That is, the theory of Fully Automated Luxury Communism (FALC). Sometimes misidentified by horizontalist critics as a kind of naive utopianism (Benanav 2019b), where technological change is imagined automatically to beget the socialist utopia, what is often missed about FALC theory is its populist strategic orientation. At its core, FALC is less a technological discourse, and more a preoccupation with the strategic possibilities for the administration of a populist democratic project afforded by modern organisational theory and technology (Phillips and Rozworski 2019). In this respect, FALC may be contrasted with the horizontalist theoretical discourses that circulated around the Occupy movement. Focused on the achievement of political transformation by prefigurative means, Occupy eschewed long-term institutionalisation in favour of the performance of immediate forms of direct democracy as a means of challenging the habits and norms of everyday consciousness (see Kiersey and Vrasti 2016). According to many leftist critics, however, the movement's refusal to institutionalise itself risked alienating ordinary people by giving its various processes an essentially ad hoc nature, and making it appear too unserious about winning power ever to be able to inflict any real damage against a vertically integrated enemy like capitalism (see Tufekci 2017; Srnicek and Williams 2015).

By contrast, FALC is a literature that errs on the side of acknowledging the rationality and interests of ordinary people, and seeks not so much to transform consciousness as to build confidence in the promise that it is only socialism that can deliver the material future we all deserve. If FALC may be said to embrace something of a Promethean vision for a technologically advanced communism, it is because it is not only confident about the potential of contemporary technological innovation, but because it also believes that this utopian vision can rally a winning electoral coalition. Crucially then, FALC expresses not only a desire to improve the prospects of the vast majority for a satisfying and dignified life, but a serious commitment to obtaining the power necessary within the state for the achievement of this goal. Thus, despite the common horizontalist characterisation of FALC as an elitist and technocratic discourse, it may well be that the reverse is true; while the prefigurative left focuses on judging and transforming the desires of ordinary people, FALC embraces an unapologetic populism.

Yet it would be incorrect to conclude from these observations that FALC and horizontalism are somehow irreconcilable. In the sections that follow, I will attempt to adjudicate this debate between FALC and horizontalism with reference to the metrics of what I will call, following Foucault, 'socialist governmentality' (2008: 92–4). Most fundamentally, the concept of socialist governmentality provides a set of basic metrics to which both a hegemonic leftist state project and a movement-based post-hegemonic project can commit, so that they might then together have a better chance of warding off the capital strike. On the one hand, I contend, this approach reveals that horizontal strategy, or what Hardt and Negri (2005) term 'the productive activity of the multitude', addresses an imperative function for socialist strategy. As Arditi (2014) contends, the activity of the multitude in voluntary parallel economies plays an especially vital role not only in generating new militant subjectivities but also in producing vital autonomous capacities for withstanding the capital strike. Nevertheless it is true, as we will see, that some horizontalist critics of FALC seem blind to questions of urgency, assuming instead that the specialised forms of subjectivity created in the movements of the multitude always already have all the answers. By way of an attempt to overcome this problem, socialist governmentality acknowledges the plight of ordinary working-class folk who may not be initiated in the arcane processes and discursive forms of horizontalism's assemblies and blockades, and who find it hard to recognise how their interests are served by participation in them.

This latter populist aspect matters, I will argue, because non-initiated folk have the right to ask hard questions of the left before they swear fealty. They have the right to ask if the left recognises the gravity of their situation, and if it has the plans and capacities to transcend the realm of the performative, and deliver meaningful improvements to their lives. With these hard questions in mind then, my core contention in this chapter is that the left needs to embrace the strategic horizon of FALC. After all, FALC comes to the table with an explicit set of policy ideas that socialist planners might commit to implementing, at the level of the state. This should matter for horizontalists, insofar as FALC's populist programme works to deepen the solidarity between the working-class base and the multitude. It achieves this not only by working within the state to improve the lives of ordinary working-class people but because, in so doing, it builds loyalty to a state-hegemonic leftist project, thereby giving the state further latitude for the implementation of policies that would strengthen *the conditions of possibility* for the development of voluntary parallel economies.

To explain how socialist governmentality can reconcile these two projects then, the claims of this chapter are laid out over three sections. In the first section, I outline the premise for my reading of FALC as a Marxist Promethean strategic orientation, as opposed to a naïve utopianism. In the second section, I show that FALC proceeds on the basis of an analysis of present world conditions that leads it to conclude that the socialist transition has not only become urgently necessary but that, due to advances in technology and planning theory, it is potentially more achievable today than at any other point in history. Here, I underline the populist pedigree of FALC's various policy positions, and note their strategic function for the left. In the same section I also offer an engagement with the critics of FALC. Broadly speaking, these theorists might be said to come from the communisation school (see Dauvé 2019). Thus, for critics like Benanav (2019b) and Wark (2015), among others, FALC amounts to little more than a naïve technological fantasy, diverting us from the real work of creating a properly communist mode of life and work.

Yet this accusation of fantastical thinking might just as equally be applied in reverse. In the third section, I thus return to the problem of the capital strike. Presented by critics like Benanav as the ultimate case study for why the left must embrace horizontalist economies, I suggest that the critics have underestimated the nature of the problem. Here, a good faith reading of FALC must necessarily note the influence of the theorist Mark Fisher (2009), who believed that one of the greatest problems facing contemporary capitalist society is chronic depression. 'Capitalist Realism', as Fisher termed it, is a condition that afflicts not only ordinary capitalist citizens, who cannot imagine a viable pathway to a life after capitalism, but also certain leftists who cannot see that the fetishisation of pure performativity is itself a symptom of this same debilitating defeatism. The stakes of Capitalist Realism are clear for our story, because it is a major barrier to effecting a successful state-hegemonic project. One hugely instructive example of this is the experience of Greece's negotiations with the EU in 2015. Thus, in the third section, I show how voluntary parallel economies were incapable of fending off the threat of an actual capital strike on their own. Moving to conclude then, I draw on the metrics of socialist governmentality to suggest that, despite the arguments of its detractors, FALC offers both a realistic assessment of our current political moment, and a strategic pathway to victory. Horizontalist movements play a role in this strategy, insofar as they provide a vital bulwark against the capital strike. Yet they need a sympathetic power within the state to fight alongside them, and secure the conditions of possibility of a liveable post-capitalism.

MARXISM AS PROMETHEAN VISION

To appreciate FALC as a strategic orientation, and not a naïve utopianism, let us start with one of the most frequently cited passages from *The Communist Manifesto*, that bourgeois society 'produces its own grave-diggers' (Marx and Engels 1848). Cited in isolation, this line seems to reveal Marx and Engels at their most deterministic; there are dynamics and forces at work within capitalism that, as sure as the sun rises, will lead the proletariat to confront and, ultimately, destroy the very same society that has called them into existence. It is worth recalling, however, that *The Communist Manifesto* was a short, polemical pamphlet, intended to educate and inspire workers, whereas any study of Marx's wider works will reveal him approaching the study of social relations with a much more nuanced framework of analysis (Vidal 2018). In these wider works, we find Marx discussing man's essential condition as that of a social animal, striving to survive in a world of material scarcity. In the historical course of his engagements with the material world, man has distinguished himself from other animals by means of the development of language, and philosophical systems. These capacities have allowed man to engage in technological development and, increasingly, to flourish. Much of this success can be attributed to man's ability, as a 'species-being' (Marx 1844), to engage in a historical progression of society-wide modes of organised production. Of course, famously, for Marx the passage between these historical modes has proceeded on the basis of class struggle. Critically, however, Marx did not insert this role for class struggle in his theory by fiat. He included it rather because, thus far, the actual history of human development has indeed yielded real class divisions, of relative degrees of coherence and power, premised in each phase upon the ability of a relatively small, dominant, master class to expropriate the surplus generated by the social production of the majority. He included it, furthermore, as Hardt and Negri (2000: 72) observe, because the record of this history of struggle bespeaks an observable and inexorable trend in the governance of production, from the transcendent towards the immanent. Or, as the Situationists express it, from 'separation' towards the full democratisation of production processes (Calder and Umland 2019).

Yet, while this progression of history may be about the movement towards democratised production and abundance, Marx did not believe that such progress was guaranteed. Classes may have an objective existence by virtue of their structural position in the economy but, as indicated in Marx's more journalistic writings, like *The Eighteenth Brumaire* (Marx 1852), they do not necessarily have an objective self-consciousness, or recognise themselves for who and what they are in history. There is a problem of strategy to be addressed, and this is where the question of changing technological conditions becomes a more political consideration. A keystone document in Marx's repertoire on technology in this sense is thus the so-called 'Fragment on Machines', from Notebooks VI and VII of the *Grundrisse*. Here, Marx appears to set out an early argument concerning the tendency towards technological innovation under capitalism, and the expected impact of automation on labour. Under the pressure of competition, capitalist firms pursue technological optimisation of their processes, 'in order to realize a maximum of labour in the maximum number of ... objects' (1993 [1939]: 701). Yet, while this view would seem to posit a role for capitalist technology as merely a tool of domination, allowing the bourgeois class to force labour to produce more output per unit of time for the same wage, the story is a little messier than that.

For Marx, technology unleashes new productive potentials as it develops and, in so doing, it can reduce the amount of necessary labour that man must undertake, in order to reproduce his being. With this potential of technology to satisfy human needs in mind, Marx and Engels (1848) express their outrage in the *Manifesto* that the private ownership of capitalism would hold back, or 'fetter', the possibility of a more humanistic regime of production. In the *Grundrisse*, however, Marx goes even further, anticipating a scenario where the productive application of technology in industry might eventually lead to a point where the worker 'steps to the side' (1993 [1939]: 705) in the production process altogether, becoming unnecessary to the reproduction of capital. The long-term upshot of capitalism's tendency towards automation is thus for Marx 'the full development of capital' (1993 [1939]: 609), where the total labour of society becomes fully objectified in machinery which, in turn, surrounds the means of production with the aura of an alien force, as being proper solely to 'the existence of circulating capital' (1993 [1939]: 701).

At this point of ultimate mystification, however, Marx believes that the future fully capitalist society will encounter an irreconcilable contradiction. Having sought to reduce 'necessary labour time' to a minimum, yet necessarily remaining bound to the use of labour time, expressed in the wage, 'as sole measure and source of wealth', something has to give. As this irreconcilable contradiction becomes irresistibly apparent for all to see, labour must realise that it was the true source of capitalist valorisation all along. The foundational myth of capitalism is thus blown 'sky-high' (1993 [1939]: 706) and it becomes possible to liberate machinery from the limited expression of its possible range of social application, subsumed within the maximalist logic of capital. In this fashion, we see that the highest phase of capital paradoxically furnishes us with the promise of an inevitable communist future, with material abundance and spare time after our necessary labours for intellectual development and edifying forms of leisure. Thus, in the 'higher phase of communist society', the use of technology is no longer about ensuring our survival, because the 'antithesis between mental and physical labour has vanished' (Marx 1875). Indeed, Marx even seems to imply that in a fully technological communist society there is no distinction between leisure and work, as all work has become akin to self-development. In such a society, the categories of useful and beautiful merge into one, and all labour becomes perfectly cooperative.

It is this relatively optimistic understanding of man's potential for technological mastery that leads some to refer to Marx as an instrumentalist (Feenberg 1991). Of course, our present moment seems quite far from that happy point of future contradiction when, like Prometheus, man is finally able to steal the mastery of nature away from the mystified forces that dominate him. Today, rather than using machines to inject objectified labour power where labour power did not or could not previously exist, and thereby improve the overall human condition, it appears we are still in the phase where capital uses machines to diminish labour, wherever there is 'an overflow of labour powers' (Marx 1993 [1939]: 702). Advanced machines appear to solidify the power of capital, in this sense, further distancing the worker from the kinds of meaningful agency over design and production that would be needed in order to wield fixed capital for the greater good. Nevertheless, recalling Marx, it would seem foolish to foreclose on the question just yet. On the one hand, as Marx tells us, we must recognise technological development as 'the condition' for labour's emancipation (1993 [1939]: 701). Read in isolation, this might be understood as suggesting a belief on Marx's part that any kind of resistance to capitalism prior to the arrival of this contradiction is futile. On the other, however, elsewhere in Marx's writings we see a thinker concerned more with immanent causality than teleology (for discussion, see Foucault 2012). Indeed, we see also a thinker so open to the question of political strategy that he even allowed for the idea of skipping through the developmental phases of history (see Shanin 2018). Thus, while Marx arguably believed that the causal order of capitalism was deeply channelled, it seems he also had an awareness of the importance of developing active strategies to resist what he saw ultimately as a cunning and recombinable opponent.

Marx was surely being modest when he suggested the task of drawing the precise blueprints of the future utopian society belonged only to 'the cook-shops of the future' (1982 [1976]: 99). Nevertheless, insofar as anyone reading this is more likely than not actually living in Marx's future, it does not seem inappropriate to want at least to test the cook-shop door, and see how far it might open. To be clear, this is not to advocate for an accelerationist project, if by accelerationism we mean a leftist project of seeking to hasten at any cost the moment of revelation of capitalism's contradiction. To the contrary, as we will explore in the next section, FALC is a populist political project, self-consciously modelled on the work of the successful right-wing group, the Mont Pelerin Society, which has worked to great effect in recent decades to promote and advance the 'common sense' of neoliberalism at multiple levels of society, from the policy realm to the university classroom, and from the op-ed page to the shop floor (Srnicek and Williams 2015). FALC starts with the question: how might the left emulate this success, today? FALC's hunch is that, with a detailed yet flexible strategic plan, capable of inspiring workers and reconnecting them with the left on the basis of an emancipatory technological promise, a formidable new left-wing subjectivity might well be possible. The achievement of this goal would be a big deal not only in terms of reinvigorating the left, however. As Phillips and Rozworski (2019) argue, it would also constitute a rupture with an established historical pattern on the left, where even the most successful revolutionary Marxists have proven weak on coming up with exact plans for the transition to a socialist economy.

DEBATING FALC

The term 'Fully Automated Luxury Communism' was coined in a video by Aaron Bastani (2014), a relatively well-known media personality on the British left, in 2014. At the centre of his argument is a claim that we should be thinking about the kinds of technological processes described by Marx as a real and present possibility, rather than a potential belonging to some impossibly distant future. Now, it would be inaccurate to limit the spirit of these comments solely to Bastani, as similar sentiments appeared contemporaneously in Srnicek and Williams (2015), Mason (2016), Frase (2017), and Phillips and Rozworski (2019). Nevertheless, as the figure who coined the term, Bastani offers a nicely synthetic summary of its basic precepts. The story here is that humanity is presently experiencing the third major technological 'disruption' of its history. The first was the shift, taking place about 12,000 years ago, towards settled agriculture. The second occurred much more recently, in the nineteenth century, and brought us industrialisation. The Third Disruption began in the 1950s, and pertains to the massive impact of modern technology not only on the cost of production, but on the way production itself is carried out. Admittedly, automation is a key issue in FALC's analysis here. The increasing role of automation in capitalist production has placed us on trajectory towards a major 'crisis of work' (Srnicek and Williams 2015). Bastani (2019), for example, even goes so far as to suggest that we may unknowingly be living in the 'peak human' period. The question, therefore, if we are indeed on the cusp of something more like a post-work society, is whether the left can leverage this development to weaken the grip of capitalism on our lives?

To be clear, however, automation is not the primary issue in this debate. To the contrary, the real issue here is the tension within the left in terms of how it imagines the relationship between democracy and process, in socialist strategy. FALC advocates, on the one hand, tend to follow a hopeful, populist reading of the opportunities for socialism inherent in capitalist technologisation. If the left is ever to succeed, the argument goes, it must persuade the masses that it is a horse worth betting on. In other words, the left must demonstrate, through its various strategies and tactics, that it is serious in its commitment to reordering the world of production, and thereby improving significantly the lives of ordinary people all around the world. On this score, however, a particular point of emphasis for FALC theorists is that the left will need to be upfront with itself, that promises of such magnitude will not be deliverable without the capacities for coordination of a technologically empowered state (Srnicek and Williams 2015). Thus, advocates of FALC insist on the centrality of entering the state, a step which will itself require the left to become a much more strategically integrated and coherent force than it is presently.

To be clear, however, when FALC speaks of entering the state, it is not doing so in the sense of seeing the state as some kind of commanding height, from which planning for the entire economy can be orchestrated. Reading Bastani's account at least, FALC sees itself very much as a break with more anti-democratic expressions of socialist strategy of the past. In keeping with its populist vision, it seeks to build legitimacy for a transitional programme towards FALC by promoting a democratic management of the economy in at least three ways (Bastani 2019). First, following examples implemented in cities like Cleveland, in the US, and Preston, in the UK, it seeks to empower local community governments to generate wealth multipliers within their jurisdictions by subsidising socially progressive forms of procurement and allowing them to introduce municipal protectionism. Second, it seeks to promote worker-owned businesses and mitigate the tendency towards local capital extraction caused by the monopoly of large banks, through the socialisation of finance and the creation of a network of local banks and credit unions. These moves will also help offset the political-economic costs of automation, says Bastani, allowing local worker-owned firms to invest in their fixed capital and training, thus increasing productivity. Finally, it seeks the introduction of a set of universal basic income (UBI) and universal basic service (UBS) packages. UBI is of course a well-known libertarian proposal to mitigate anticipated job loss from automation (see also Sculos 2019). UBS on the other hand refers to services that belong more in the social wage column. Some of these are provided in a more cost-effective manner at the national level, says Bastani, such as in the British health care model, which remains one of the most efficient such systems on the planet. While others, such as housing, transport, and education, might be provided more locally. The key, however, is that the Third Disruption means these services no longer have to be provided according to a logic of artificial scarcity, or in an environmentally destructive manner.

As already noted, opponents of FALC express caution about what they perceive as hyperbolic claims about the empirical impact of automation technologies. Wark (2015), for example, contends that FALC is simply too optimistic, believing in the possibility of a grand post-capitalist future when such an outcome is simply untenable in the face of irreversible environmental catastrophe and the death of the industrial workers' movement. For others, like Koshy (2019), the problem is more ideological, insofar as FALC appears to be 'in thrall to the story Silicon Valley likes to tell about itself'. In similar vein, Sadowski (2018) and Galloway (2017) prefer the terms 'Potemkin AI' and 'Bromethanism', respectively, to evoke the over-hyped fairy-tale nature of automation discourse. And, indeed, in a particularly detailed extension of this critique, Benanav (2019a, 2019b) scrutinises the data about the extent of actually existing automation and finds that the robots are hardly coming for our jobs anytime soon. Tracing the long history of effervescent expectations for automation, Benanav shows that such thinking has been around for a long time. And while it has always believed that the optimised flying-car society of the Jetsons is just around the corner, history shows that we are in fact no closer to a revolutionary crisis of unemployment. Indeed, says Benanav (2019b: 118), in the present context what actually seems to have happened instead is a crisis of 'under-employment', associated with Late Capitalism's ongoing economic stagnation and collapse in demand for industrial goods.

Automation theorists are correct, Benanav elaborates, that there is a diminishing demand for labour in Late Capitalist societies. Yet, while we can see evidence of substantial deployment of automation in the retail, apparel and electronics industries, as 'first links' in global supply chains, there is no sign as yet that automation is the major issue confronting labour (Benanav 2019b: 120). As he elaborates, the real story is 'inadequate output demand' (2019b: 121). On the one hand, we tend to think of deindustrialisation in terms of jobs moving overseas. Reviewing the data, however, while industrial output has increased dramatically in low- and middle-income countries between 1970 and 2017, the fact remains that manufacturing output value has shown significant, if sluggish, growth in the rich countries, over the same period (Benanav 2019a: 18). Today, indeed, overcapacity in manufacturing is becoming a worldwide phenomenon, affecting even poorer and emerging economies (2019a: 24). As such, our appraisal of the impact of automation must be tempered by a recognition of the lack of sufficient demand for the quantity of goods that existing global industry is already capable of creating.

On the other hand, while automation theorists often seem to suggest that automation is the main villain of our current unemployment crisis, and that we should expect it soon to affect the service sector the same way it affected industry, there is good reason to doubt the data on productivity increases in rich countries (Benanav 2019a: 19). The upshot is that industrial workers might not be quite so caught in the pincer of offshoring plus automation as is sometimes thought. Globally then, we seem to be entering an era not so much of automation-driven unemployment, but of stagnation-driven under-employment and 'dead-end service jobs' (Benanav 2019b: 145).

Now, admittedly, Benanav's argument is focused primarily on rebutting right-wing and capitalist automation discourse. However, in the same breath, he also caricatures FALC advocates as saying 'little' about the problem of manufacturing overcapacity. Of course, left-wing automation proponents are also frequently advocates of technocratic, marginal interventions, like UBI. For Benanav (2019b: 134), such proposals merely set us on course for a 'zero-sum conflict between labour and capital' over diminishing spoils, while the ship of capitalism continues to crash into the great iceberg of its own productive overcapacity. We should be crystal clear here, however. While it is true that FALC is largely preoccupied with the impact of automation upon labour, Benanav's critique of FALC as merely an automation discourse constitutes something of a theoretical sleight of hand. FALC theorists actually identify a number of different crises ongoing in the current moment, not least among which is the pervasiveness of neoliberalism's 'low-inflation ideology' (Bastani 2019). Mason (2016), indeed, makes clear that wages in Late Capitalism have failed to keep up with inflation, and the whole global capitalist system is indeed stagnant. Equally, FALC theorists discuss a wide range of policy proposals beyond UBI and their applicability in different contexts and scales, from worker ownership to municipal protectionism, and from the re-politicisation of supposedly independent central banking to a mass jobs programme under the Green New Deal (Bastani 2019). Conversely, we should be clear about what FALC theorists mean when they talk about the Third Disruption. Automation, for FALC, is an expression of the increasingly reproducible nature of the knowledge (or 'instructions') that determines how we manage production in the first place. Drawing inspiration from Rifkin (2014), James Livingston (2016) describes this as a kind of 'primitive disaccumulation'. Today, as he puts it, 'a diminishing proportion of socially necessary transactions' can even be captured in market data. This is bad news for capitalism, insofar as the arrival of zero-cost reproduction of information has consequences for the scarcity-based price mechanism that sustains it. But it is potentially good news for socialism, insofar as it opens up the possibility for the governance of a 'new commons', with new computational possibilities for planning the production and distribution of goods and services, based on a more humanistic measurement of what we need, and where.[1]

The point here is not to suggest, contra Benanav, that FALC really does possess the plan for some kind of magical leftist 'fix' for capitalism's overcapacity problem. To the contrary, it is to suggest that Benanav has painted a misleading picture. Unlike the facile futurism of Silicon Valley propagandists, FALC is not an attempt to predict the future. To the contrary, FALC is guided by a sense of duty to the ideal of restoring the left as a mass movement. FALC is a wager that the best way to achieve this is to show the world that the left offers the best policy agenda to improve general human welfare. By caricaturing FALC as concerned solely with the problem of 'robots taking our jobs', and as starry-eyed for technocratic fixes like UBI, Benanav risks throwing the FALC baby out with the libertarian UBI bathwater. A fairer assessment would show that the argument for FALC does not stand or fall on the veracity of Silicon Valley myths. To the extent that automation plays a role in FALC, it is a future-oriented and political question. FALC hardly denies the problem of stagnation, or its horrible repercussions for labour. The question is, what is to be done about it?

If the fully automated future that breaks the value relation is not here just yet, it is hardly the case that there are no jobs to be done in the meantime. Given Benanav's concern about industrial overcapacity, he might at least express some curiosity about the possibilities for commandeering this capacity and putting it to use, for example, in the context of a Green New Deal programme (see Aronoff 2019). Such programmes have massive popularity among voters throughout the Western world, and their successful implementation would surely promote legitimacy among workers for further, comparable programmes, helping us build the political momentum we will need in order to secure an environmentally sustainable post-scarcity and post-work world. Puzzlingly, however, anti-FALC commentators like Benanav insist on catastrophism, hand-waving in one breath about the death of the industrial labour movement (2019b: 144–5) and the failures of the Keynesian state (2019b: 136), while in the next extolling the virtues of horizontalist blockades (2019b: 145). What is never made clear is how the critique of FALC should logically lead us to an embrace of horizontalism, or how these horizontalist techniques are supposed to help the left ward off the very real problem Benanav claimed we had to overcome in the first place: the capital strike.

CAPITALIST REALISM AND THE CAPITAL STRIKE

In previous sections of this chapter, we established that with the information revolution, or the 'Third Disruption' as it is known in management literature, humanity may be arriving at the point where it has the technological capacity to ensure that all are fed, that work hours can be radically diminished, that all can have access to a basic modicum of luxury, and that the planet's atmosphere can be repaired. However, as we noted at the start of this chapter, there is a general consensus among socialists that none of these dreams can become a reality so long as we have no plan for escaping the threat of the capital strike. Benanav clearly shares this appraisal, insofar as he invokes the capital strike as the ultimate reason why FALC, which he sees ultimately as a state-based Keynesian strategy, and therefore insufficiently attuned to the need for class struggle, should be regarded as deficient. However, despite Benanav repeatedly suggesting that the capital strike is the most serious challenge facing left strategy, it is clear neither why he thinks that FALC has no hope against it nor why he believes we should join him in thinking that spontaneous horizontalist blockades, à la Piqueteros (2019b: 145), should necessarily be thought of as the safer bet. Why, after all, should ordinary people commit to one kind of act, and not the other? What is missing here, as Bratsis (2015) puts it, is serious consideration as to 'what kinds of activity it takes to produce a new political power'.

It is worth pausing here to reflect on what is arguably the key political problem of contemporary capitalism. For Mark Fisher, a figure frequently cited in FALC literature, this is the problem that our collective intuitive understanding has an easier time imagining the end of the world than imagining a future without capitalism. For Fisher, this logic suggests a sort of widespread reluctant acceptance of our fate, as both the victims and the perpetrators of a slow-burn catastrophe. In his book, *Capitalist Realism* (2009), Fisher suggests that Capitalist Realism is partly synonymous with the advent of neoliberalism. A political programme with an extremist vision for a complete anthropological reinvention of humanity as *Homo economicus*, or economic man (see also Foucault 2008), neoliberalism became ascendant in the 1970s as the intellectual blueprint for many of the policy makers and pro-capitalist intellectuals of our time. Yet, notes Fisher, neoliberal ideology is far from the main issue here. We have not been brainwashed, or fallen victim to some kind of economic false consciousness. Rather, the issue is how shifting trends in global production are affecting the relationship of ordinary people to their own political power. In this respect, Fisher is preoccupied with what he sees as the gaslighting logic of Late Capitalist management culture. We live today in a regime of production where we are urged increasingly to find the solutions to our problems within ourselves: to smile, to 'practise gratitude', to 'lean in', to 'find our bliss', to 'become resilient', and to have 'difficult conversations' about our daily struggles, all while simultaneously having the basic conditions of our self-reproduction pulled out from under us.

The upshot, says Fisher, is the generalisation of a social phenomenon called 'hedonic depression' (2009). We seek joys, as all humans must, according to the philosopher Spinoza, by means of the channels available to us. But such channels today are limited, and increasingly permit only individualistic kinds of joy. Thus, for example, we might seek to engage in politics by posting on social media platforms, like Twitter. We might even become addicted to the hormonal surge of the 'likes' we receive from such activity. But, as Fisher notes, the depressive aspect of this practice cannot be ignored. We are perfectly aware, even as we seek this kind of recognition, that what we are experiencing is 'sad passion'. That is, we know that real technological possibilities exist today that would, if appropriated within a properly democratic programme, allow us to overcome widespread poverty and radically increase the opportunities for everyone in our species to experience genuine, truly collective kinds of joy. Today, however, for lack of concrete institutions like organised labour to channel our collective power and effect real change, we return over and over to the well. Indeed, Fisher laments, it is not only the ordinary citizen who suffers this performative affliction. The exact same condition affects much of the left, explaining thereby much of the 'call-out' culture and 'witch-hunting moralism' that seems to afflict the online left today, as it pursues the politics of what Fisher (2013) terms 'the vampire castle'.

How can the theory of Capitalist Realism guide our judgement in evaluating this debate between FALC and its critics? Let us recall that, for Benanav (2019b: 135), the capacity of horizontalist volunteer economies to fend off the capital strike constitutes the superlative argument in favour of communisation theory. To give him the benefit of the doubt, it is possible that, like Ginden and Panitch (2015), discussing the 2015 Grexit crisis, Benanav believes that the existence of vibrant 'solidarity networks' provides a necessary bulwark for resisting the will of capital. Critically, however, despite their recognition of the existence of a relatively advanced voluntary parallel economy in

Greece, even Ginden and Panitch did not believe that the movements there were sufficiently developed in 2015 that they could go it alone, without the help of the state. The movements needed more time to develop. In the fateful summer of 2015, however, time was the one thing the people of Greece did not have. Following a positive 'Oxi' referendum, which rejected the terms of the EU's Third Memorandum, Alex Tsipras was faced with a real dilemma. With the powers of capital refusing to honour the Greek vote, Tsipras could either listen to the voices of the so-called 'Plan B' movement, and attempt to set Greece on a course to depart the EU, 'no matter the cost' (Gourgouris 2015), or listen to the polls, which suggested that an overwhelming percentage of the population, including 66% of his own party, would prefer to remain within the EU (Ginden and Panitch 2015).

As Gourgouris (2015) puts it, the situation was such that 'the field of historical action ... exceeded the theoretical armory'. Ultimately, in deciding not to press for Grexit, it appears that Tsipras was guided by a sense of the impossibility of the choices before him. On the one hand, as Bratsis (2015) argues, despite being able to muster some 30 general strikes in the months leading up to the referendum, the power of the Greek social movements was simply not commensurate to the task of pressuring Europe's financial institutions. On the other hand, neither was the Greek solidarity economy in a position to enable a viable Grexit, and sustain the country through the likely ensuing all-out capital strike. Critically, on balance, this meant that Greece had no real counter-threat to use as leverage in the struggle to bend the will of the EU. Ultimately, then, given the great pain that Grexit would inflict on the very same subjects that his party, Syriza, was sworn to defend, and the risk that these same subjects might, out of desperation come to rationalise a rightward political turn, Tsipras chose finally to respect the wishes of the Greek electorate, and capitulate (Ginden Panitch 2015).

In terms of the question of political power then, as posed above by Bratsis, it seems that Tsipras ultimately made the correct choice. As Balibar and Mezzadra express it, the decision was a victory in terms of 'time and space' (Watson 2015). *Time*, that is, for the composition of new militant subjectivities elsewhere in Europe and, hopefully, some electoral victories for forces opposed to the EU's ongoing regime of austerity. And *space*, equally, for a broader political engagement with Greece's public institutions, where clientelism and corruption remain rampant. This victory thus placed on the table the possibility of a strategic partnership with the social movements. In this scenario, on the one hand, Syriza might have engaged with Greece's impressively capable parallel economic networks, even going so far as to commandeer military capacities in order to shore up its conditions of possibility, and help those suffering under austerity (Gindin and Panitch 2015). Externally, meanwhile, the Greek government had a range of legal options it could have pursued within the institutions of the EU, allowing it to work with allies in other austerity-stricken European countries to expose and obstruct the Troika's agenda (Varoufakis 2018). In the end of course, with the situation compounded by the effects of a burgeoning refugee crisis, the Greek government did not even attempt to leverage this victory. Instead, it opted to become a relay for the imposition of the very agenda it had set out to oppose (Lapavitsas 2016). Tsipras's ultimate decision not even to try to pursue this avenue is not something that can be easily explained in terms of strategic calculation, and may even have come down to personal factors (Varoufakis 2018). Yet it certainly does not invalidate the argument that the plan was the least worst option for Greece.

The point here is not to dismiss Benanav for drawing our attention to the potential role of a large and vibrant parallel economy, in resisting the capital strike. To be sure, the multitude approach possesses a tried and trusted capacity for tactical, network-based auto-generation that more traditional hegemonic models seem to lack (Arditi 2014). It is to suggest, however, that the power of such economies should not be idealised. This is why the Greek case is instructive. By all accounts, in 2015 the country had a relatively advanced parallel economy compared to most Western countries, but even this proved insufficient to the task of supporting the country through a capital strike. Benanav (2019b: 138) draws inspiration from great thinkers, including Marx and Kropotkin, to suggest we should just go ahead and set up work-sharing communities, as if we lived already in utopia. Indeed, Benanav suggests that it is an open question how populations may respond to such proposals, and that they might even embrace them, just as they might 'the wonders of a child's experience in the world' (2019b: 139). Yet there is a certain condescension in Benanav's idea that we should somehow expect uninitiated folk living under Capitalist Realism, struggling to pay the bills and keep a roof over the heads of their loved ones, and with little by way of spare time for the study of abstract anarchist theory, automatically to warm to the prospect of long evenings debating quotidian issues such as the arrangement of 'garbage collection' (Benanav 2019b: 138). Indeed, unaccompanied by any kind of critique of the political realities facing most ordinary people, such sentiments ring jarringly of unseriousness.

CONCLUSION: FALC AS SOCIALIST GOVERNMENTALITY

Foucault once suggested that while socialist theory expresses clear historical and economic values, it has no theory of its own 'way of governing' (2008: 94). For this reason, he concluded, a real left governmentality has yet to be 'invented' (2008: 94). As to what such a governmentality might look like, however, Foucault did not say much. He merely pointed out two criteria. First, that it should be focused on the 'transformation of economic conditions'. Second, that it should eschew the temptations of sovereign power and refuse any dangerous romanticisations of its own historical purpose with notions like 'class enemy' (Foucault 2003: 262).[2] From the first criterion, we can infer from Foucault the need for a pragmatic plan to govern for economic transformation. Thus, we can envision something similar to Gramsci's hegemonic political model. That is, the pursuit by the left of a 'war of movement' (for discussion, see Worth 2013) within society in order to leverage the vertically integrated capacities of the state in order to secure the conditions of possibility for a flourishing of socialism. Conversely, from the second criterion, we can infer the parallel need for a 'post-hegemonic' model. Here, inspired by FALC, we can recognise that the skills and imaginative capacities of open and welcoming movements, or what Hardt and Negri term the multitude, are the self-organising engine of leftist transformation. Crucially, however, as Gourgouris (2015) notes, the point of the idea of socialist governmentality is that while neither of these two forms or expressions of socialist power is subservient to the other, each is nevertheless 'responsible for each other'.

In this chapter, we have shown that FALC makes a uniquely powerful contribution to this debate. Refusing the blackmail of having to choose between hegemony and post-hegemony, FALC is actually a powerful distillation of the relationship between these two tendencies within the theoretical envelope of socialist governmentality. FALC recognises that solidaristic movements cannot go it alone. By placing the problem of Capitalist Realism at the centre of its analysis, FALC realises that the only real option for the left to steer humanity towards a socialist post-capitalism is a strategy of 'populist Marxism' (Bastani 2019). That is, a left politics which eschews all forms of elitism, including that inherent in its own tendency for performativity and purity, in order to articulate a theory of rupture that is 'understandable to most people in an idiom that they readily understand' (Bastani 2019). It is a leftist politics that is willing to compromise, and is prepared to start thinking instead about the kinds of positive propositions that will be needed in order to assemble a coalition of sufficient power that the future can be put back in play. It is a politics, in other words, that has the audacity at least to consider the possibility that workers want us to appeal to them with convincing arguments about what's in it for them. In this sense, FALC seeks explicitly to expand the loyalty of the working-class base to the multitude.

NOTES

1. The reader familiar with the socialist calculation debate will know that it is a massive literature, and impossible to summarise in a short chapter like this. For a good overview, see Morozov (2019).
2. To be clear, socialism for Foucault is within its rights to seek to eliminate its adversaries, 'in economic terms', and even to take away their 'privileges'. Whenever socialism goes beyond this point, however, and essentialises its opponent as an 'enemy' in order to justify killing him, this for Foucault is tantamount to 'racism'.

REFERENCES

All URLs referred to were checked on 17 December 2020.

Arditi, B. (2014) 'Post-hegemony: Politics Outside the Usual Post-Marxist Paradigm', in A. Kioupkiolis and G. Katsambekis (eds) *Radical Democracy and Collective Movements Today: The Biopolitics of the Multitude versus the Hegemony of the People*. Abingdon: Routledge, pp. 17–44.

Aronoff, K. (2019) 'Bernie Sanders's Climate Plan More Radical than Opponents', *The Intercept*, available at: https://theintercept.com/2019/08/22/bernie-sanders-climate-policy/

Bastani, A. (2014) 'Fully Automated Luxury Communism!', Novara Media, available at: https://youtu.be/dmQ-BZ3eWxM

Bastani, A. (2019) *Fully Automated Luxury Communism*. London: Verso.

Benanav, A. (2019a) 'Automation and the Future of Work – 1', *New Left Review* 119: 5–38, available at: https://newleftreview.org/issues/II119/articles/aaron-benanav-automation-and-the-future-of-work-1

Benanav, A. (2019b) 'Automation and the Future of Work – 2', *New Left Review* 120: 117–146. Available at: https://newleftreview.org/issues/II120/articles/aaron-benanav-automation-and-the-future-of-work-2

Bratsis, P. (2015) 'The Materiality of Power and the Physics of Change: Lessons from Henri Lefebvre, Nicos Poulantzas, and the Greek Crisis', paper presented at Democracy Rising conference, University of Athens, available at: https://www.academia.edu/14259245/The_Materiality_of_Power_and_the_Physics_of_Change_Lessons_from_Henri_Lefebvre_Nicos_Poulantzas_and_the_Greek_Crisis

Calder, J. and C. Umland (2019) 'Beyond a Spectacular Image of the Working Class', *New Political Science* 41(4): 1–15.

Dauvé, G. (2019) *From Crisis to Communisation*. Oakland, CA: PM Press.

Feenberg, A. (1991) *Critical Theory of Technology*. Oxford: Oxford University Press.

Fisher, M. (2009) *Capitalist Realism*. Ropley: Zero Books.

Fisher, M. (2013) 'Exiting the Vampire Castle', available at: https://www.opendemocracy.net/en/opendemocracyuk/exiting-vampire-castle/

Foucault, M. (2003) *Society Must be Defended: Lectures at the Collège de France, 1975–76*, edited by M. Senellart. New York: Picador.

Foucault, M. (2008) *The Birth of Biopolitics: Lectures at the Collège de France, 1978–1979*, edited by M. Senellart. New York: Picador.

Foucault, M. (2012) 'The Mesh of Power', *Viewpoint Magazine*, available at: https://www.viewpointmag.com/2012/09/12/the-mesh-of-power/

Frase, P. (2017) 'What It Means to Be on the Left', *Jacobin*, available at: https://www.jacobinmag.com/2017/07/socialism-liberalism-left-frase

Frost, A.A. (2017) 'All Worked Up and Nowhere to Go', *The Baffler*, available at: https://thebaffler.com/outbursts/all-worked-up-nowhere-to-go-frost

Galloway, A.R. (2017) 'Brometheanism', Communication and Culture Blog, available at: http://cultureandcommunication.org/galloway/brometheanism

Ginden, S. and L. Panitch (2015) 'The Syriza Dilemma', *Jacobin*, available at: https://www.jacobinmag.com/2015/07/tsipras-debt-germany-troika-memorandum/

Gourgouris, S. (2015) 'The Syriza Problem: Radical Democracy and Left Governmentality in Greece', available at: https://www.opendemocracy.net/can-europe-make-it/stathis-gourgouris/syriza-problem-radical-democracy-and-left-governmentality-in-g

Hardt, M. and A. Negri (2000) *Empire*. Cambridge, MA: Harvard University Press.

Hardt, M. and A. Negri (2005) *Multitude*. New York: The Penguin Press.

Kalecki, M. (2018) 'Political Aspects of Full Employment', *Jacobin*, available at: https://www.jacobinmag.com/2018/05/political-aspects-of-full-employment-kalecki-job-guarantee

Kiersey, N. and W. Vrasti (2016) 'A Convergent Genealogy? Space, Time and the Promise of Horizontal Politics Today', *Capital & Class* 40(1): 75–94, doi: 10.1177/0309816815627733.

Koshy, Y. (2019) 'Cookshops of the Future', *The Baffler*, https://thebaffler.com/latest/cookshops-of-the-future-koshy

Lapavitsas, C. (2016) 'One Year On, Syriza Has Sold Its Soul for Power', available at: https://www.theguardian.com/commentisfree/2016/jan/25/one-year-on-syriza-radicalism-power-euro-alexis-tsipras

Le Blanc, P. and H.C. Scott (eds) (2015) *Rosa Luxemburg: Socialism or Barbarism*. London: Pluto Press.

Livingston, J. (2016) *No More Work*. Chapel Hill, NC: University of North Carolina Press.

Marx, K. (1844) *Economic and Philosophic Manuscripts of 1844*, Marxists Internet Archive, available at: https://www.marxists.org/archive/marx/works/1844/manuscripts/labour.htm

Marx, K. (1852) *18th Brumaire of Louis Bonaparte*, Marxists Internet Archive, available at: https://www.marxists.org/archive/marx/works/1852/18th-brumaire/

Marx, K. (1875) 'Critique of the Gotha Programme', Marxists Internet Archive, available at: https://www.marxists.org/archive/marx/works/1875/gotha/ch01.htm

Marx, K. (1982 [1976]) *Capital*, vol I. London: Penguin Books.

Marx, K. (1993 [1939]) *Grundrisse: Foundations of the Critique of Political Economy (Rough Draft)*, trans. M. Nicolaus. London: Penguin Books.

Marx, K. and F. Engels (1848) *Manifesto of the Communist Party*, Marxists Internet Archive, available at: https://www.marxists.org/archive/marx/works/download/pdf/Manifesto.pdf

Mason, P. (2016) *PostCapitalism*. New York: Farrar, Straus and Giroux.

Morozov, E. (2019) 'Digital Socialism?', *New Left Review* 116: 33–67.

Phillips, L. and M. Rozworski (2019) *The People's Republic of Walmart: How the World's Biggest Corporations are Laying the Foundation for Socialism*. London: Verso.

Rifkin, J. (2014) *The Zero Marginal Cost Society: The Internet of Things, the Collaborative Commons, and the Eclipse of Capitalism*. New York: Palgrave Macmillan.

Rossignol, J. (2020) 'Apple Loses $2 Trillion Status Following Largest One-day Loss in Market Value of Any Company Ever', MacRumors, available at: https://www.macrumors.com/2020/09/04/apple-loses-2t-status/

Sadowski, J. (2018) 'Potemkin AI', *Real Life*, available at: https://reallifemag.com/potemkin-ai/

Sculos, B.W. (2019) 'Changing Lives and Minds: Progress, Strategy, and Universal Basic Income', *New Political Science* 41(2): 234–247, doi: 10.1080/07393148.2019.1595286.

Shanin, T. (2018) '1881 Letters of Vera Zasulich and Karl Marx', *Journal of Peasant Studies* 45(7): 1–20, doi: 10.1080/03066150.2018.1536370.

Shure, N. (2020) 'Uber and Lyft Are Threatening a Capital Strike', *Jacobin*, available at: https://www.jacobinmag.com/2020/08/uber-lyft-capital-strike-california-reclassify

Srnicek, N. and A. Williams (2015) *Inventing the Future*. London: Verso.

Tufekci, Z. (2017) *Twitter and Tear Gas, The Power and Fragility of Networked Protest*. New Haven, CT: Yale University Press.

Varoufakis, Y. (2018) *Adults in the Room: My Battle with the European and American Deep Establishment*. New York: Farrar, Straus and Giroux.

Varoufakis, Y. (2020) 'Something Remarkable Just Happened This August: How the Pandemic Has Sped Up the Passage to Postcapitalism', Lannan Foundation virtual talk, Yanis Varoufakis: Thoughts for the Post-2008 World, https://www.yanisvaroufakis.eu/2020/08/21/something-remarkable-just-happened-this-august-how-the-pandemic-has-sped-up-the-passage-to-postcapitalism-lannan-institute-virtual-talk/

Varoufakis, Y. and D. McWilliams (2020) '"There Is a Glimmer of Hope": Economists on Coronavirus and Capitalism', available at: https://www.theguardian.com/world/2020/may/06/there-is-a-glimmer-of-hope-economists-on-coronavirus-and-capitalism

Vidal, M. (2018) 'Are Workers the "Gravediggers" of Capitalism?', *Jacobin*, available at: https://www.jacobinmag.com/2018/10/working-class-gravediggers-marx-theory-revolution

Wark, M. (2015) 'Inventing the Future', Public Seminar, available at: http://publicseminar.org/2015/10/inventing-the-future/

Watson, M. (2015) '"Syriza Wins Time – and Space" by Étienne Balibar and Sandro Mezzadra', Verso Books Blog, available at: https://www.versobooks.com/blogs/1885-syriza-winstime-and-space-by-etienne-balibar-and-sandro-mezzadra

Worth, O. (2013) *Resistance in the Age of Austerity*. London: Zed Books.

7
Belaboured Markets: Imagining a More Democratic Global Economic Order

Jonathon W. Moses

This chapter imagines a world beyond capitalism. By capitalism, I mean the private ownership and control over the means of production; that is, capital. To go beyond capitalism, we must secure public control over capital, and this can only be done when capital is held accountable to political authority. This, in a nutshell, is my argument.

My proposal is hardly new or utopian, but it is not without challenges. The first challenge is the need to create a world of democratic states with the capacity to secure reliable and productive employment, thereby minimising social and economic inequalities. Our current economic order fails miserably in this regard. We live in a world where capital enjoys free rein, and communities have remarkably few means by which to influence social investment. Elected officials are unable to satisfy popular expectations because they have lost the tools they need to manage the domestic economy in ways that can satisfy the broader political community. Consequently, one hears growing calls for technical, as opposed to democratic, solutions to economic challenges.[1] These developments are fuelling a populist movement that has the force (and fury) to overturn democratic institutions.

To address these deficiencies, we need to secure political control over social investment – and each community should enjoy the freedom to control investments in its own way. In other words, controlling capital doesn't need to mean confiscating the means of production – although it can – it simply means that the community must have the capacity to influence decisions that are necessary for its material survival.

The second challenge is to find a way to integrate democratic states in ways that can protect their political autonomy, while allowing for a more just distribution of the world's bounty. This challenge is not new, but it used to attract much more attention. The need to balance autonomy and integration lay at the heart of political debate at the turn of the twentieth century, when we argued over whether it was possible to secure socialism in one country. In the post-war period, the world experimented with a handful of international regimes, in sundry attempts to secure that balance. But today's international system has given up on the effort: we limit democratic autonomy in the name of free markets, and we prioritise efficiency over justice.

This chapter offers a vision of an alternative international economic order: one that facilitates and encourages economic exchange (in order to secure the goods and services that people need and desire) while leveraging the democratic influence of workers and citizens. Finally, in a world beyond capitalism, we should prioritise the individual's freedom of mobility over that of goods, services and investment portfolios. In short, imagining the end of capitalism requires us to re-think the nexus of global markets and democratic polities.

Most contemporary attempts at harnessing globalisation have aimed to restrict global labour and trade flows. This chapter proposes several different scenarios, each of which is possible, and many of which have been tried before. In short, these are more practical than utopian scenarios. In the most attractive scenario, democratic states embrace free migration and (mostly) free trade in goods and services, while severely limiting international capital flows. This scenario offers several advantages over the existing capitalist order: (a) it allows for greater democratic influence over social investments; (b) it improves labour's bargaining position, relative to capital, within each domestic setting; (c) it encourages trade-based economic growth, rather than more destructive (and speculative) capital flows; and (d) it strengthens the voice of individual denizens, by providing them with a threat of exit in the face of unresponsive (or captured) political authority.

THE WORLD AS IT IS

Today's democratic states are enmeshed in a global economic order that severely limits their scope for political autonomy and democratic accountability. Since the 1970s, and under the banner of increased efficiency, the free trade movement has expanded significantly. National regulations and procurement arrangements – initially introduced by democratic legislatures in response to popular demands, and used to protect workers, their communities, and the surrounding environment – have been jettisoned in the name of comparative advantage, equal access and level playing fields. A broadening array of bilateral and multilateral trade and investment agreements set real limits (and penalties) on those who wield protective regulations (e.g. Investor–State Dispute Settlement – ISDS]) or prioritise local producers (e.g. Agreement on Government Procurement – GPA). Only agricultural products and labour markets seem to be immune to the spread of free trade.

The logic of free trade has even been extended to the most fictitious of all commodities: capital (Polanyi 2001 [1944]). By lifting restrictions on cross-border capital movements, we have made it almost impossible for elected officials to discipline and control productive investment for the needs of the community. Capital owners wield the threat of exit: when local conditions and/or regulations are seen to be too arduous, they seek better terms elsewhere.[2] But the free movement of capital also undermines the capacity of states to manage the domestic economy, by hobbling every country's capacity to conduct autonomous fiscal and monetary policies.

In a world with free capital mobility, it is increasingly difficult for countries to impose an autonomous (or even effective) income tax. Absent this important source of revenues, states find it difficult to sustain popular redistribution policies and social benefits. Unable to control the amount of capital entering/leaving their country, policy makers are unable to allocate it in a socially optimal manner. Worse, increased capital mobility has made it very difficult for states to employ autonomous monetary policies in response to costly crises that regularly impact capitalist economies. When elected representatives are no longer able to manage their local economies, workers must fend for themselves during economic downturns (Moses, forthcoming).

The only market that remains under stringent regulation is the one for labour: there are significant restrictions on immigration that limit worker mobility internationally. Consequently, workers do not enjoy the same threat of exit (as does capital), and workers are confined to states with few tools left to bring about substantial change and/or manage the domestic business cycle. In those areas where labour mobility is allowed (e.g. in common currency areas, such as the US and the EU), migration is often used as a means of economic adjustment, rather than as an opportunity (see e.g. Moses, forthcoming). To facilitate that mobility, European states have cut back on protections and support, while wages are made 'flexible'. The result has been stagnant real wages, increased inequalities, and dwindling support for democratic institutions.

ALTERNATIVE WORLD ORDERS

The current world order is only one of several possible economic world orders. Through countless decisions, unfolding over time and across countries, we have arrived at a global political economy that largely embraces the free exchange of goods and services. This norm, our default understanding of 'liberal capitalism', embraces the free movement of goods, services and capital, while restricting the free movement of people. This norm is hegemonic, but not unique: it is easy to imagine different world orders or different ways to operationalise liberal capitalism.

Indeed, at different times, and in different places, it is possible to find examples of international agreements that reflect different priorities (while still encouraging economic exchange and increased efficiencies). Some regimes have allowed free trade in goods but restricted international labour and capital mobility; other regimes have allowed for free trade and labour mobility but restricted international capital mobility. This section considers some of these variants, and the interests associated with each.

By pointing to these options, we can see that countries *decide* how to engage the international economy, and they should do so in full recognition of the costs/benefits involved. Some modes of economic integration prioritise the needs of economic exchange over those of political autonomy and stability: too much economic integration can erode local political authority and the community that we cherish. For example, volatile in/outflows of capital and labour can destabilise local markets, and the capacity of political authority to provide adequate regulation or control. Other modes of integration allow sovereign governments more control over economic production and exchange: they allow political authorities to protect against the crises that are endemic to capitalism and to secure more just (if not always more efficient) outcomes. In deciding which mode of integration is suitable, we need to assess how different modes of integration affect the distribution of opportunities and the scope for political sovereignty.

At the most general level, we can depict three main paths to economic integration: (a) the integration of goods/services markets (trade-based); (b) the integration of factor markets[3] (international factor mobility); and/or (c) a combination of both. In effect, these paths result in what I will call three different *modes of integration*: (1) trade-based; (2) labour-based; and (3) capital-based. A trade-based regime is one that facilitates free trade in goods and services; a labour-based regime facilitates free migration; and a capital-based regime supports free capital mobility over international borders. When combined in different ways, these three modes of integration produce eight possible combinations, or regime types (see Table 1). Each mode of economic integration delivers an equivalent economic result: they all deliver some form of factor price convergence (produced by increased efficiencies based on comparative advantage). But each of the resulting regimes benefits some asset holders more than others. Also, it is important to note that several of these regime types have existed in practice (see right-hand column), while others are more hypothetical.

These international regimes allow for sufficient variation in how economies might be managed, for the benefit of different groups of people. Variants of most regime types have existed before, in smaller regions, or for shorter periods of time, and each regime type is viable, given sufficient political will. My preferred regime, the People's regime (#4), allows for significant social control over investment, free labour mobility, along with trade in some goods and services. This sort of international regime nurtured the modern social democratic movement in northern Europe. It allows member states to control the domestic capital supply and allocate it for political purposes (e.g. choosing to prioritise education, rural development or home ownership). The Trader's regime (#3) attracts many others, who seek a return to the managed capital regime found in the Bretton Woods system. But the Trader's regime provided little opportunity to escape from unjust polities, and contributed to interstate inequality, as labour mobility was severely restricted.

Table 1 Regime types

#	Type	Content	Historical example
1	Liberal	K,L,T	Pre-First World War
2	Protectionist	k,l,t	Great Depression
3	Trader's	k,l,T	Post-Second World War (Bretton Woods)
4	People's	k,L,T	Nordic Common Market
5	Privileged	K,l,T	Contemporary world
6	Rentier's	K,l,t	Hypothetical
7	Worker's	k,L,t	Hypothetical
8	Asset holder's	K,L,t	Hypothetical

Note: 'K' denotes 'capital'. Upper-case letters denote open markets; lower-case letters denote protected markets. Hence in the Liberal regime (#1), there is free trade in goods, services, capital and labour. In the Protectionist regime (#2) each of these markets is protected.

Each regime benefits different groups of asset holders, and we can expect that vested interests will support beneficial regimes. It is for this reason (not on grounds of efficiency or justice!) that the current regime benefits capital owners and traders at the expense of workers. The first step in bringing about a regime change is to make people aware of how these different regimes benefit/harm their interests, and to mobilise support accordingly. This awareness and collective action can bring about both the crisis, and the preferred (if not necessarily utopian) response.

From an economic perspective, then, it matters little which mode of integration is chosen. After all, in traditional economic analyses there are only three factors of production: labour, capital and land, and they are interchangeable with one another. It doesn't matter which factor is prioritised, as they can achieve (in different combinations) the same outcome. This is most evident in the classic production functions used by economists, for example Cobb-Douglas, but is also evident to most travellers. When travelling in Norway, tourists will see relatively few workers laying pipes in the ditch alongside the road. The cost of labour is so high in Norway that employers invest in machinery to save on labour costs. In effect, employers substitute capital for labour when laying pipes. When travelling in Bangladesh, by contrast, tourists will see many workers, but less machinery laying pipes, as capital in Bangladesh is scarce (and hence relatively expensive), whereas labour is cheap. Market integration is equally agnostic with regard to the choice of factors. Factor price convergence can occur even in the absence of factor (labour or capital) mobility – as economists expect the equalisation of factor prices to result from international specialisation and the division of labour made possible by trade. The origins of this argument can be traced back to Robert Mundell's (1957) equivalence proposition and Paul Samuelson's (1948, 1949) Heckscher-Ohlin analyses. In short, to the extent that the gains of economic integration are derived from factor price convergence, it does not matter how markets are integrated – the same effect can come from labour market integration, capital market integration or trade in goods and services.

From a political or social perspective, however, the differences are significant. Each mode of integration delivers radically different consequences with respect to distributional concerns, as well as to the stability and scope of policy autonomy. For these reasons, it matters how we choose to integrate national economies.

Forms of integration

To consider who benefits from different forms of integration, we can turn to the abundant literature on trade. The trade-based mode of economic integration is the most established. It is entirely possible for a country to enjoy the benefits of integration without liberalising capital and labour markets, by simply engaging in trade. Indeed, economists have long recognised that trade can function as a substitute for limited (international) factor mobility. This was, after all, the foundational logic of the Bretton Woods system: economic development was to be driven by trade, while international capital and labour flows were severely restricted. Neo-Ricardian trade theory, upon which much economic integration theory is based, does not require international factor mobility to facilitate factor price convergence. These approaches begin by assuming the absence of factor mobility internationally; yet they still yield a complete equalisation of factor prices through the international specialisation and division of labour made possible by trade. Hence, when a farmer in Kansas sells her soybeans to a buyer in China, the land, labour and capital required to produce that soy is (in effect) moved from Kansas to China. In practice, of course, the factors of production (the farmer, her capital and her land) don't need to move to China – just the products of those factors. If our intent is to secure factor price convergence, and to enjoy the benefits derived from comparative advantage, it is (in theory) sufficient to limit international integration to trade in goods and services.

For many observers, trade-based integration has never been sufficient. After all, there are many competing motivations to liberalise factor markets. For one, trade is never completely free, and its potential is often hindered by vested interests that limit trade to certain sectors. When this occurs, international factor mobility might act as a substitute for international trade in goods and services (Mundell, 1961). This recognition drives our understanding of alternative modes of integration that rely on capital or labour market integration.

After all, some states may suffer from a shortage of capital or labour. Others may enjoy an abundance of one or the other. The same variance of interests is found among asset holders. If given a chance, asset holders might be willing to move their assets when attractive opportunities lie elsewhere, in order to maximise returns on investment (or job opportunities for workers). Given their very different natures, capital (investment) is obviously more mobile than labour (workers) – but the same logic and incentives hold for both groups. Factor mobility happens all the time in closed economy examples[4] – but the exact same thing can occur across national borders. In other words, it is possible to secure integration effects – at least in theory – by liberalising factor flows, even if the trade in goods and services remains restricted.

As seen in Table 1, global economic regimes can prioritise one, the other, or some combination of these modes of integration. While the economic effects of integration are more or less the same, regardless of the mode, the political effects can vary significantly. These political effects can be organised into two main types: distributional effects and policy effects.

Distributional effects

To understand the distributional effects, we can follow Ronald Rogowski (1989: xiii), who draws from Stolper and Samuelson (1941). In this framework, increased trade integration affects domestic factor interests (and political cleavages) in predictable ways. If you own an asset that is relatively abundant (relative to the rest of the world), then you will benefit from increased integration: capitalists in capital-rich (read developed) economies will benefit from increased capital mobility, while workers in labour-rich (read less developed) countries will benefit from increased labour mobility. Traders who produce goods and services that depend on the intensive use of abundant factors will benefit along with the asset holders: t-shirt producers (both workers and owners) in Bangladesh (a labour-rich, capital-poor, state) will benefit from free trade, because their t-shirts are made with abundant (read cheap) labour. As long as national borders maintain existing inequalities of factor distribution, trade will benefit the abundant asset holders.

Of course, the opposite is also true: scarce factor owners benefit from protection. So if you are a worker in Norway (where labour is relatively scarce), you would prefer that labour markets remain protected, and that poor workers from the developing world are kept at bay. It is because Norwegian workers are so few that they are so powerful (relative to capital in Norway); because they are so powerful (not to mention productive), Norwegian workers enjoy higher wages.

Although originally developed to infer interests related to trade, the argument is easily extended to factor mobility. In general – and at the global level – free trade in capital benefits capital holders, at the expense of workers, while free trade in labour (free migration) will benefit workers at the expense of capital.[5] To the extent that national regulations still limit the factor mobility of asset holders, then free capital mobility will benefit (developed) countries abundant in capital (relative to the rest of the world), while free migration will benefit (underdeveloped) countries, that suffer under an abundance of labour.

Hence, free trade regimes allow (relatively) abundant asset holders to benefit more than (relatively) scarce asset holders. Developed countries (that enjoy an abundance of capital) benefit from trade in capital-intensive goods and services and international capital mobility; while developing countries (suffering under an abundance of labour) will benefit from free trade in labour-intensive goods and services and free international migration. When the other factor, land scarcity/abundance, enters the equation the calculation becomes slightly more complicated, but the resulting lessons are clear (see Rogowski, 1989: 12, Figure 1.3).

Policy effects

It is not uncommon to consider the distributional effects of various modes of economic integration, as we did earlier in the chapter. We are mostly aware of these effects, if not always able (or willing) to protect against them.[6] The effects on policy from each mode of integration are less well understood, and yet have the largest consequences. The remainder of this section will consider the effects of different modes of integration on the capacity of governments to respond to, manage, or avoid economic downturns. Let us consider each mode in turn.

Trade

As we have seen, increased trade can have dramatic distributional consequences, but its impact on political stability or policy autonomy is relatively minor. Still, the relevance of these effects differs significantly for different types of economies (whether developing or developed). After all, the utility of managing trade flows varies with the level of economic development: liberalising trade flows benefits developed economies, more than it does developing counties, ceteris paribus.[7]

By participating in a liberal trade regime, countries suspend their use of controls, tariffs, and non-tariff barriers to trade. These policy instruments are most often used to secure important national policy objectives (e.g. food and/or military security) or to protect infant industries from international competition. The latter (infant industry protection) is the primary means by which countries establish and nurture domestic competence.[8]

In recent decades, the international trading regime has required states to jettison even more policy tools, many of which are especially important for protecting popular (read democratic) interests. We see this trend in the World Trade Organization's slow extension of free trade into new areas such as services (GATS – the General Agreement on Trade in Services) and intellectual property (TRIPs – Trade-Related Aspects of Intellectual Property Rights); in the growing effort to restrict local procurement procedures that might benefit indigenous producers (e.g. the Agreement on Government Procurement, or GPA); and in the expanded use of ISDS (investor–state dispute settlement) and other contractual constraints (e.g. 'stabilisation clauses') to scuttle sovereign regulatory control in national investment sites. By undermining sovereign policy tools, the trade-based mode of integration can hurt both developing and developed countries in that they tend to benefit large global firms at the expense of smaller local firms.[9]

In short, by embracing free trade, states lose some scope for sovereign policy. This loss of autonomy is especially pronounced in the developing world, as it is essential to protect and nourish economic growth in the early stages of economic development. But it is important to realise that the scope of that loss can be managed by influencing the way in which trade is secured. Trade can be limited to particular areas (e.g. agricultural produce), and certain types of states can be protected from competition as they build up their capacity to compete (for example, via a generalised system of preferences [GSP]). When transfer and transportation costs are large, then trade is only attractive in those sectors suffering from very large price differentials. Because trade regimes can be telescoped in and out in this way, trade-based integration can be engineered in ways that protect sovereign institutions and political stability.

Labour

Labour markets are less volatile, given the inherently immobile nature of labour, and the integration of national labour markets is unlikely to fuel significant economic and/or political crises (unless grievances are inflated by populist leaders). After all, in the free migration context before the First World War, international labour mobility was seldom associated with large-scale crises or conflicts. Most people, given the opportunity, prefer to stay at home (Moses, 2006).
But when opportunities at home are meagre, and the differences in market benefits (wages, protections, etc.) are large, we should expect significant pressure for international labour migration. If these movements are large, one can expect crowding problems, with the potential for destabilisation – as we see today in large urban centres across the developing world.[10]

In short, global labour mobility would clearly impact the capacity of political authorities, especially if the global labour flows are on a large scale. But this impact benefits the world's most desperate residents (who are voting with their feet), at the expense of the world's most developed states. In this light, it doesn't seem like a particularly unjust trade-off. In a free (fully integrated) labour market, workers will enjoy the opportunity to exit. By voting with their feet, repressed workers have an effective signalling device to broadcast their dissatisfaction with both political and economic conditions at home (Moses, 2006, 2011, 2012, 2017b). Hence, this mode of integration limits sovereign autonomy, but mostly from the bottom up: people will flee abusive contexts and seek attractive ones, and sovereign authority will need to adjust accordingly.

As with trade, it is possible to scale global migration up and down, in order to secure better outcomes and to avoid potential crises. States now compete with one another to attract high-skilled migrants, and future demographic pressures may prompt freer migration of lower-skilled workers as well. But because labour markets are sticky – the costs of mobility are large – it is relatively easy to manage these flows.

To conclude, the effects of migration on sovereignty and political autonomy are greater than we saw in the trade-based mode of integration, but these costs are manageable in light of the inherent immobility of labour. Global differences in opportunity must be substantial and long-lasting before workers are willing to leave home, family and friends. When these conditions exist, however, migration may be the most just and efficient means of lessening those differences (Moses, 2006).

Capital

Of the three modes of integration, capital market integration has *by far* the most damaging effect on political sovereignty. This effect stretches across several policy areas, as internationally mobile capital undermines the capacity of political authority to employ several common tools of economic policy.

First and foremost, the potential for capital flight forces political authorities to decide between embracing a fixed exchange rate regime or maintaining an autonomous monetary policy.[11] In other words, the authorities must decide on a monetary policy that either satisfies external constituents (via the exchange rate) or domestic constituents (via the interest rate). This effect is significant when one realises that an autonomous monetary policy was the primary means by which most developed countries steered their national economies in the post-war period (see e.g. Moses, 2000). When countries liberalise their capital markets, they lose control over the quantity of money in circulation, and with it the capacity to affect its price (the interest rate) and allocation.

Second, free capital mobility makes it impossible to commit to tax and regulatory policies that differ significantly from those of a country's main competitors. The reason for this is clear: the threat of capital flight. Any country planning to fund a welfare state will find it difficult to tax income/wealth. Consequently, political authorities will need to transfer the tax burden over to other (less mobile) asset holders (land and labour). Attempts to maintain more rigorous environmental, safety and/or labour regulations are easily 'voted' down by the threat of capital's exit (a so-called 'capital strike'). In addition, those countries with highly organised income policies (e.g. corporatist income policies), find that the relative bargaining power of capital increases, relative to labour, as any negotiated outcome is susceptible to the threat of a capital strike (exit). On each of these fronts – money, fiscal, regulatory and incomes policies – increased capital mobility hinders the hand of government.

If this were not worrisome enough, financial markets are inherently unstable and prone to crisis. Roving herds of investors have challenged fixed exchange rates (and systems), projecting phenomenal costs on domestic markets. (In the early 1990s, Sweden was forced to raise its interest rates to 500% to fight off an investor attack during Black Wednesday: see Moses 2017a: 7.) The global integration of financial markets is connected to a series of international crises, and has brought the world economy to its knees at least twice in the past hundred years. This volatility affects both economic and political worlds, but is very difficult to constrain, given the enormous concentration of wealth and power in the financial sector.

While any capitalist market needs access to capital for continued productive activity, the productive investment share of global capital flows is minuscule: most global capital flows are speculative and highly leveraged in nature. In the past, it has been possible to cordon off different types of capital, or to limit international flows that were not directly linked to trade in goods and services. Given sufficient political will, we could do this again. But the fungible and speedy nature of capital makes it more difficult to manage/control (than either trade or migration flows).

Summing up

From this examination of the political consequences of different modes of economic integration I conclude with three observations. First, many of the gains from economic integration can be secured by trade alone – without encouraging the more complex and destabilising effects of labour and capital market integration. The political ramifications of trade liberalisation are of an entirely different magnitude than those of labour and (especially) capital market liberalisation. This is less so for developing countries, who will need special allowances to integrate their economies on their own terms (or risk that their infant industries will be overrun), but the instruments of trade are flexible enough to be adapted to specific country needs.

Second, the integration of capital markets is by far the most costly in terms of political and social risks. There are several reasons for this. First of all, these markets are most prone to crisis (with broader economic effects that stretch beyond the financial markets):

> all 14 of the largest postwar crises took place after the mid-1970s. The three decades beginning in 1946 were unusually free of financial catastrophe. (That likely resulted from the tight controls on international flows of capital that formed part of the Bretton Woods system, a reminder that although open global capital markets bring major benefits, they also produce volatility.) But the crises after the mid-1970s show how much economic output can be lost when capital flows come to a sudden stop – and how hard it can be to recover from the downturn. (Reinhart and Reinhart, 2018: 86)

In addition, significant segments of these (financial) markets are tangential to society's productive and exchange needs: they feed speculative, rather than socially constructive, purposes. Worse yet, capital markets are one of the most important sources of economic inequality within countries – and this has serious political consequences. Finally, and perhaps most importantly, increased capital mobility undermines the public's capacity to steer the economy toward collective ends: it undermines autonomous tax, monetary, regulatory and incomes policies and it limits the community's ability to determine how productive investments should be allocated. Simply put: capital market integration undermines democracy. For all these reasons, the economic gains from capital market integration would need to be enormous if they are to be justified politically. They are not.

This leads me to my final observation: in deciding how to integrate a country's economy, policy makers need to balance the political costs against the anticipated economic benefits. How can a country maximise the economic gains from integration, while protecting its political autonomy and the people who must live and work in the shadow of this market? It seems to me that that there is a hierarchy of integration, where trade market integration is the least costly (in terms of its effect on political sovereignty); where labour market integration is somewhat more intrusive – but the scope of that intrusion will always be limited by the stickiness of labour (it is costly to move); and where capital market integration is the most costly and destabilising – it represents the biggest threat to political sovereignty.

THE WORLD AS IT SHOULD BE

When we imagine a better world, we need to consider how states can enjoy the benefits of economic integration, without sacrificing the capacity to manage the economy to secure popular outcomes. As described earlier, each mode of economic integration can deliver the sort of efficiency gains that modern states expect; but they differ widely in their distributional and policy effects.

In imagining that world, it is necessary to design a global economic order that will make the market subservient to politics. To paraphrase Thomas Piketty (in a quote widely circulated, but never actually referenced):[12] 'We want capitalism and market forces to be the slave of democracy rather than the opposite.' In a post-capitalist scenario, it behoves us to focus on three democratic objectives.

First, it is necessary for elected officials to regain control over social investment (private property, borrowing Marx's terminology) and to secure an international system that can provide states with sufficient autonomy to decide for themselves how to control their investments. We all depend upon productive enterprise, and our individual welfare depends upon a well-paying job. Because of our reliance on productive investment, it is necessary that elected officials have the capacity to allocate capital to projects that are assessed in terms of their political and social value, not just their returns on investment. Political control over the capital supply is absolutely necessary to secure democratic objectives.

State-ownership is not necessary to secure this control, but elected officials must be able to steer social investment. This means elected officials need control over the domestic money supply, its price and its allocation. To do this it is necessary to limit international capital mobility, such that elected officials are able to control the amount of capital in circulation (and with it, its price). When this is done, the state will be free to allocate cheaper capital to (politically) prioritised sectors, such as education, or rural development; and more expensive capital to less important sectors (e.g. luxury items and second homes). In a democracy, social returns should be balanced against fiscal returns.

Second, elected officials need to be able to control the business cycle and protect against economic disruptions. As long as we rely on paid employment for our survival – because the state cannot possibly support a population that is unemployed, and because workers at the bottom of the skill chain are hurt most by economic downturns – it is essential for the state to secure a strong, full-employment, economy. Doing so will improve the relative balance of power between workers and capital within each economy, making it less likely that workers will be forced to accept substandard wages and working conditions. As we have seen, by limiting international capital mobility (in particular), it is much easier for states to manage the business cycles (using autonomous fiscal and monetary policies) and avoid devastating crises.

Finally, it is necessary to return regulatory authority to democratically elected officials. If a host population wishes to protect its environment, community or workforce (for example), and it recognises that doing so may put it at an economic disadvantage relative to other states that do not secure these protections, then the international economic order should not be able to limit those popular preferences.

On each of these fronts it is important to recognise that different states will prefer different outcomes and different policy solutions to achieve those outcomes. A world order made up of democratic states cannot assume that one (policy) size will fit all. After all, that is the main point of democracy: state policy should reflect local (democratic) interests. But in granting this significant power to state officials, it is necessary to provide a guarantee, or back door, to protect individuals from potential abuses of power. Voting by ballot has proven entirely insufficient; voting with one's feet shows more promise.

The international regime that can best secure these outcomes is one that limits international capital mobility but encourages labour mobility and (limited) trade in goods and services. I called this the People's regime (#4) in Table 1. As we saw during most of the Bretton Woods period, an international regime that supports trade with limited capital mobility can secure export-based growth with significant scope for national policy autonomy. If that trade is directed toward agricultural production, it could even minimise global income inequalities. When capital mobility is restricted, government officials can manage the domestic economy, providing greater stability and employment opportunities for workers. By limiting capital mobility, and returning policy autonomy to states, we can generate a set of incentives that forces elected officials to respond to the needs of the people, more than those of capital owners. Finally, if workers have the possibility of exit, they can use it in response to abusive employers and political officials. Elected officials will be forced to compete with one another to provide more attractive working/living conditions, or risk losing their workforce to a neighbouring (more attractive) political community.

This sort of global regime is not a pipe dream: something similar existed within the Nordic Common Labour Market, from 1954 to the mid-1980s (as seen in Table 1). Under this regime, workers from any one of the Nordic countries could freely move to any other; economic growth was driven mostly by the export of and trade in goods; and international capital mobility was severely restricted (through the Bretton Woods arrangement). As a result, Nordic states were able to develop sophisticated welfare states and secure democratic accountability, economic growth and relative income equality – while still participating in the global economy. Not only were these states able to manage their domestic economies in a way that minimised the need for market-forced migration, but workers were able to secure protections that allowed them to retrain during economic downturns (rather than be forced to move). In effect, Nordic workers were able to move to other countries to avail themselves of better opportunities rather than out of economic necessity.

In imagining a better world, we need to construct an international economic regime that can provide states with the policy autonomy that democracy requires. The current regime does not have this capacity, but it is easy to imagine a future regime that does.

NOTES

My thanks to Michael Alvarez and the two editors for their useful comments on earlier drafts.

1. Consider, for example, Brennan (2016). But consider also recent events in Europe, when the elected prime (sic) ministers of both Italy and Greece were pushed aside and replaced with 'technocrats', for fear of upsetting markets. See: https://www.theguardian.com/commentisfree/2011/nov/13/europe-rise-technocracy-editorial
2. When investments are sunk, this type of immediate capital strike is more difficult, but the threat of future exit remains a powerful lever in the investors' negotiations with labour, community representatives, and elected officials.
3. As land is not mobile, the relevant factor markets are the labour market and the capital market.
4. Consider how factor mobility facilitates economic development within a given country. This is the simple closed-economy model that animates introductory macroeconomic textbooks, and it is obviously a gross simplification: with no exports, imports or cross-border factor flows. As countries become more economically developed, capital accumulates in urban cities, invests in productive activity, and attracts idle labour from the countryside (think Arthur Lewis, 1954). As peasants are drawn to the city to work, rural landowners are forced to invest in new technology (e.g. a harvesting machine), to replace the missing (and cheap) peasant labour. In effect, the landowner uses capital (in the form of technology) to replace the missing farmhands. When this labour floods into the city, worker incomes rise (relative to their farm income), allowing for greater consumption of local goods (and any excess is remitted back home). This allows them to buy the goods they help to produce (think Henry Ford).
5. Although I don't have space to elaborate here, this argument should be tempered by the recognition that labour mobility will always be more cumbersome than capital mobility, given the nature of labour as a commodity (i.e. these are friends and family moving, not investment portfolios). Consequently, the scope of global labour mobility will always be smaller than that of global capital mobility.
6. Economists have long recognised that there are exposed pockets of the economy that are negatively affected by free trade; but as the overall gains to consumers outweigh the relatively smaller losses to particu-

lar sectors, it makes economic (and political) sense to transfer some of those (general) gains to compensate those who have been negatively affected. In the US, this policy is referred to as 'trade-adjustment assistance'. In addition to compensating the losers, countries have a number of other options they can use to soften the blow, including the use of tariff and non-tariff barriers.
7. The theory of comparative advantage has us examine the benefits of increased trade, as opposed to not trading. This theory does not help us understand the effects of trade on relative gains across countries (i.e. that some countries benefit more than others from trade). To do this, we need to move beyond the theoretical models of mainstream economic textbooks and examine the actual lessons of history.
8. This tradition of economic nationalism has deep roots and can be traced back to Hamilton (1791) and List (1855). More recent examples include Chang (2003) and Reinert (2007).
9. Of course, the country might benefit from the increased efficiency associated with the larger firms – but if this production doesn't benefit local wage-earners and/or contribute to the local tax base, then it is of questionable benefit.
10. In a context of free labour migration, the most attractive labour markets may be overwhelmed by migrants, making it difficult for states to maintain high protective standards (regulations) and wages. Even in countries that have strong regulatory traditions and organised labour markets (such as in Norway), it has proven difficult to fight social dumping – and this is under conditions of relatively limited labour migration (mostly from within the EU).
11. I am referring to the Unholy Trinity argument, also known as the Mundell–Fleming conditions, or the monetary policy trilemma. See Mundell (1961), Fleming (1962), Obstfeld and Taylor (2017), but also Moses (2000, 2017a). For an influential counter argument, see Rey (2018).
12. See e.g. Prasad (2018: 855).

REFERENCES

Brennan, Jason (2016) *Against Democracy*. Princeton, NJ: Princeton University Press.
Chang, Ha-Joon (2003) *Kicking Away the Ladder*. London: Anthem Press.
Fleming, J. Marcus (1962) 'Domestic Financial Policies under Fixed and under Floating Exchange Rates', *IMF Staff Papers* 9(3): 369–380.

Hamilton, Alexander (1791) 'Report on Manufactures', Communicated to the House of Representatives, 5 December.

Lewis, W. Arthur (1954) 'Economic Development with Unlimited Supplies of Labour', *The Manchester School* 22(2): 139–191.

List, Friedrich (1885) *The National System of Political Economy*, trans. from the original (1841) edn by Sampson Lloyd. London: Longmans, Green and Company.

Moses, Jonathon W. (2000) *OPEN States in the Global Economy: The Political Economy of Small State Macroeconomic Management*. Houndmills: Macmillan.

Moses, Jonathon W. (2006) *International Migration: Globalization's Last Frontier*. London: Zed.

Moses, Jonathon W. (2011) *Emigration and Political Development*. New York: Cambridge University Press.

Moses, Jonathon W. (2012) 'Migration and Political Development: Exploring the National and International Nexus', *Migration and Development* 1(1): 123–137.

Moses, Jonathon W. (2017a) *Eurobondage: The Political Costs of Monetary Union in Europe*. Colchester: ECPR Press.

Moses, Jonathon W. (2017b) 'Sparrows of Despair: Migration as a Signalling Device for Dysfunctional States in Europe', *Government and Opposition* 52 (2): 295–328

Moses, Jonathon W. (forthcoming) *Workaway: The Human Costs of Europe's Common Labour Market*. Bristol: Bristol University Press.

Mundell, Robert A. (1957) 'International Trade and Factor Mobility', *American Economic Review* 67: 321–335.

Mundell, Robert A. (1961) 'A Theory of Optimum Currency Areas', *American Economic Review* September: 657–665.

Obstfeld, Maurice and Alan M. Taylor (2017) 'International Monetary Relations: Taking Finance Seriously', *Journal of Economic Perspectives* 31(3): 3–28.

Piketty, Thomas (2014) *Capital in the Twenty-first Century*. Cambridge, MA: Harvard University Press.

Polanyi, Karl (2001 [1944]) *The Great Transformation*. Boston, MA: Beacon.

Prasad, Ajnesh (2018) 'When Is Economic Inequality Justified?', *Business Horizons* 61(6): 855–862.

Reinert, Erik (2007) *How Rich Countries Got Rich ... and Why Poor Countries Stay Poor*. London: Constable.

Reinhart, Carmen and Vincent Reinhart (2018) 'The Crisis Next Time: What We Should Have Learned From 2008', *Foreign Affairs* 97(6): 84–96.

Rey, Hélène (2018) 'Dilemma not Trilemma: The Global Financial Cycle and Monetary Policy Independence', NBER Working Paper 21162. Original paper May 2015, revised February 2018, available at: www.nber.org/papers/w21162

Rogowski, Ronald (1989) *Commerce and Coalitions: How Trade Affects Domestic Political Alignments*. Princeton, NJ: Princeton University Press.

Samuelson, Paul A. (1948) 'International Trade and Equalisation of Factor Price', *Economic Journal* 58: 163–184.

Samuelson, Paul A. (1949) 'International Factor-price Equalisation Once Again', *Economic Journal* 59: 181–197.

Stolper, Wolfgang Friedrich and Paul A. Samuelson (1941) 'Protection and Real Wages', *Review of Economic Studies* 9: 58–73.

8
Post-capitalism and Associated Reactions: Mapping Alternative Routes and Transcending Strategic Certainty

David J. Bailey

The onset of neoliberal stagnation in 2008 prompted a new wave of post-capitalist literature to emerge (Srnicek and Williams 2015; Bailey 2019; Ranis 2016; Monticelli 2018; Mason 2015). As the urgency with which we need to replace capitalism is increasingly recognised, the unanswered question of how to achieve such a social transformation continues to preoccupy us. There is, arguably, a broad consensus regarding what a post-capitalist society might feature – a socialisation (or 'commoning') of the means of production, with some form of deliberation (rather than exchange) determining the allocation of resources, and some degree of voluntary association between subjects in a form that transcends the coercive pressures of capitalist scarcity, especially that of competition and exploitation (Albert 2004; Chatterton and Pickerell 2010; Gibson-Graham 2006). As Marx and Engels (1967 [1888]: 105) put it, this requires the creation of a society in which, 'the free development of each is the condition for the free development of all'. It will also entail an eradication of the 'background' inequalities and pathologies upon which it rests – gendered patterns of social reproduction, racialised exclusions, and the stubborn disregard for the environmental well-being upon which we each depend (Fraser, in Fraser and Jaeggi 2018). There is an absence of certainty, however, regarding how we might achieve a transition to such a society. We *appear* to be fundamentally uncertain about ways in which to proceed from the capitalist present to the post-capitalist future. Contrary to appearances, however, this chapter argues that much of the current post-capitalist debate remains committed to many of the political certainties of the twentieth century. These certainties, which used to be positioned as resting on the need to choose between the dichotomy of reform and revolution, and/or between the need to either embrace or to reject the state, have now come to be viewed by many commentators as outdated. Nevertheless, this chapter argues that the current wave of post-capitalism continues to reflect, and thereby consolidate, the certainties they claim to transcend. The post-capitalist debate remains wedded to the idea that we can act with certainty, and that in doing so we might overcome the barriers to post-capitalist transition. The present chapter more fundamentally rejects the certainty informing debates on post-capitalist trajectories, and instead replaces it with an uncertainty that recognises the immovability of obstacles to post-capitalism. In short, we benefit from recognising that there is no straightforward exit route towards a post-capitalist society, built upon strategic certainties, and that in adopting such a perspective we might become more effective in our efforts to destabilise, disrupt and transcend contemporary capitalist society.

UNCERTAIN CERTAINTY: THE RAPID SHIFT FROM ANTI-POWER TO STATE-FOCUSED LEFT POPULISM

> Uncertainty is how we experience the possibilities arising from the multiple relationships between fear and hope. (Santos 2018: 293)

In the past decade we have seen a rapid shift in left circles – especially among those in the Global North-west – between what might be considered opposed left strategies. At the risk of caricaturing this shift, what started in 2011 with a commitment to 'change the world without taking power' had, by 2015 morphed into a plan for state-focused left populism. We can trace this transformation by considering a number of theorists of left strategy.

One of the most prominent theorists of the anti-globalisation movement, which was a hegemonic force on the radical left in the years leading up to the onset of the global economic crisis in 2008, was John Holloway, and especially his text, *Change the World without Taking Power*. Holloway (2005) sought to theorise some of the problems and solutions that (especially) the anti-globalisation left had been dealing with during the 1990s and early 2000s. Much of this work was inspired by an engagement with the thinking of the Zapatistas, around slogans such as 'one no, many yeses', the need for a 'movement of movements', and a commitment that 'whilst asking we walk'. This represented a conviction that, for much of the twentieth century, many on the left had been excessively focused on seizing state power – an aim which Holloway and other Open Marxists theorised as being (either implicitly or explicitly) locked into the reproduction of capitalist forms, and especially the form of the capitalist state. Thus, for Open Marxists, the state is a capitalist state (Dinerstein and Pitts 2018: 477). It only came fully into existence as part of the historical development of capitalism, and its form – which seeks to separate the political from the economic – is a central component of capitalism as a commodity-producing society (Holloway and Picciotto 1977). For Holloway, therefore, it is necessary for anti-capitalist activity to occur in-and-against the state, but also (and perhaps especially) *beyond* the state. Indeed, it is beyond the state that movements such as the Zapatistas could generate alternative social relations focused around deliberation, democracy, prefiguration, horizontalism and cooperation – all of which are central to visions of post-capitalist society, and which were also subsequently taken up within many of the groups that considered themselves to be part of an anti-globalisation left.

This commitment to horizontalism and prefiguration was hegemonic among much of the radical left at the time of the eruption of the public square movements of 2011. Like David Graeber, who is widely viewed as one of Occupy Wall Street's key intellectual and organisational contributors, that movement rejected much of the more hierarchical methods of doing politics: 'After the Global Justice Movement, the old days of steering committees and the like were basically over. Pretty much everyone in the activist community had come around to the idea of prefigurative politics: the idea that the organizational form that an activist group takes should embody the kind of society we wish to create' (Graeber 2013: ch. 1). This saw a broad attempt to identify ways in which to organise social initiatives and forms of resistance in an explicitly egalitarian, participatory and democratic fashion. This, in turn, was informed by a broader concern that to do otherwise would inadvertently risk reproducing hierarchies that were considered undesirable, reflecting long-standing principles of the anarchist movement that are captured by the preamble to the Industrial Workers of the World (IWW) constitution: 'building the new society in the shell of the old'. This prefigurative consensus reflected both a widespread scepticism towards state-led communism, which was associated with leaders, events and political systems such as Stalin, the crushing of the Prague Spring, and the Soviet bloc. It was also informed by the legacy of the New Left movement(s) of 1968 (Yates 2015). As Maeckelbergh (2009) describes, these experiences created a 'distrust of Communism and traditional political parties', and a general tendency for political practice to be 'infused with discussions about what constitutes a democratic way to organise meetings', as well as 'an aversion to fixed structures of authority; [and instead an effort to seek political formations in which] there are no officers or positions of power; and there is a deep distrust of representation' (2009: 13). For many, the outpouring of popular protest witnessed across multiple places around the globe during 2011, and especially those adopting the method of occupying public squares, represented the culmination of this growing commitment to horizontal and prefigurative politics which had been developing at the core of the so-called anti-globalisation movement since (at least) the launch of the Zapatista rebellion in 1994 (Flesher Fominaya 2017; Roos and Oikonomakis 2014).

Yet, no sooner had horizontalism appeared to have reached its zenith, as the main ideological underpinning of the movements that emerged out of the post-2008 context, than questions began to be raised regarding the efficacy of the horizontalist approach. This can perhaps be most clearly witnessed in the work of Srnicek and Williams (2015), in which they questioned the degree to which horizontalism can be 'scaled up'. This articulated a frustration, experienced by many who had taken part in the wave of protests during 2011, that horizontalist protest was neither able to reverse austerity, nor to maintain a lasting presence, as it encountered difficulties in terms of challenging the more concrete and organised capacity of the neoliberal state. As Srnicek and Williams describe, the commitment to horizontalism and prefigurativism had, by 2011, become a 'folk politics' for the left. This folk politics was focused on the local, the informal, direct democracy, and a spatial immediacy. As such, it failed to consider ways in which to extend beyond the local scale of horizontalist activists: 'The problems of scale and extension are either ignored or smoothed over in folk-political thinking' (Srnicek and Williams 2015: 11). In articulating a general sense of disappointment regarding the lasting effects of this kind of 'folk politics', Srnicek and Williams described what they considered to be a common cycle: that, due to its inability to move beyond the immediate, this kind of politics inevitably results in demobilisation and disappointment. In their own words, there is a common pattern:

> resistance struggles rise rapidly, mobilise increasingly large numbers of people, and yet fade away only to be replaced by a renewed sense of apathy, melancholy and defeat. Despite the desires for a better world, the effects of these movements prove minimal. (2015: 5)

Similar words of caution were also voiced by others initially sympathetic to the strategies of horizontalism, but who remained concerned that mobilisation might not lead to social change. As Kiersey and Vrasti (2016: 83) perceptively warned, the question remains: 'how to marshal these prefigurative energies, converting them into an effective revolutionary force while shielding them from the disciplinary machinations of the capitalist state'. Their response was to advocate a cautious and pragmatic engagement with the institutions of the state, in order to gain the 'time and space' necessary to be able to generate a more thoroughgoing assault on vertical authority, while at the same time continuing to foster the development of horizontal movements across those societies bearing the pain of austerity.

This move away from horizontalism was consolidated later still, as part of an apparent shift towards left populism. Having sought initially to 'change the world without taking power', by 2015 the radical anti-austerity left were increasingly moving towards an explicit attempt to conquer the state, in part on the basis of a renewed strength that could be gained by tapping into the mobilisation of anti-austerity activism. This could be witnessed, politically, with the emergence of Podemos in Spain and the rapid ascendance of Syriza in Greece, and with the rapid rise to prominence of Bernie Sanders and Jeremy Corbyn as outsider left populists in the United States and United Kingdom (Charalambous and Ioannou 2019). It can also be witnessed in the turn towards a rejection of horizontalism by thinkers such as Mouffe (2018), Sunkara (2019) and Dean (2016).

Reflecting on similar dilemmas, in their recent book *Assembly*, Michael Hardt and Antonio Negri (2017) discuss the way in which horizontalism had for many within social movements become a fetishised principle that prevented effective action. This is perhaps surprising as, for many, Hardt and Negri's earlier work, especially *Multitude*, represented a canonical statement in support of the principle of horizontalism, prefigurativism, grassroots politics, and the rejection of the politics of representation and the state (which were typically considered to be 'constituted' power, to be rejected in favour of 'constituent' power) (Hardt and Negri 2005). In what might be considered a recanting, or perhaps a nuancing or clarification, of an earlier position, therefore, in their more recent work, Hardt and Negri (2017: 3) proclaim, 'the movements tend to be short-lived and seem unable to bring about lasting transformation'. As a result, they assert, there remains the need for 'vertical' politics, with leadership, hierarchy, and representation: 'under present conditions, a dynamic between verticality and horizontality, between centralised and democratic decision-making structures, is still necessary' (2017: 18). As such, Hardt and Negri advocate a rejection of a 'pure' focus on horizontalism and prefigurativism: 'prefigurative experiences in themselves lack the means to engage the dominant institutions, let alone overthrow the ruling order and generate a social alternative' (2017: 276).

What is perhaps surprising about these political, strategic and theoretical developments is the degree to which they reveal a rapid shift between different forms of certainty. This is puzzling. The rapid move between different positions suggests a fundamental uncertainty regarding the question of which route is most efficacious. Yet, despite this apparent uncertainty, positions *were* held with certainty at the time at which they were predominant, despite the rapid moving *between* different (strongly held) strategic convictions. As such, it might not be the case, as Esteva (2017: 2565) puts it, that we see an 'uncertainty created by the fact that old rationalities and sensibilities are obsolete and the new ones are not yet clearly identified'. By 'uncertainty', we commonly mean a contrast with 'risk'. Whereas risk is known and predictable, uncertainty is unknown and cannot therefore be foretold, measured or predicted (Scoones 2019: 6–8; see also the discussion in Blyth 2006). Under conditions of risk, it is sensible to proceed with caution; under conditions of uncertainty we are forced to embrace the need to adapt. In this sense, 'uncertainty refers to unknown probabilities and therefore implies a form of indeterminacy that expands the creative possibilities for human agents' (Lyng 2008: 110). When uncertainty is acknowledged and embraced, the likely response is an attitude marked by experimentation, non-linearity, improvisation, deliberation, and disruption (Scoones 2019: 26–8). In contrast, in considering the political moves outlined, from horizontalism to populism, we have seen a shifting between different positions of *certainty*: from a certain commitment to prefigurativism, through a certainty that such 'folk politics' is unlikely to produce desired outcomes, towards a certainty that a populist recapture of the state might, after all, be politically necessary and/or fortuitous. As such, rather than consider the political present as an era marked by uncertainty, it is more accurate to conclude that what we witness is a cycling between different positions each of which is drawn from the spectrum of old rationalities, and which continue to be held with a strong degree of certainty, only to be jettisoned remarkably rapidly once they have proven unable to resonate with the current (and rapidly changing) political and socio-economic context.

MAPPING ROUTES OF STRUGGLE AND FAILURE: TWENTIETH-CENTURY CERTAINTY AND OBSTACLES TO POST-CAPITALISM

As I have suggested, this rapid shifting between different certainties reflects, to a degree, some of the key debates within the left that have characterised the twentieth-century period. In particular, it speaks to two of the major debates that preoccupied the left: between reform and revolution; and between an embrace or rejection of the state (for a good summary of some of these debates, see Townshend

1996). Throughout much of the twentieth century, left parties and protest movements continued to return to these two key questions, which in turn underpinned many of the differences and debates that divided them (Bailey 2017). For those seeking social transformation through decentralised and democratic grassroots radicalism it was widely considered necessary for revolutionary activity to be located at the level of the grassroots, outside of large-scale capitalist institutions such as the state, as the alternative would be to contribute to a tyranny imposed from above. We might think of the experience of the anarchist revolution in Spain as an instance that exemplifies this view (Peirats 1974). In contrast, for those who feared that a radical politics of the everyday would result in discoordination, lack of direction and therefore an inability to defend hard-won gains from the inevitable pressures of counter-revolution, the answer was the securing and stabilising of the power of the subordinate classes, through the capture of the state, or, in Marxist terminology, by producing a dictatorship of the proletariat (Lenin 1918). Similarly, the schism between gradualist social democracy and revolutionary communism pitted those who feared, on the one hand, that gradualism would amount to little more than the reproduction and perpetuation of established social inequalities, against those, on the other hand, who considered goals of radical social transformation to be a recipe for utopianism and impracticality (for one of the best accounts of these debates, see Berman 2006). In sum, these debates were underpinned by two interlinked questions or strategic decisions – between those who sought macro-social change, in contrast to those seeking gradual and piecemeal reforms; and between those who sought to channel their efforts within established institutions of authority, and especially the state, and those who considered it necessary to construct alternative and rival social relations outside of the relations of the state, capital and/or money (see Figure 1 for a summary).

Yet each of these strategic options brought with them corresponding pitfalls, as is and has been repeatedly pointed out by those adopting positions at opposite ends of the spectrum across which these strategic dilemmas range. As Figure 1 attempts to visualise, each of these different alternative post-capitalist routes has been associated with its own corresponding pitfalls. As Figure 1 tries to

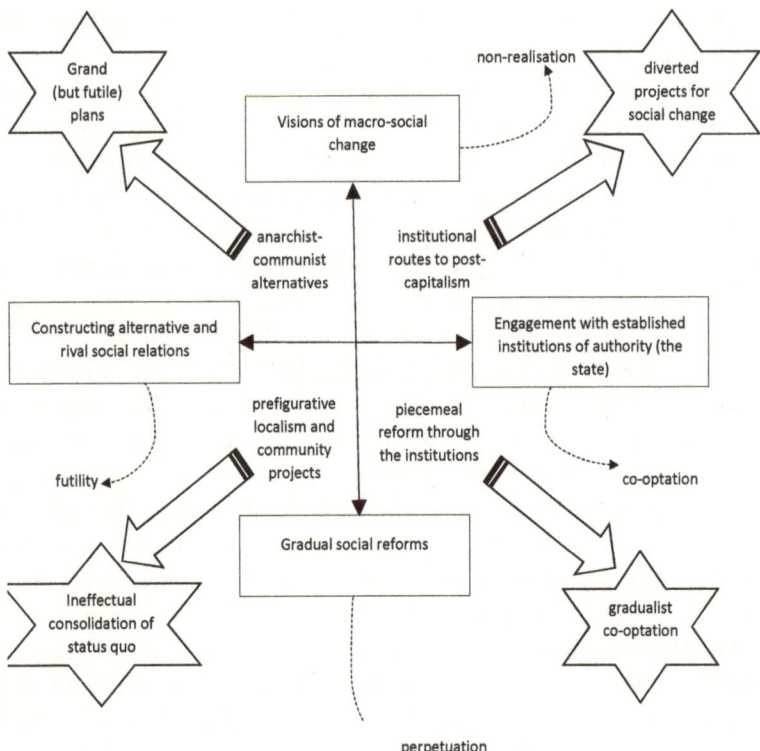

Figure 1 Trajectories of change and associated pitfalls: a gloomy reading

show, while anti-capitalist strategies have a tendency to diverge over key questions of scale and organisation, nevertheless each option is also arguably associated with different types of failure, which those on opposing sides of the debates have tended to highlight. Indeed, the history of the twentieth century left in many ways confirms each of these criticisms, and as such can be read as a history of failures and dead-ends. This includes the degeneration of the Soviet Union, the defeat of the anarchist movement in the Spanish civil war, the coup that ended the Chilean socialist government of Allende, the U-turn of the Mitterrand government, and the jailing and repression faced by the 1970s post-Operaismo social movements in Italy. This list of defeats goes on and on. Rather than identifying a 'correct' route towards a post-capitalist society, we have arguably instead witnessed moves along alternative exit routes, each of which has displayed an inability to result in a post-capitalist trajectory. As Hardt and Negri (2017: 70) put it: 'It seems that we are caught in a double bind – we can't take power and we can't not take power.'

DEADLOCK, AMBIGUITY, DISRUPTION

Such a gloomy reading of the history of the twentieth-century left prompts a consideration of both the likely consequences of alternative routes towards post-capitalism, and what appear to be inevitable obstacles wherein any particular exit route prompts its own set of pitfalls, without any apparently successful exit route 'out' of capitalism. Rather than adopt such a gloomy conclusion, however, we might instead draw on a number of more nuanced theorists of left strategy, for whom the type of problems, difficulties and dilemmas that we have thus far considered in this chapter have arguably been thought of as problematic, but nevertheless not insurmountable. The choice is not, in Hardt and Negri's words, 'between ineffective horizontality and undesirable leadership' (2017: 227). Perhaps central to such an analysis is the observation that, while the route out of capitalism appears difficult to envisage, nevertheless, the prospect that capitalism is able to stabilise its systems of control and authority is equally improbable. There is both no clear route out of capitalism, *and* no clear means by which to maintain it. It is for this reason, therefore, that we should consider capitalism *both* as marked by a seeming absence of viable exit routes *and* as continually generating opportunities to contest, disrupt and dislodge the apparatuses of control which constitute it. In this sense, even though the exit route from capitalism is not immediately apparent, we nevertheless always have available to us means by which to test and tease mechanisms of authority and stasis which seek to uphold it. This represents, for Hardt and Negri (2017), the development of 'counterpowers'; these 'cannot be conceived as harmonious or linear, but instead they must always function antagonistically, in an effort to subvert capitalist sovereignty' (2017: 257). This, moreover, remains without certainty – 'there is nothing assured about this process' – and instead represents a 'wager', that is, 'based on the accumulation of resistances, struggles, and desires for liberation' that exist within the present (2017: 258).

Through such experimental acts of resistance, and without a search for certainty or guaranteed pathways, we can perhaps begin to re-envisage (non-linear) trajectories towards a post-capitalist society (Deleuze and Guattari 1988). In doing so, what remains of this chapter draws on the work of three thinkers and activists who have sought to grapple with some of these kinds of problems, and in doing so have outlined what we might consider to be suggestions and ideas that provide opportunities for hope: Rosa Luxemburg, Frantz Fanon and Veronica Gago.

These three thinkers in particular are chosen because, as we shall see, they each in their own way seek to deal with the kinds of dilemmas and contradictions with which we began this discussion. They each recognise that the question of resistance, subversion, or 'counterpower', begins from a position of, and response to, structural weakness. Yet, an attempt to challenge (or even simply survive) a position of structural weakness is, clearly, hampered from the start, precisely by the condition of being structurally weak. This obviously has the potential to be a fundamental constraint. In different ways, however, as we shall see, Luxemburg, Fanon and Gago, each suggest approaches to agency that emerge from a recognition of this problem, but in a way that avoids being rendered incapable of action. For this reason, perhaps, they provide insights that merit their consideration.

Luxemburg

In her work, *The Mass Strike, the Political Party, and the Trade Unions*, Rosa Luxemburg (2008 [1906]) starts with a similar difficulty to that which we have been focused on in the present chapter. In doing so, she considers the role of mass dissent, the mass strike (especially in the 1905 Russian Revolution) and the role of revolutionary left parties and intellectuals and trade unions within the broader process of class struggle and revolutionary activity. In setting out a set of difficulties that resonates with our discussion thus far, Luxemburg describes the context in which struggle happens. This can be re-stated as a paradox:

class struggle is necessary because the proletariat is dominated and therefore needs to build the capacity to overturn that domination, but at the same time any acts which move the proletariat closer to an increased capacity for struggle are equally likely to be challenged by the ruling class, and – given the balance of class of forces as they currently exist – that ruling class is likely to be successful. Indeed, if the capacity of the proletariat was sufficient to challenge the ruling class then there would be no need for that challenge to occur in the first place, as domination would already have been overturned. As Luxemburg puts it, albeit in a passage which she subsequently goes on to reject:

> either the proletariat as a whole are not yet in possession of the powerful organization and financial resources required, in which case they cannot carry through the general strike or they are sufficiently well organized, in which case they do not need the general strike. (Luxemburg 2008 [1906]: 112)

A similar paradox is noted with regard to the attitude of trade unionists, especially at the level of trade union officialdom. Luxemburg considers trade union officials to display a tendency to always put off trade union activity and disputes until a later point – a point during which trade union density, organisation and militancy is increased sufficiently to enable conflicts to be guaranteed of success. Thus, Luxemburg describes how, 'The attitude of many trade-union leaders to this question is generally summed up in the assertion: "We are not yet strong enough to risk such a hazardous trial of strength as a mass strike"' (2008 [1906]: 156). Yet, as Luxemburg points out, it is never possible to determine in advance what level of organisational strength would be necessary in order for a mass strike to be successful. As such, she concludes:

> The tacit assumption is that the entire working class of Germany, down to the last man and the last woman, must be included in the organisation before it 'is strong enough' to risk a mass action, which then, according to the old formula, would probably be represented as 'superfluous'. (2008 [1906]: 156)

It is in seeking to overcome these kinds of constraining dilemmas that Luxemburg advocates what we might consider to be a strategy of 'struggle-without-guarantees'. That is, in recognising that the odds are stacked against the proletariat, we can also recognise that unexpected and unpredictable events do occur, and that they have the surprising capacity to advance the strength, in this case, of the proletariat. Thus, Luxemburg goes to great lengths to highlight the way in which those seeking to ensure the 'correct' direction of class struggle will inevitably find themselves in a situation whereby the complexity of events has overrun their capacity to offer a meaningful plan of action. As she observes, it is beyond the scope of any political activist to determine in one particular context what form the class struggle takes at that particular time:

> If anyone were to undertake to make the mass strike generally, as a form of proletarian action, the object of methodological agitation, and to go house to house canvassing with this 'idea' in order to gradually win the working class to it, it would be as idle and profitless and absurd an occupation as it would be to seek to make the idea of the revolution or of the fight at the barricades the object of a special agitation. (Luxemburg 2008 [1906]: 118)

Likewise, in considering the development of the 1905 Russian Revolution, Luxemburg considers how earlier events and disputes over wages and working conditions, as well as mass demonstrations, and the responses of the authorities (and especially the massacre in St Petersburg in January 1905) all contributed to the uprising that occurred throughout 1905. In this sense, the capacity for earlier forms of resistance to feed into and empower later forms, in unpredictable ways, highlights the unplannable nature of social change: '*it is impossible for anyone to reckon upon it with any degree of certainty*' (2008 [1906]: 140, emphasis added). As a result, moreover, 'it is extremely difficult for any directing organ of the proletarian movement to foresee and to calculate which occasions and factors can lead to explosions and which cannot' (2008 [1906]: 148).

It is on the basis of these reflections that Luxemburg advocates a non-linear strategy of uncertainty. In this sense, engagement in struggle and resistance must be done *without* a clear and linear strategy for social change, in order to take advantage of the unexpected opportunities for empowerment that do, and will, arise. This might occur in the context of a mass strike or revolutionary context: 'The worker, suddenly aroused to activity by the electric shock of political action, immediately seizes the weapon lying nearest his hand for the fight against his condition of economic slavery' (2008 [1906]: 146). But it also might occur in the less dramatic context of union mobilising and socialist campaigning. For instance, Luxemburg describes the development of German trade unions in the late nineteenth century. Here, despite being insufficiently strong to take on the German anti-socialist laws, nevertheless, the trade unions:

> weak as they were at the time, did take up the struggle ... and showed that they were 'strong enough', not only to emerge from the struggle victorious, but to increase their strength fivefold.... It is true that the methods by which the trade unions conquered in the struggle against the antisocialist laws do not correspond to the ideal of a peaceful, beelike, uninterrupted process: they went first into the fight absolutely in ruins, to rise again on the next wave and to be born anew. But this is precisely the specific method of growth corresponding to the proletarian class organizations to be tested in the struggle and to go forth from the struggle with increased strength. (Luxemburg 2008 [1906]: 157–8)

Perhaps the most important lesson that Luxemburg takes from all of this, therefore, is that no particular form of struggle should be prioritised, as it is simply not possible to determine in advance which form will be most effective. For instance, in seeking to decide between what she refers to as 'economic' and 'political' struggle, she claims that we should decide *not* to decide, as each route is anyway inseparable from, and interconnected with, the other: 'cause and effect continually change places' (2008 [1906]: 145). For the purposes of our present discussion, the lesson is perhaps that, faced with seemingly intractable difficulties in terms of deciding on the best exit route out of capitalism, it would be better to embrace a rejection of claims to certainty regarding the best way forward, and instead to seek to test, through experimentation with different and alternative types of struggle, the different opportunities that are made available at any one point in time and place, abandoning overly rigid and pre-given restrictions or preconceptions.

Fanon

In his most mature work, *The Wretched of the Earth*, Frantz Fanon (1967 [1965]) also begins with a similar set of difficulties with which we are seeking here to consider; albeit now applied more directly to strategic questions relating to decolonisation. As Fanon describes, decolonisation rests on a contest between 'settlers' and 'natives', in which both categories are necessary for the existence of the other: 'it is the settler who has brought the native into existence and who perpetuates his existence. The settler owes the fact of his very existence, that is to say his property, to the colonial system' (1967 [1965]: 28). In seeking to overturn the colonial system, therefore, decolonisation stirs up a number of contradictions that arise from the interconnected nature of the colonial settler and the 'native'. This raises a number of dilemmas that are not straightforwardly resolved. One area where this can be seen is in Fanon's discussion of violence. For Fanon, violence is so constitutive of colonialism that the native is induced to take up violence themself, as a means of expression. In this sense, the violence of the native is created by the colonial system. Decolonial violence itself is a product of colonialism: 'the settler has shown him the way he should take if he is to become free […] and by an ironic turning of the tables it is the native who now affirms that the colonialist understands nothing but force' (1967 [1965]: 66).

This intrinsic relationship, between the violence of the colonial system and the identity of the movement for decolonisation, also creates further intractable dilemmas that speak to our questions of strategic choices and unavoidable difficulties. This is perhaps most evident in considering the demand for decolonisation. This is often grounded upon a demand for the return to the 'natives' of ownership of a country that in many cases never existed prior to colonisation – 'In their speeches the political leaders give a name to the nation' (1967 [1965]: 53) – although, again ambiguously, Fanon nevertheless sees this as a progressive act. The leaders of decolonial struggles have already, therefore, conceded that territories created by colonisation now have become concrete to the extent that the ambition is to replace the rulers of colonial territories with decolonial rulers of post-colonised territories. This represents a somewhat contradictory form of peaceful negotiation. The threat that the leaders of decolonial struggles pose is that of mass mobilisation by the oppressed and colonised 'natives', as a bargaining tool that remains in the background. The demands of decolonial leaders – seeking to rule over those decolonialised territories – is therefore already ambiguous from the start: 'the national political parties never lay stress upon the necessity of a trial of armed strength, for the good reason that their objective is not the radical overthrowing of the system' (1967 [1965]: 46). Indeed, Fanon is explicit about the ambiguity of this nascent political elite: 'On the specific question of violence, the [nationalist] *élite* are ambiguous' (1967 [1965]: 46).

This contradictory role of both leadership figures and violence, within struggles for decolonisation, clearly speaks to a number of the problems of post-capitalist strategy that we have been discussing in this chapter. In particular, it highlights further still the intractable difficulties that are associated with any forms of radical political action. In this case, this arises from the fact that the leaders of decolonial struggles – and especially the nationalist parties that adopted a leadership role within them – were typically based within the urban centres of colonised territories. This created a situation in which those who had been partially empowered by the colonial system were also those who began to make the most explicit demands for decolonisation. As Fanon puts it, these are people who 'have begun to profit – at a discount, to be sure – from the colonial set up'. As a result, the 'leaders' of the native insurrection sought to adapt to the colonised world. Thus, Fanon describes the 'native intellectual' who 'clothed his aggressiveness in his barely veiled desire to assimilate himself to the colonial world' (1967 [1965]: 47). As such, the demand for assimilation rendered decolonial struggles paradoxical, in a way that resonates with the dilemmas facing multiple forms of anti/post-capitalist strategies. This is highlighted further still when we come to view the position of the colonialists themselves, who would oftentimes welcome the demands of decolonial leaders: 'Their purpose is to capture the vanguard, to turn the movement of liberation towards the right and to disarm the people: quick, quick, let's decolonize' (1967 [1965]: 55).

It is in seeking to consider ways to respond to these various paradoxes, dilemmas and contradictions that Fanon offers some important insights that can help to inform a response to the difficulties associated with the question of post-capitalist exit routes. Thus, Fanon appears to propose a kind of hopeless violence, which, while unable to promise efficacy, can nevertheless contain the potential for liberation. In his consideration of the decision to volunteer to join the decolonial struggle and to take up arms and engage in insurrectional activity, Fanon describes how, 'confidence was proportional to the hopelessness of each case' (1967 [1965]: 67). At the same time, a commitment to (hopeless) violence enabled insurrectionary decolonialists to liberate themselves from the constraints of the colonial system. Once they took this step, the option of continuing to consent to, and collaborate with, colonialism, was ended. In this sense, 'The colonized man finds his freedom in and through violence' (1967 [1965]: 68). This was the case, not only in the sense of avoiding a return to colonial relations, but also in terms of restoring dignity. For Fanon, violence provided the opportunity to restore to colonised subjects the capacity for agency: 'At the level of individuals, violence is a cleansing force. It frees the native from his inferiority complex and from his despair and inaction; it makes him fearless and restores his self-respect' (1967 [1965]: 74).

In terms of our present discussion, what we can perhaps take from Fanon's work is his consideration of the intractable difficulties that those engaged in decolonial struggles faced. It is in this context, moreover, faced with dilemmas and obstacles whichever the strategic direction of political activity, that Fanon considers the role of violence. While we do not need to accept Fanon's argument for violence per se, nevertheless we can take it as a further elaboration of Rosa Luxemburg's argument that we considered earlier in this chapter: faced with an intractable dilemma, in which no strategic choices promise a linear route towards the absenting of domination, we can instead adopt strategies of experimental struggle that are *without* a clear outcome, and which nevertheless have the potential to open opportunities through which to develop subjectivity, disruption and the capacity for experimentation with struggle.

Gago

In a more recent contribution to similar discussions, Veronica Gago has introduced a number of important insights into the experience of neoliberal subjects in what she considers to be Argentina's post-neoliberal context of the 2000s (Gago 2017). This is a context in which neoliberal subjectivities remain in place, despite the end to the political legitimacy of neoliberalism, and especially following the experience of the 2001 crisis in Argentina. As Gago describes, in seeking to adapt to the insecurity and hardship of neoliberal society, in which jobs are unavailable and/or unreliable, individuals are forced to find alternative ways in which to live, in the gaps outside of the formal economy and through forms of association that simultaneously both constitute *and* challenge the domination of neoliberal capital. These ways of existing, Gago terms, 'baroque economies in which the persistence and confrontation with the neoliberal dynamic from above and from below are simultaneously negotiated' (2017: 3). In mapping the forms of subjectivities that develop both as part of, and in resistance to, neoliberal dynamics, Gago sets out a perspective that can help us to understand and consider the forms that resistance takes in contexts where the possibility of organised resistance appears absent. For Gago, therefore, we see a context in which neoliberal subjects are forced into subversive forms of association and agency, as individuals adapt, cooperate and associate in different and innovative ways, in interaction with the efforts made by capital and the state to restructure society along neoliberal lines, and which is done in pursuit of a new mode of accumulation. As Gago shows, this can be seen in a number of different contexts, including *La Salada*, the largest illegal market in Latin America, which is interlinked with a network of 'clandestine textile workshops' in which (especially Bolivian) migrant workers make up a large majority of the workforce (2017: 16). In describing this context, Gago highlights the combination, at the same time, of both brutal exploitation and the construction of new communities and solidarities, as the market's population is required to find ways to live outside of the formal economy, and in doing so to create new forms of 'self-management'.

Likewise, Gago considers the context of *Villa 1-11-14*, which is effectively a shanty town in Buenos Aires, in which migrant workers, mainly from Bolivia, exist in ways which necessitate forms of association and cooperation that enable survival, including through forms of house sharing, community decision making, and a loan system that enables funding to rotate between members of the loan pool so that each person can at a certain point in time afford sufficient resources to invest in setting themselves up with a livelihood. It is in this sense that neoliberal domination brings with it the scope for the conversion of neoliberal social relations into sources of survival *and* resistance (for a similar perspective, see also Fishwick and Connolly 2018). Importantly, this is not always overt resistance, and as such illustrates the complexities of post-capitalist subjectivities, in that the novel forms of resistance that emerge are not necessarily openly in pursuit of post-capitalist outcomes. As Gago describes, we see 'forms of doing and calculating, that use neoliberalism tactically, putting it into crisis in an intermittent but recurring way'. In other words, even when neoliberal society appears to have created the necessity to adopt neoliberal subjectivities, these nevertheless remain open to the capacity to act (experimentally) in ways which challenge those conditions which constitute neoliberal society.

CONCLUSION

We live in a time in which the need for a post-capitalist trajectory, or exit route, is both widely recognised and yet feels unobtainable. Many of the strategic certainties that underpinned the twentieth-century debates around post-capitalist strategy are often considered to have been abandoned in the post-1989 era. Nevertheless, many of the debates that have exercised the radical left, especially since the onset of the so-called 'age of austerity' that followed the 2008 crisis, have tended to echo the same certainties that informed those debates, albeit in a way that has witnessed a rapid cycling between different positions. It is the claim of this chapter that the apparent failure to resolve the strategic debates of the twentieth-century left, as well as the rapid moving between alternative positions in the present, can each be understood to reflect the fundamental difficulties that are associated with the pursuit of a post-capitalist exit. Some have sought to respond to these difficulties through a strategy of hybridity. For Hardt and Negri (2017), for instance, we need 'a subversion that transfers the struggle and the perspective of transformation from the horizontal axis of social struggles to the vertical axis of the struggle for power' (2017: 257). Yet this might only represent an attempt to combine previously contradictory certainties. Rather than search for a certain strategy or a trajectory, therefore, we might be better served by accepting that each route will be uncertain and difficult, if not impossible, to follow. Faced with these kinds of uncertainties and difficulties, the chapter has argued, we can draw on a tradition of left theorising that is more willing to accept that such intractable problems exist. Faced with such a realisation, we can perhaps consider ways in which experimental attempts to associate, organise within, and challenge, structures of domination can provide unexpected opportunities for resistance and social change to arise, all of which has a tendency to occur in an unpredictable manner, and which therefore demands that we acknowledge *and* embrace the necessary uncertainty that unavoidably informs our efforts to bring such change about (and which will probably be unsuccessful, but with unintended yet disruptive consequences).

REFERENCES

Albert, M. (2004) *Life after Capitalism*. London: Verso.

Bailey, D.J. (2017) *Protest Movements and Parties of the Left: Affirming Disruption*. London: Rowman and Littlefield International.

Bailey, D.J. (2019) 'Extra-capitalist Impulses in the Midst of the Crisis: Perspectives and Positions Outside of Capitalism', *Globalizations* 16(4): 371–385.

Berman, S. (2006) *The Primacy of Politics: Social Democracy and the Making of Europe's Twentieth Century*. Cambridge: Cambridge University Press.

Blyth, M. (2006) 'Great Punctuations: Prediction, Randomness, and the Evolution of Comparative Political Science', *American Political Science Review* 100(4): 493–498.

Charalambous, G. and G. Ioannou (eds) (2019) *Left Radicalism and Populism in Europe*. London: Routledge.

Chatterton, P. and J. Pickerell (2010) 'Everyday Activism and Transitions towards Post-capitalist Worlds', *Transactions of the Institute of British Geographers* 35: 475–490.

Dean, J. (2016) *Crowds and Party*. London: Verso.

Deleuze, G. and F. Guattari (1988 [2004]) *A Thousand Plateaus: Capitalism and Schizophrenia*, trans. B. Massumi. London: Continuum.

Dinerstein, A. and F.H. Pitts (2018) 'From Post-work to Post-capitalism? Discussing the Basic Income and Struggles for Alternative Forms of Social Reproduction', *Journal of Labor and Society* 21(4): 471–491.

Esteva, G. (in conversation with A. Escobar) (2017) 'Post-Development@25: On "Being Stuck" and Moving Forward, Sideways, Backward and Otherwise', *Third World Quarterly* 38(12): 2559–2572.

Fanon, F. (1967 [1965]) *The Wretched of the Earth*. London: Penguin.

Fishwick, A. and H. Connolly (2018) 'Working-class Resistance in Hard Times: An Introduction', in A. Fishwick and H. Connolly (eds) *Austerity and Working-class Resistance: Survival, Disruption and Creation in Hard Times*. London: Rowman and Littlefield International.

Flesher Fominaya, C. (2017) 'European Anti-austerity and Pro-democracy Protests in the Wake of the Global Financial Crisis', *Social Movement Studies* 16(1): 1–20.

Fraser, N. and R. Jaeggi (2018) *Capitalism: A Conversation in Critical Theory*. Cambridge: Polity.

Gago, V. (2017) *Neoliberalism from Below: Popular Pragmatics and Baroque Economies*. Durham, NC: Duke University Press.

Gibson-Graham, J.K. (2006) *A Postcapitalist Politics*. Minneapolis, MN: University of Minnesota Press.

Graeber, D. (2013) *The Democracy Project: A History, A Crisis, A Movement*. New York: Spiegel and Grau.

Hardt, M. and A. Negri (2005) *Multitude: War and Democracy in the Age of Empire*. London: Penguin.

Hardt, M. and A. Negri (2017) *Assembly*. Oxford: Oxford University Press.

Holloway, J. (2005) *Change the World without Taking Power: The Meaning of Revolution Today*, new edn. London: Pluto.

Holloway, J. and S. Picciotto (1977) 'Capital, Crisis and the State', *Capital and Class* 1(2): 76–101.

Kiersey, N. and W. Vrasti (2016) 'A Convergent Genealogy? Space, Time and the Promise of Horizontal Politics Today', *Capital & Class* 40(1): 75–94.

Lenin, V.I. (1918 [1992]) *The State and Revolution*. London: Penguin.

Luxemburg, R. (2008 [1906]) *The Mass Strike, the Political Party and the Trade Unions*, in H. Scott (ed.) *The Essential Rosa Luxemburg: Reform or Revolution and The Mass Strike*. Chicago: Haymarket Books, pp. 111–182.

Lyng, S. (2008) 'Edgework, Risk, and Uncertainty', in J.O. Zinn (ed.) *Social Theories of Risk and Uncertainty: An Introduction*. Oxford: Blackwell, pp. 106–137.

Maeckelbergh, M. (2009) *The Will of the Many: How the Alterglobalisation Movement is Changing the Face of Democracy*. London: Pluto.

Marx, K. and F. Engels (1967 [1888]) *The Communist Manifesto*. London Penguin.

Mason, P. (2015) *Postcapitalism: A Guide to our Future*. London: Allen Lane.

Monticelli, L. (2018) 'Embodying Alternatives to Capitalism in the 21st Century', *tripleC* 16(2): 501–517.

Mouffe, C. (2018) *For a Left Populism*. London: Verso.

Peirats, J. (1974) *Anarchists in the Spanish Revolution*. London: Freedom Press.

Ranis, P. (2016) *Cooperatives Confront Capitalism: Challenging the Neoliberal Economy*. London: Zed Books.

Roos, J. and L. Oikonomakis (2014) '"They Don't Represent Us": The Global Resonance of the Real Democracy Movement from the Indignados to Occupy', in D. Della Porta and A. Matoni (eds) *The Transnational Diffusion of Protest from the Indignados to Occupy Wall Street*. Colchester: ECPR Press, pp. 117–136.

Santos, B.d.S. (2018) *The End of the Cognitive Empire: The Coming of Age of Epistemologies of the South*. Durham, NC: Duke University Press.

Scoones, I. (2019) 'What is Uncertainty and Why Does it Matter?', STEPS (Social, Technological and Environmental Pathways to Sustainability) Centre Working Paper 105, available at: https://opendocs.ids.ac.uk/opendocs/bitstream/handle/20.500.12413/14470/STEPSWP_105_Scoones_final.pdf (accessed 30 November 2020).

Srnicek, N. and A. Williams (2015) *Inventing the Future: Postcapitalism and a World without Work*. London: Verso.

Sunkara, B. (2019) *The Socialist Manifesto: The Case for Radical Politics in an Era of Extreme Inequality*. London: Verso.

Townshend, J. (1996) *The Politics of Marxism: The Critical Debates*. Leicester: Leicester University Press.

Yates, L. (2015) 'Rethinking Prefiguration: Alternatives, Micropolitics and Goals in Social Movements', *Social Movement Studies* 14: 11–21.

9
Mapping Post-capitalist Futures in Dark Times

Adam Fishwick

The deepening crises of contemporary capitalism have been heralded in a new turbulence of violence, collapse and decline. In Isabelle Stengers' (2015) 'catastrophic times', McKenzie Wark's (2014) 'mode of production of non-life', or in Wolfgang Streeck's (2014, 2016) depiction of global (or perhaps European and North American) capitalism as a 'social system in chronic disrepair', the future (or ending) of capitalism is one in which its (self-) destruction wreaks havoc and denies the right to life across the globe. These are portrayed as dark times in which capitalism as mode of production and social reproduction is in a terminal phase, for itself and for most of the 7 billion subjects existing in its mode of life. As Wark notes, the question driving politics now is no longer how to 'manage biopower' – that living component required for the reproduction of global capitalism – but rather: 'from whom is the maintenance of life to be withdrawn first?' (Wark 2014). This is hideously exemplified in recent times. Violent border regimes in Europe and North America oversee those fleeing intersecting crises, withdrawing any 'maintenance of life' as they die in deserts or at sea, while the pandemic crisis of Covid-19 has seen governments neglect marginalised communities through reckless approaches to public health, leaving hundreds of thousands dead.

These examples, though, are only the most visible recent forms of exclusion, which are at the core of both the crisis and reproduction of contemporary capitalism. Exclusion, for those in the majority world of the Global South – and in unequal and impoverished cities of the Global North – has long been the norm. As Mustafa Dikeç (2017) notes, the 'unprecedented' rise of urban uprisings of the last decade in both 'their intensity ... [and] their geography' captures the increasing prevalence – and continuing failure to address – processes of exclusion across the globe (Dikeç 2017: 4). Exclusion is fundamental to capitalist development, either in violent processes of accumulation by dispossession (Harvey 2004) or in the construction of 'urban informality' in the management of populations in growing cities across the Global South (Roy 2005). What, then, does the end of capitalism look like if we consider first this exclusion? And, beyond this, how might we begin to conceptualise ways of mapping post-capitalist futures from this starting point of increasingly dark times?

Drawing on the 'decolonising dialectic' of George Ciccariello-Maher (2017), I argue that we can fruitfully rethink routes toward an uncertain post-capitalist future from the starting point of these dynamics of exclusion. The drive to exclude, and its centrality to capitalism's own self-reproduction, creates sites and spaces in which excluded actors organise through the particularism of their exclusion to engender a rupture in and against the prevailing political order. It is, I argue, this understanding of dialectical motion that can better help us to situate possible routes toward post-capitalism in the lived realities of excluded populations in the Global South and beyond. Doing so moves away from the inclusive technological utopianism and Western-centric universalisms of the post-capitalist literature and towards a multiplicity of agency rooted in diverse particularisms. The aim of this chapter, therefore, is, through this argument, to propose we locate the paths to post-capitalism from inside its contested outside.

RETHINKING POST-CAPITALISM FROM 'OUTSIDE'

Prominent literature on post-capitalism begins from an understanding of the resources made available by capitalism to a new age of prosperity and abundance. These are centred on the potential emancipatory hope provided by advanced technologies – either in the collectivities of the internet (Mason 2015), the post-scarcity politics of the communal exploitation of space exploration (Bastani 2019), or the promise of post-work utopias and Universal Basic Income (Srnicek and Williams 2015). Various technological innovations are to be captured in the development of a post-capitalist future, through a universalising centripetal logic that runs counter to the centrality of capital's own fragmentary and centrifugal violence.

For example, as Srnicek and Williams (2015) argue:

> Populism thus involves a continual negation of differences and particularisms, seeking to establish a common language and programme *in spite of any centrifugal forces* ... the mobilisation of a populist movement around post-work politics would require articulating a populism in such a way that a variety of struggles for social justice and human emancipation could see their interests being expressed in the movement. (Srnicek and Williams 2015: 160, emphasis added)

But to what extent does this overstate the potentiality of collective dynamics that could develop in the current moment, situating their critique of 'folk politics' and their alternative universalism in an emergent centripetal process? Can an emergent post-capitalist future be derived in opposition to capitalism's tendency to fragment and divide? As I show in what follows, we can, and perhaps should, locate pathways from capitalism instead within these centrifugal, exclusionary violences that typify the lives of the majority – not as something to work against – but to work through, embracing particularisms *as the site of the universal.*

As Srnicek and Williams (2015) note, the local, the particular – the experience of the everyday – is a starting point, 'a necessary component for any successful political project' (2015: 12). Yet their analysis of the current conjuncture of global capitalism, despite emphasising patterns of exclusion and the 'management' of surplus populations by the state and capital (2015: 98–103), returns the particularity of various exclusions to an important, but perhaps generalised 'crisis of work' that, in practice, subsumes these experiences under a narrower technologically driven universalism that grows out of a very specific lived universalism experienced, primarily, in the

Global North. For example, it is the increasing role of technology and automation in capitalist production that they understand as driving processes of violent exclusion (Srmicek and Williams 2015: 101–2), rather than the lived experience of exclusion as an already-existing prior condition as it is experienced across much of the Global South. In emphasising the role of technology in 'crumbling' the 'very social basis of capitalism' by undermining waged employment, they emphasise a relatively narrow tendency in the global economy (2015: 92). Even in depicting urban marginalisation in the Global South, the dashed hopes of the 'surplus humanity' residing there are directly determined by a so-called 'premature deindustrialisation' driven by the rise of automation and new technologies (2015: 96–8). Consequently, the problem for them lies with the expulsion – the externalisation – of these 'surplus' populations by technological innovation as a shared, universal experience across the globe. The continuing, everyday and prior experience of violent exclusion under capitalism that both pre-dates and perhaps even prefigures these trends that they focus on, is then marginal to the overdetermining logic of contemporary technological developments.

It is against this tendency in the post-capitalism literature, then, that I propose to articulate the possible pathways towards a post-capitalist future in and from a prefiguring (international) political economy of exclusion that foregrounds this tendency as a dominant one and which, I would argue, would look very different to that envisaged in this section. It is from the following depiction of the violent, exclusionary logics of contemporary capitalism that I seek to build, conceptually, an understanding that is rooted in these centrifugal dynamics that continue to expel millions from the means to survive in the ravages of the current moment. The aim, then, is to explore how – by beginning from these always-already, or pre-existing, processes of exclusion – new pathways toward post-capitalism may then come into view. Moreover, this begins from an expanded definition of exclusion that incorporates not just the violent processes of expulsion from circuits of capital accumulation, but also the contradictory ways in which capitalism includes but also withdraws, to quote Wark, the 'maintenance of life'.

THE (INTERNATIONAL) POLITICAL ECONOMY OF EXCLUSION

Re-centring the dynamics of exclusion is, in this chapter, my starting point for rethinking paths to post-capitalism from the majority world of the Global South and beyond. Exclusion is a historical constant in the formation of global capitalism, expelling swathes of the population from the means of life. This process has been understood as a 'primitive accumulation' that strips places of natural resources and human lives, as a moment of enclosure and the formation of the proletarian working class, as the violent constitution of the gendered spaces of social reproduction, as an ongoing process of dispossession that enables capital accumulation, or as the racialised exclusions that enforce and reproduce its racist borders (Marx 1990 [1867]: ch. 26; Wood 1995; Federici 2018; Harvey 2004; Bhattacharya 2018). It is simultaneously a process of expulsion and life-sapping (re)incorporation into the circuits of capital accumulation that underpin and overdetermine the institutional configurations of contemporary capitalism. As Ronaldo Munck (2005) illustrates, drawing on the extensive historical debates in Latin America on marginalisation and exclusion, this dialectic of the spatial integration of global capitalism with the direct and ongoing exclusion of its populations is the dominant trend. As a concept, exclusion is 'powerful term ... [that] allows us to break with the economistic and individualistic parameters of contemporary concepts of poverty' and situate these lives in a dynamic relation with the expansion of global capitalism (Munck 2005: 24–5). Exclusion takes on concrete forms in specific moments that represents the grounds of capitalism's re/decomposition (see Fishwick and Kiersey in this volume) on which potential new social formations can develop. This is not to fetishise the often-impossible conditions under which communities survive, but to render visible the violence of exclusion that, in the present moment, makes improbable a post-capitalism built on a world of abundance, refocusing on one made in the violent redistribution of scarcity.

This is most clearly apparent when we trace the current conjuncture of capitalist development in the Global South. Here the notion of 'accumulation by dispossession' (Harvey 2004) is a useful entry point into understanding the continued centrality of violent exclusion to contemporary capitalist development. Used across a range of settings to make sense of the varying levels of 'extra-economic' coercion accompanying global capitalist expansion (see, for example, Spronk and Webber 2007 on Latin America; Benjaminsen and Bryceson 2012 on sub-Saharan Africa; and Prudham 2007 on North America), it goes beyond simple primitive accumulation to the present functioning of the global capitalist economy. Harvey argues that features Marx associated with primitive accumulation have 'remained powerfully present within capitalism's historical geography' (Harvey 2004: 74). It is not that violent practices associated with original patterns of accumulation have simply been displaced by the abstract, alienated functioning of the capitalist mode of production, but that the former remains integral to the latter. In fact, as has been shown, the methods of accumulation by dispossession have only expanded, incorporating various financial, technical and legal mechanisms for violent dispossession (Harvey 2004: 75; Prudham 2007; see, also, Gago and Mezzadra 2018 for a rethinking of this as 'extractivism'). As Bin (2018) explains, dispossessions do not automatically or necessarily expand processes of capital accumulation, but also serve a range of different functions. Violence and exclusion remain central to the expansion of global capitalism, but in diverse and – importantly for what follows – continually contested ways.

Exclusion is the expulsion through either physical or more insidious structural violence – aimed at the removal of subjects from a status, location or mode of living. This violence is – and always has been – at the core of global capitalist accumulation. It is this paramount centrifugal tendency that characterises the current conjuncture and which, as such, is how capitalism as a social formation is commonly experienced. Dispossession and exclusion, as Bin (2018) argues, is not simply about the commodification of land and labour, but acts also to disenfranchise and 'render as many people as superfluous as possible' (Mbembe 2019). Rather than the entrepreneur or the landlord, as Kamola (2018) argues, it is the 'pirate' that embodies capitalist expansion – in its violence, pillaging and worse. Consequently, utilising the resources – material, affective and otherwise – that capitalism has engendered and subsumed to forge a meaningful universalism is insufficient if it is those very resources themselves that remove the capacity of the majority to live.

Furthermore, it is also the manner in which global capitalism integrates populations – the ways in which it includes as well as excludes – that also often relies upon violent social and political practices that reduce the capacity to reproduce our selves. This has been expressed in the notion of 'adverse incorporation' (Phillips 2011, 2013) to comprehend this tendency in capitalist expansion in the Global South, particularly in relation to global value chains and the exploitative practices of transnational corporations. For example, the form of expansion by transnational corporations into the Global South through the dynamics of global value chains has been reconceptualised as 'global poverty chains' (Selwyn 2019). Here, Selwyn argues that forms of inclusion in global value chains – networks of capitalist firms that characterise the contemporary organisation of global production – heighten exploitation and worsen the already poor living standards of those throughout the majority world of the Global South (see also Tricontinental 2019 on rates of exploitation). Hence it is the specific modalities of inclusion within capitalist accumulation that exclude individuals from rights – rights at work, rights to decent and dignified wages, rights to reproduce themselves and their communities.

From feminist International Political Economy perspectives, Shirin Rai et al. (2014) further extend this idea by using the concept of 'depletion' to explain the gendered effects of crisis as a steepening decline in the capacity to engage in socially reproductive activities. Here, they define depletion as when 'resource outflows exceed resource inflows in carrying out social reproductive work over a threshold of sustainability, making it harmful for those engaged in this unvalued work' (Rai et al. 2014: 88–9). They note three sites – the individual, the household, and the community – where this depletion is occurring at increasingly rapid rates and where multiple forms of 'gendered harm' are occurring (2014: 90–2). In this sense, it is not expulsion that is creating such harm, but the structural inclusion into harm-inducing forms of socially reproductive practice, at once integral to expanding capital accumulation and destructive to those very forms of everyday life required for that process of expansion.

These patterns simultaneously induce an expulsion of swathes of the population from the means of reproducing life and intensify the conditions under which life is itself reproduced under contemporary capitalism.

Yet these exclusions also offer ways to consider possibilities of moving away from the deleterious effects of these forms of capitalist inclusion. Taking debt as a starting point and building on the work of Lazzarato and Butler, Sigridur Thorgeirsdottir (2015) demonstrates this logic in response to the function of indebtedness, particularly in the wake of the global financial crisis. Here, the gendered dimensions of 'disempowering or empowering conditions' rendered by the global financial system are brought to the fore (Thorgeirsdottir 2015: 570). The 'political economy of exclusion and repression' in this case is the deepening indebtedness that transforms individuals into competitive, indebted subjects, reproducing a deepening crisis of social reproduction via what development theorists would term a gendered adverse incorporation (2015: 571). Importantly, for Thorgeirsdottir, this restriction of the indebted, excluded subject is a starting point for rethinking the possible subjects that can emerge in this relationship. She elaborates on the 'relational subject ... in the care-ethical tradition' (2015: 573) to propose pathways to figuring out an exit from the vagaries of global debt, offering possible sites for mapping post-capitalist futures in these dark times.

Mustafa Dikeç (2017) argues that the increasing prevalence of 'exclusion' as a lived reality can be identified through the growing presence of moments of 'urban rage'. Mapping these across the US, Europe and Turkey, he explores the 'political' significance of these moments as 'products of violence inflicted on excluded urban citizens' (Dikeç 2017: 15). It is, he argues, the presence of systemic exclusion – experienced across cities in the Global North as 'forms of everyday violence' (2017: 128) – that render political what is often dismissed as the mere 'pathological' violence of riots, revolts and urban uprisings. As he draws out in his representation of these moments, it is the solidarity that emerges from these inherently political moments of urban protest that is crucial. In discussing recent urban uprisings in Sweden, for example, he highlights how 'the feeling of exclusion is strong, but so is the feeling of community ... built on shared experiences and frustrations' (2017: 149). It is, for Dikeç, the process of making visible the patterns of exclusion and the dissent of the excluded that characterises these dynamics of urban rage – they are 'reminders of the presence of a body of citizens who feel wronged by the working of the established order ... asserting themselves as equals in urban space' (2017: 173–4). Exclusion, for Dikeç, presents the grounds upon which seemingly spontaneous moments of violent urban protest manifest, revealing the inner workings of a political economy that deprives and marginalises.

Yet, at the same time, while this reading of exclusion and its intimate interconnection with urban uprising is invaluable, it also privileges the notion that the excluded are mobilising with an explicit aim of equal inclusion into the 'established political order'. For Dikeç, urban rage is 'destructive' and not emancipatory (2017: 216), and seeks not to craft anew the political order in the tumult of violence and crisis, but to assert equality – as fully *included* citizens – into a political order that already exists. It is difficult, for example, to see how a demand for full and equal inclusion into a political order that reproduces the 'everyday violence' that Dikeç identifies would resonate with those upon whom this violence is enacted. Dikeç, of course, focuses his analysis on cities primarily in the Global North – those which putatively represent liberal democratic systems based on the veneer of inclusion. But, as his argument makes clear, the intensification of violent urban uprisings only illustrates the systematic classed, gendered and racialised exclusions upon which these systems are intrinsically based. Alternatively, and as for example has been argued by Chris Hesketh (2016) and others, excluded communities in the Global South do not seek inclusion, rather they operate in and reproduce 'non-capitalist' spaces that, although subsumed within the established political and economic order, explicitly do not seek to be included within it.

POST-CAPITALIST FUTURES IN DARK TIMES

In the face of this brutal demise of the conditions of life under capitalism, then, the possibility of forging a pathway towards a post-capitalism might seem improbable. Yet against this, Lebowitz

(2003) and De Angelis (2017), for example, write of two political economies or two social forms of organisation – a 'political economy of the working class' (Lebowitz 2003) or an autopoietic 'commons' (De Angelis 2017) – that persist within and against capitalism. It is from these – characterised by collective social labour of the working class or the self-reproducing 'commoning' social practices – that both consider the possibility of an emergent post-capitalist alternative of common and collective ownership. They argue that capital exploits this activity in the process of accumulation, but in this subsumed social sphere new social forms of organisation continually can and do emerge.

In this section, I turn to two main contributions that, in combination, can allow us to go further and place these post-capitalist dynamics explicitly in the brutal contradictions of its possible endings. In this way, we might think about mapping post-capitalist futures through an understanding of the collective, utopian post-capitalist experiments that prevail and the rupture on which their extension must then be predicated. First, I elaborate on the significance of Ana Dinerstein's (2014, 2016b) concept of 'concrete utopia' as a specific reading of collective, social prefigurative practice in constructing a post-capitalist future. I highlight how this reading of utopia and prefiguration offers a unique way of comprehending possibility. Second, I show how this can be fruitfully read alongside George Ciccariello-Maher's (2017) 'decolonised dialectics' for understanding how the violence endemic in the crises and ending of capitalism can be a site that is mobilised for constructing pathways and possible exits that may already be percolating in the current conjuncture within, against and beyond capitalism.

This reading of post-capitalist futures emerging from prefigurative, utopian practice has circulated in autonomist (Böhm et al.2010; Dinerstein 2014; Berardi 2017), feminist (Motta 2013; Dinerstein 2016a), and anarchist (Shukaitis 2014; Springer 2016) literatures. It stems, essentially from an effort to read social change from the bottom up, considering explicitly how the everyday practices that are engaged in distinct contexts provide a means of beginning to construct alternatives within and against capitalism. It considers these not in terms of success or failure, but rather as containing immanent sources of social change that emerge and persist in unexpected and unknowable ways. In contrast to reading autonomous social praxis as a fully formed, external alternative, it is 'an antagonistic political demand ... a site of struggle' (Böhm et al. 2010: 28). It is praxis continuously appropriated and subsumed into the existing social formation(s) by powerful actors – at once a 'possibility' and an 'impossibility', rather than a parallel social formation (2010: 18). This is a crucial idea, as it posits autonomous mobilisation as bound up with the concrete realities of the present. Rather than an ontological formation outside or alongside capital or the state, it is bound up in continuing dialectical contestation, building possibility in the existing societal conditions.

For Ana Dinerstein, particularly in articulating the notion of 'concrete utopia' (Dinerstein 2016b), this is a means to comprehend emergent possibility in living, everyday alternatives. As a means for understanding prefigurative practice, concrete utopia represents a concerted effort to capture the combined dynamics of struggles characteristic of these experiences:

> Conceived in the currents of the River of Capital, concrete utopia is compelled to navigate its open veins, its canals and passageways, stop at its stations, fall into its vessels, swim against its current.... Concrete utopia is shaped by those relations and dynamics, oppressions and social forms that she wants to obliterate. (Dinerstein 2016b: 52–3)

These are continuously (re)shaped by 'the context and material conditions provided by the context and relations that produce the utopian demand ... [they] cannot remain intact as abstract utopias do, for they belong to the material world and are constantly reshaped by struggle' (Dinerstein 2014: 142). It is this representation of utopia that makes this perspective invaluable for interpreting their possibility. Both for situating post-capitalist possibility in the messy contradictions of the present, but also for identifying the kernel of possibility in combination with 'the existence of an excess that does *not yet* exist' (Dinerstein 2016b: 51).

This approach explicitly connects prefigurative practice and utopia to exclusion and the devastation wrought by the decomposition of collective forms of social organisation that predicate capitalist accumulation. Moreover, it also helps to articulate the limits of a universalism bound up in the centripetal dynamics of the post-capitalism literature, as already outlined. Focusing a critique on the centrality of Universal Basic Income and 'post-work', Pitts and Dinerstein (2017) argue for the need to engage rather than 'falsely' resolve working-class struggle. The perspective derived from this concept of concrete utopia is, then, about 'harnessing the legal and political weaponry at hand to expand space for alternatives through and not in spite of the present state of things' (Pitts and Dinerstein 2017: 16). Harnessing this in the really-existing – the concrete – context of dramatic and often violent centrifugal forces then situates the possibility of utopian, prefigurative practice – and of post-capitalism – explicitly within this ongoing lived experience of contemporary capitalism.

The key question that follows on from this, then, is how the possibility of this 'not yet' is transmitted and forces a rupture with the 'context and relations' that shape the formation of this concrete utopian form without its continuing or expanding subsumption. On the one hand, Massimo De Angelis (2017: 291) proposes that a critical mass of 'commoning' – social practices that would comprise such utopias – would bring a tipping point at which the multiplication of commons will spread without friction as they become viewed as the best form of societal organisation. But this perhaps overstates the importance of the volume of commoning practices over their form and content. Alternatively, can we not read the exit from the capitalist model of social organisation as derived from a moment of force, a disruption of the 'force field' (De Angelis 2017: 113) on which he predicates his understanding of conflict and change? This would enable the revelation of that not yet existing excess as bound to this rupture within, against and beyond the exclusionary dynamics of contemporary capitalism.

Conceptualising this rupture – this opposition to the universalism of prominent perspectives on post-capitalism – is the next step. Here, George Ciccariello-Maher's (2017) approach to 'decolonising dialectics' offers a way towards comprehending this rupture. His perspective of the rupture, with its multiple sites of exclusion, enables a reading of the various means by which a process of de-excluding can be drawn through the encounter with the excluded in a process of making known the practices of survival in which they are engaged. It is not necessarily violence in a physical form, but a disruption of the ordering of exclusion with sufficient force to open the way to new pathways towards the expansion of utopian forms of possibility. What, then, is required are specific constellations of societal dis-ordering that operate to disrupt and begin to make impossible the continued social order.

In *Decolonizing Dialectics*, George Ciccariello-Maher (2017) focuses in part on the question of rupture, on dialectics in motion against the 'totalising unity' ascribed to 'the dialectic'. This notion of rupture is particularly significant as it enables us to extend our understanding of the significance of local forms of social practices in two ways. First, and linked to a prefigurative praxis, it allows for an understanding of failure that does not preclude the wider impact of radical, experimental practice. Second, it foregrounds excluded actors and their practices that exist between external and internal logics of rupture in ways that can exceed the totality of the social formation we understand as global capitalism.

From here, Ciccariello-Maher draws together the thought of radical thinkers on dialectics whose experience and insights are informed directly by the unique antagonisms they faced – George Sorel, Frantz Fanon and Enrique Dussel. At the core of each there is, he argues, a concern with what he terms a radicalised or 'micro-dialectics' (Ciccariello-Maher 2017: 49), premised not on a unitary totality, but rather a localised confrontational moment of rupture in which radical social transformation can be set in motion. From Sorel, he draws out the importance of confrontation – of violence even – in making the inequalities of class known in the setting of his west European Marxist thought (Ciccariello-Maher 2017: 48). From Fanon, this necessity of violent rupture – an idea that is widely associated with his work both academically and politically – is decolonised in the context of Fanon's own anti-colonial praxis. Here, this rupture is associated with escape from the realm of 'non-being', in which the colonised peoples make themselves and become known in the violent rupture of anti-colonial struggle (Ciccariello-Maher 2017: 54-8). Moreover, this local, micro rupture is then rendered global through his handling of the question of anti-colonial identity – the space of non-being is posited as the colonised world, which, through the confrontational rupture, enters into dialectical motion once again.

It is from Dussel, though, that Ciccariello-Maher draws the most important contribution to this decolonial dialectics. Bringing out the rejection of orthodox dialectics in Mariátegui and Fanon, the turn to reject both the reformist and orthodox Marxist logic of cross-class alliance and stage-ist developmentalism is a crucial one that helps us to better understand the process of dialectical motion as infused by the local conflicts and multiple axes of struggle in the colonised world. It is in the 'complex, multiple, and dynamic' relational understanding of 'exteriority' – or exclusion – that these multifaceted sites of conflict enter into dialectical confrontation and motion, incorporating 'all those groups that are systematically excluded' (Ciccariello-Maher 2017: 112). This is significant as it opens the realm of possibility internally and externally with an 'analectical moment' – essentially a rupture of the existing order led by those outside the existing totality – as the first step to motion (2017: 114). It foregrounds the excluded actor and shows how the external rupture intersects with the internal, dialectical motion, thereby transforming – decolonising in Ciccariello-Maher's terms – the immanent possibility that is promised to us by the logic of dialectics. The rupture that is brought on by the realisation of the outside reshapes the totality of the dialectical unity, opening up alternate trajectories borne out of transformed internal relations.

Central to this, moreover, is a decolonised notion of 'the people' or, drawing on the work of Dussel and the context of Venezuela, '*el pueblo*', which is used very differently from 'the people' in Srnicek and Williams' work on left populism. Instead, it is an attempt to pinpoint the concrete emergence of a radical subject that derives internally from the totality as a moment of rupture: '*the people is not unity but division*' (Ciccariello-Maher 2017: 130, my emphasis). It is this radical notion of the people as based in division that situates the dialectical movement simultaneously outside and within the totality of capitalism. It is the beginning of a rupture in which the people, conceptualised in and through this division, mobilise and again set into motion a dialectical movement against the enforced unity of the prevailing social formation. In a vital turn, Ciccariello-Maher also addresses the question of going beyond the negative dialectic of the rupture through the 'illegible' character of the exterior, or of the excluded (2017: 158–60). The expansion of utopian praxis then derives from the observation that its illegibility is central to a movement from a 'negation of the negation' to the emergence of a 'positive program' grounded in that exteriority (2017: 161). Again, this is not to fetishise or romanticise those who are excluded, but to recognise the grounding of an alternative social formation in their materiality and to locate it in dialectics set into motion by an emergent recognition and overcoming of that state.

For Ciccariello-Maher, while it is the rupture that intersects – often violently – with the totality of the dialectically ordered capitalism, this perhaps leaves open two key features of this engagement. The first is the ostensible stasis of the dialectics – the notion that the totality of capitalism is relatively stable prior to the rupture. Although in his explication of Dussel he is careful to not romanticise Dussel's emphasis on exteriority, he does posit the agent of social change as that *beyond* the dialectically ordered social formation of capitalism. Yet, as autonomists have shown, that motion – the rupture that for Ciccariello-Maher (and Dussel) derives from the engagement of the inside and outside of capitalism, be it in the colonised world or in those systemically excluded elsewhere – is always-already existing. The unified totality is a necessary fallacy, both as revolutionary outcome (as Ciccariello-Maher posits) and as contemporary social form. It is a fallacy inasmuch as it itself derives from the logic of conflict and it is necessary inasmuch as that conflict must be continually concealed to secure the conditions of its own reproduction. The question is about the strength of that internal antagonism as a motor for societal transformation. While it may be that the rupture from the outside engagement is most powerful, a diminished space of conflict is not an absent one.

The second is the source of that external agency itself. The turn to Fanon and the question of 'non-being' is crucial to understand the emergence of the force of motion of those that are excluded in the construction of the state of non-being and to understand the 'analectical moment' Ciccariello-Maher draws from Dussel. The question that then arises, however, is how that often violent moment of recognition and rupture translates into the context of wider societal change. As Ciccariello-Maher importantly notes, the axes of exclusion derive from more than simply the narrow dialectic of class struggle, but what can translate the moment of rupture along one of these multiple axes to a kick-starting of the immanent possibilities that lie dormant or unrealised in the existent totality? Also, as he notes, the category of exteriority is broad, being 'individual, collective, and global' (Ciccariello-Maher 2017: 120). It is here that the engagement of interiority and exteriority must be developed, as well as the 'concretisation' of the exterior, to explicate the roots of the agency of Dussel's 'people' (Ciccariello-Maher 2017: 121) and to comprehend this relational movement that can construct a path to an unknowable post-capitalist future.

Consequently, by locating this forceful moment of rupture in the multiplicity of micro-dialectics, this pushes us towards identifying the distinctiveness of various post-capitalist futures that they may engender. As the exclusionary dynamics of contemporary capitalism extend throughout the everyday lives of individuals and communities across the globe, the shared experiences of this process can become imbued with a new collective possibility. To this end, and rather than seek the universalism of a post-capitalism produced from within capitalism itself, we might instead begin to see the possibility and the rupturing potential of multiplying prefigurative practices that emerge in the process of exclusion via a diverse and collective constitution of alternate modes of living against but within the current crises of capitalism.

CONCLUDING REMARKS

The emergence of a post-capitalism that transforms the world for the better cannot rely on an uneven abundance produced under capitalism. The living experience of global capitalism in the majority world of the Global South and beyond is one of deepening exclusion – a process of multiple violences in which increasing swathes of the world's population are rendered superfluous as they become less valuable for capitalism's unstoppable expansion. As I have argued, in this (international) political economy of exclusion, the possibilities of a way out, alternatively, lie with the forms of organisation constructed by those communities that face this exclusion every day. It is here we see the experimentations with concrete utopias that provide a source of prefigurative practices for another world. At the same time, these are constrained, subsumed or submerged within and under the violent dynamics that underpin capital accumulation. It is within a forceful confrontation grounded in but against these logics that a path to a post-capitalist future might be located, that is, a rupture with the universalising character of capitalist expansion, which is a universalism that leads not to a post-capitalist future of abundance, but to scarcity, or the 'reproduction of non-life'.

This chapter provides an engagement between exclusion in contemporary capitalism, the concrete character of utopian, prefigurative praxis, and the centrality of the forceful rupture to the mobilisation of dialectical motion. This, perhaps, presents the beginnings of a dynamic pathway to a post-capitalist future more hopeful than the one we see before us. Though to achieve this, it is essential to begin by centring the violent dynamics, the destructive exclusions of global capitalism and confrontational ruptures that can disrupt the normal functioning of capitalist social relations from within and outside its unity. Consequently, it looks to present a means of placing the contemporary (self-) destruction of capitalism at the very heart of identifying the reality – and necessity – of local, utopian forms of prefigurative practice, considering how their pathways to a post-capitalist future rely on efforts to disrupt the prevailing order by producing new sites of conflict and confrontation that rebuild anew.

REFERENCES

All URLS were last checked on 24 November 2020.

Bastani, Aaron (2019) *Fully Automated Luxury Communism: A Manifesto.* London: Verso.

Benjaminsen, Tor and Ian Bryceson (2012) 'Conservation, Green/Blue Grabbing and Accumulation by Dispossession in Tanzania', *Journal of Peasant Studies* 39(2): 335–355.

Berardi, Franco (2017) *Futurability: The Age of Impotence and the Horizon of Possibility*. London: Verso.

Bhattacharya, Gargi (2018) *Rethinking Racial Capitalism: Questions of Reproduction and Survival*. London: Rowman and Littlefield International.

Bin, Daniel (2018) 'So-called Accumulation by Dispossession', *Critical Sociology* 44(1): 75–88.

Böhm, Steffen, Ana C. Dinerstein and André Spicer (2010) '(Im)possibilities of Autonomy: Social Movement in and beyond Capital, the State and Devclopment', *Social Movement Studies* 9(1): 17–32.

Ciccariello-Maher, George (2017) *Decolonizing Dialectics*. London: Duke University Press.

De Angelis, Massimo (2017) *Omnia Sunt Communia: On the Commons and the Transformation to Postcapitalism*. London: Zed Books.

Dikeç, Mustafa (2017) *Urban Rage: The Revolt of the Excluded*. New Haven, CT: Yale University Press.

Dinerstein, Ana C. (2014) *The Politics of Autonomy in Latin America: The Art of Organising Hope*. Basingstoke: Palgrave.

Dinerstein, Ana C. (2016a) *Social Sciences for an Other Politics: Women Theorizing without Parachutes*. Basingstoke: Palgrave.

Dinerstein, Ana C. (2016b) 'Denaturalising Society: Concrete Utopia and the Prefigurative Critique of Political Economy', in Ana C. Dinerstein (ed.) *Social Sciences for an Other Politics: Women Theorizing without Parachutes*. Basingstoke: Palgrave Macmillan, pp. 49–62.

Federici, Silvia (2018) *Witches, Witch-hunting and Women*. Oakland, CA: PM Press.

Gago, Verónica and Sandro Mezzadra (2018) 'A Critique of the Extractive Operations of Capital: Toward an Expanded Concept of Extractivism', *Rethinking Marxism* 29(4): 574–591.

Harvey, David (2004) 'The "New" Imperialism: Accumulation by Dispossession', *Socialist Register* 40: 63–87.

Hesketh, Chris (2016) 'The Survival of Non-capitalism', *Environment and Planning D: Society and Space* 34(5): 877–894.

Kamola, Isaac (2018) 'Pirate Capitalism, or the Primitive Accumulation of Capital Itself', *Millennium: Journal of International Studies* 47(1): 3–24.

Lebowitz, Michael (2003) *Beyond Capital: Marx's Political Economy of the Working Class*. Basingstoke: Palgrave.

Marx, Karl (1990 [1867]) *Capital*, vol. 1. London: Penguin.

Mason, Paul (2015) *PostCapitalism: A Guide to Our Future*. London: Allen Lane.

Mbembe, Achille (2019) 'Thoughts on the Planetary: An Interview with Achille Mbembe, by Sindre Bangstad and Torbjørn Tumyr Nilsen', *New Frame*, available at: https://www.newframe.com/thoughts-on-the-planetary-an-interview-with-achille-mbembe/

Motta, Sara (2013) 'Teaching Global and Social Justice as Transgressive Spaces of Possiblity', *Antipode* 45(1): 80–100.

Munck, Ronaldo (2005) *Globalization and Exclusion: A Transformationalist Perspective*. Boulder, CO: Kumarian Press.

Phillips, Nicola (2011) 'Informality, Global Production Networks and the Dynamics of "Adverse Incorporation"', *Global Networks* 11(3): 380–397.

Phillips, Nicola (2013) 'Unfree Labour and Adverse Incorporation in the Global Economy: Comparative Perspectives on Brazil and India', *Economy and Society* 42(2): 171–196.

Pitts, Frederick H. and Ana C. Dinerstein (2017) 'Postcapitalism, Basic Income and the End of Work: A Critique and Alternative', *Bath Papers in International Development and Wellbeing* 55, available at: https://researchportal.bath.ac.uk/en/publications/postcapitalism-basic-income-and-the-end-of-work-a-critique-and-al

Prudham, Scott (2007) 'The Fictions of Autonomous Invention: Accumulation by Dispossession, Commodification and Life Patents in Canada', *Antipode* 39(3): 406–429.

Rai, Shirin, Catherine Hoskyns and Dania Thomas (2014) 'Depletion: The Cost of Social Reproduction', *International Journal of Feminist Politics* 16(1): 86–105.

Roy, Ananya (2005) 'Urban Informality: Toward an Epistemology of Planning', *Journal of the American Planning Association* 71(2): 147–158.

Selwyn, Benjamin (2019) 'Poverty Chains and Global Capitalism', *Competition & Change* 23(1): 71–97.

Shukaitis, Stevphen (2014) 'Learning Not to Labor', *Rethinking Marxism* 26(2): 193–205.

Springer, Simon (2016) *The Anarchist Roots of Geography: Towards Spatial Emancipation*. Minneapolis, MN: University of Minnesota Press.

Spronk, Susan and Jeffrey Webber (2007) 'Struggles against Accumulation by Dispossession in Bolivia: The Political Economy of Natural Resource Contention', *Latin American Perspectives* 34(2): 31–47.

Srnicek, Nick and Alex Williams (2015) *Inventing the Future: Postcapitalism and a World without Work*. London: Verso.

Stengers, Isabelle (2015) *In Catastrophic Times: Resisting the Coming Barbarism*, trans. Andrew Goffey. London: Open Humanities Press. Available at http://openhumanitiespress.org/books/download/Stengers_2015_In-Catastrophic-Times.pdf

Streeck, Wolfgang (2014) 'How Will Capitalism End?', *New Left Review* 87: 35–64.

Streeck, Wolfgang (2016) *How Will Capitalism End: Essays on a Failing System*. New York and London: Verso.

Thorgeirsdottir, Sigridur (2015) 'Dependency and Emancipation in the Debt-economy: Care-Ethical Critique of Contractarian Conceptions of the Debtor–Creditor Relation', *Hypatia: A Journal of Feminist Philosophy* 30(3): 564–579.

Tricontinental (2019) *Rate of Exploitation: The Case of the Iphone*. Available at: https://www.thetricontinental.org/the-rate-of-exploitation-the-case-of-the-iphone/

Wark, McKenzie (2014) 'The Birth of Thanaticism', *Public Seminar*. Available at: http://www.publicseminar.org/2014/04/birth-of-thanaticism/

Wood, Ellen (1995) *Democracy against Capitalism: Renewing Historical Materialism*. Cambridge: Cambridge University Press.

10
The Distance Between Two Dreams: Post-neoliberalism and the Politics of Awakening

Japhy Wilson

Dreaming and awakening are abiding themes of radical thought and action. The utopian visions of William Morris's *News from Nowhere* are disclosed in a dream, while for H.G. Wells the realities of modern capitalism are only revealed when *The Sleeper Awakes*. Popular uprisings are replete with revolutionary wake-up calls, from the 'Ya Basta!' of the Zapatistas to the 'Time for Outrage!' that inspired the Indignados. In the words of a placard at Occupy Wall Street: 'We fell asleep for a while. *Just woke up*.' But even Lenin, that most austere of revolutionaries, emphasised the 'need to dream', and argued that '*the rift between dreams and reality* causes no harm if only the person dreaming ... works conscientiously for the achievement of his fantasies' (quoted in Stites 1989: 41, 42, emphasis added). Yet something is missed in the back-and-forth between this clutter of dreams, and this clamour of calls to awaken. There is an almost imperceptible gap between the two, located precisely in 'the rift between dreams and reality'. I would like to pause, for a moment, in this rift.

In his forthcoming monograph, *The Riskiest Moment*, Mladen Dolar draws our attention to the significance of this space between sleep and waking life.[1] Focusing on the work of Franz Kafka, Dolar notes a recurrent theme in stories including *The Trial*, *The Castle* and *The Burrow*, in which the protagonist becomes trapped 'at the edge of awakening', on this 'threshold where for a moment the relation between the subject and the world wavers ... which is no longer a dream, but is not yet the familiar and constituted reality in which one can find one's bearings' (Dolar 2017: 2). From this point onwards, for Kafka's characters, life becomes a nightmarish struggle to escape from this uncanny edge. Yet Kafka's message, according to Dolar, is to do the very opposite: not to find a way out of this space, but to strive to persist within it:

> Kafka's guideline could be stated in these terms: 'don't give up on the edge', the edge of what is neither the dream nor reality but the impossible in-between.... What is at stake is not an awakening to reality, but an awakening to something that gets lost in reality once it has been constituted and made ontologically consistent. (Dolar 2017: 2, 10)

Dolar develops his argument in relation to modern literature and philosophy. But what is the *political* significance of this 'edge of awakening', of this 'rift between dreams and reality'? And what might it mean, in political terms, to maintain fidelity to Kafka's refusal to give up on the edge? This chapter approaches these questions through an exploration of a peculiar mixture of metaphors at the heart of one of the most significant leftist political experiments of recent times: the post-neoliberal government of Rafael Correa Delgado in Ecuador, which held power from 2007 to 2017. The 'Citizens' Revolution', as it was known, called on the people to awaken from the 'long neoliberal night'. Yet Correa campaigned on the promise to build 'the nation that we dream of', and once in power, the government declared that 'dreams are transformed into reality with the Citizens' Revolution'. The twin imperatives of radical praxis – to dream utopian dreams, and to wake up to reality – were thus implicitly condensed into a single oxymoronic message: '*Wake up into a dream!*' Drawing on field research conducted in Ecuador in 2015 and 2016, this chapter seeks to make sense of this seemingly incongruent exhortation. Like the displacement at work in a dream, I argue, the apparent nonsense of this message expressed a repressed truth. More specifically, it betrayed a desire to retroactively suture a rift that had opened between one dream and another.

In what follows, I explore this distance between two dreams, as a means of addressing the politics of awakening. The first section locates the origin of the Citizens' Revolution in a seemingly radical response to the chaotic breakdown of Ecuadorian neoliberalism. The second section argues that this post-neoliberal project was less radical than it appeared: instead of constituting an awakening from the neoliberal night, it promised an escape into a fantasy space of harmonious integration within the dynamics of global capital. The third section begins again from a different starting point, disclosing a hidden history of blockades and uprisings in the Ecuadorian Amazon. In contrast to the Citizens' Revolution, these struggles confronted the crisis of neoliberalism, not by escaping from this edge of awakening, but by remaining within it. The fourth section argues that the Citizens' Revolution's call to awaken from the neoliberal night was effectively a call for the awakened population to submit themselves to the slumber of ideological interpellation, organised by the dream machine of the post-neoliberal state. The fifth section suggests that the dream of the Citizens' Revolution eventually produced a Real more traumatic than the neoliberal reality from which it offered an escape, triggering a return to the abyss between two dreams. I conclude by considering what insights this might hold regarding the relationship between crisis and hope at the end of capitalism.

THE NEOLIBERAL NIGHT

Ecuadorian neoliberalism began with an airplane exploding into a mountain. In 1981, President Jaime Roldos proposed a new hydrocarbons law, which included measures to nationalise the oil industry, on which the economy had depended since the early 1970s. A few weeks later, he died in a plane crash that was widely considered to have been orchestrated by the CIA (Perkins 2005: 153–7). His replacement, Osvaldo Hurtado, cancelled the hydrocarbons law and embarked upon the first of many structural adjustment programmes agreed with the International Monetary Fund (IMF), based on the dismantling of Import Substitution Industrialisation (ISI) policies of prior administrations, in exchange for balance of payments support in the context of collapsing oil prices and soaring debt obligations. Further neoliberal reforms were implemented by subsequent regimes throughout the 1980s, including the withdrawal of subsidies, the deregulation of labour, the reduction of the public sector, and the liberalisation of trade and investment (Acosta and Falconi 2005; Gerlach 2003).

The impoverishment and instability produced by these policies led indigenous social movements from the highlands and the Amazon to form the Confederation of Indigenous Nationalities of Ecuador (CONAIE). In 1990, CONAIE organised the *Levantamiento* (Uprising) – a national campaign of marches, blockades and protests demanding the abandonment of neoliberalism. Neoliberal reforms, however, continued apace, including increases in value-added tax and fuel, electricity and telephone prices, in exchange for further bailouts from the IMF. Matters finally culminated in February 1997, when 2 million people participated in a general strike that eventually forced the corrupt and incompetent president Abdala Bucaram from office (Becker 2011; Lucero 2001).

In 1998, in the midst of a deepening economic and social crisis, the presidency was assumed by the Harvard-trained economist Jamil Mahuad, who responded to the failure of four national banks by transferring US$6 billion to the banking sector – 23 per cent of annual GNP. The bailout was financed by further cuts in social spending, which fell in real terms by 50 per cent in 1999 alone. In a desperate attempt to restore stability to the financial system, Mahuad announced the replacement of the national currency with the US dollar. This symbolic capitulation to US power provoked another indigenous *levantamiento*, which received widespread national support. Mahuad was deposed by the uprising on 21 January 2000, and the president of CONAIE, Antonio Vargas, briefly assumed control of the state as part of a Junta of National Salvation, together with a Supreme Court judge and an army colonel Lucio Gutierrez. Within hours, however, the coalition had collapsed under pressure from the USA. The vice-president Gustavo Noboa then assumed the presidency and completed the dollarisation of the Ecuadorian economy, in exchange for a further tranche of IMF financing.

In the run-up to the 2002 election, Pachakutik, the political wing of CONAIE, renewed their ties with Colonel Gutierrez, by supporting his bid for the presidency. Gutierrez ran on a left-populist platform that promised an end to neoliberalism. Once in office, however, he immediately agreed to a further structural adjustment programme with the IMF, and opened negotiations for a Free Trade Agreement with the USA. Pachakutik withdrew from the Gutierrez administration in August 2003, amid mounting popular anger at the betrayal of the political programme on which he had been elected. But their initial complicity with his capitulation to the neoliberal agenda had destroyed the credibility of CONAIE and fragmented the radical left. All that remained, it seemed, was rage. In April 2005, a spontaneous uprising took to the streets of Quito. Gutierrez dismissed the demonstrators as *forajidos* (outlaws), but after a week of massive protests, the 'Outlaw Rebellion' succeeded in removing him from office (Acosta and Falconi 2005: 39, 70; Becker 2011: 83–90).

Gutierrez was replaced by his vice-president, Alfredo Palacio, and the neoliberal project lurched forward once again. By this point, however, the Ecuadorian political system had lost all legitimacy. Three presidents had been deposed by popular uprisings in the space of seven years; Congress had an approval rating of 2 per cent; and the main leftist party had been discredited (Muñoz et al. 2014: 175–6). It was in this context of 'profound crisis' that 'the figure of [Rafael] Correa erupted into the history of the nation' (Harnecker 2011: 7). Correa, a heterodox economist with a PhD from the University of Illinois, had worked as an adviser to Palacio during his period as vice-president, and was now appointed Minister of Economy and Finance. In stark contrast to his predecessors, Correa publicly challenged neoliberal orthodoxy, calling for the nationalisation of the oil industry and the reversal of IMF reforms. The World Bank responded by cancelling a US$100 million loan to the country, which was followed by Correa's forced resignation two weeks later, in August 2005. His supporters reacted to his removal from office by taking to the streets in protest against what they perceived as Palacio's submission to the demands of the foreign oil companies and the International Financial Institutions (OSAL 2005: 180). At a demonstration outside the Finance Ministry, the people began to chant 'Correa for President!'[2]

Following Correa's departure from government, the neoliberal status quo swiftly resumed. But the popular support for Correa had convinced Alberto Acosta – another heterodox economist – of the electoral viability of a post-neoliberal political project, built around the charismatic figure of Correa himself, and based on 'a governmental team committed to a single agenda of structural reforms.... It is not only the agenda that is at stake. Power is now up for grabs' (Acosta and Falconi 2005: 35). This realisation led Acosta to invite a select group of dissident economists, including Correa, to a series of private meetings at his house in Quito. Huddled around the dining table, they began to formulate an economic programme to challenge neoliberalism, and to launch themselves into power.[3]

AWAKENING INTO A DREAM

The meetings at Acosta's house resulted in the publication of a book entitled *Besieging the Impossible* (*Asedios a lo imposible*), which served as the 'point of departure' for their political project.[4] The book summarised the social and economic consequences of the neoliberal night: deindustrialisation, the collapse of the internal market, increasing dependency on primary commodity exports, persistent low growth, intensified poverty and inequality, the collapse of public services, a massive increase in the foreign debt burden, profound economic instability, endemic corruption, and the ecological destruction wreaked upon the Amazonian region of the country by the transnational oil industry (Acosta and Falconi 2005: 29–33). *Besieging the Impossible* depicts this dark panorama in terms of 'economic terrorism', and 'a tortuous adjustment', resulting in an 'atmosphere of profound crisis', and culminating in 'a moment of desperation' (Acosta and Falconi 2005: 22–9). The severity of the crisis demanded a radical response, and the book was intended as a call to act in precisely this way, as Acosta explains:

> We were laying siege to a city. That was the idea. The impossible as a city. We were laying siege to the impossible in order to make it possible.... The impossible was a free society, a just society, an equal society, an economy that serves humanity.... We believed that it was possible.[5]

This insistence on the possibility of radical transformation under apparent conditions of its objective impossibility seemed to embody the revolutionary courage required to 'embrace what, prior to the act, appears as impossible. Only in this way will our act touch the Real' (Žižek, quoted in Bosteels 2011: 170). However, as Slavoj Žižek (2008a) argues:

> When the normal run of things is traumatically interrupted, the field is open for ideological competition.... The danger is that the predominant narrative ... won't be the one that awakens us from the dream, but the one that will enable us to continue to dream. (Žižek 2008a)

In practice, faced with the catastrophic conditions of the neoliberal night, the architects of the Citizens' Revolution adopted a narrative of precisely this kind. This narrative was based on neo-structuralism, an economic policy programme promoted by the Economic Commission for Latin America and the Caribbean (ECLAC). During the 1970s, ECLAC had been the intellectual centre of structuralism and ISI, based on an overtly politicised understanding of the power relations of the world market, and an interventionist set of policies designed to industrialise Latin America and to liberate the region from its dependent position within the core–periphery structure of the global economy. The failure of ISI, the rise of neoliberalism, and the brutal social consequences of this transition led to the breakdown of this symbolic framework, and confronted ECLAC with the overwhelming power of global capitalism unleashed from all ideological and geographical constraints and revealed as 'a monstrous formation whose very "normal" state is permanent dislocation ... a social system caught in a vicious superego cycle of incessant expansion' (Žižek 1999: 376).

In response to this collapse of its cognitive coordinates, ECLAC developed neo-structuralism, which was conceived as a 'pragmatic' new policy paradigm capable of constructive engagement with the economic realities of neoliberal globalisation. Instead of deepening the structuralist critique of global capitalism, neo-structuralism abandoned the core–periphery paradigm, and replaced it with 'the highly seductive notion that international competitiveness, social integration, and political legitimacy can synergistically be attained by swimming along, not against, the swift currents unleashed by globalization' (Leiva 2008: xx). In doing so, ECLAC retreated from questions concerning the production of economic surplus and the nature of international power relations, and set out an agenda for an 'intelligent insertion into international markets'. This agenda sought to overcome the worst excesses of neoliberalism, not by challenging the dominant model of export-led development, but through a state-led transition from a 'spurious competitiveness' based on cheap labour and natural resources, to a 'systemic competitiveness' based on the comprehensive organisation of society around increased economic productivity and improved social equity. As Fernando Leiva explains in his comprehensive critique of neo-structuralism, the destructive dynamics of global capitalism revealed by the crisis of neoliberalism were therefore not confronted but disavowed:

> After enduring wrenching ... restructuring under neoliberal policies ... political leaders and public opinion eagerly welcomed neo-structuralism's discursive innovation: Latin America's dynamic integration into a changing global economy did not have to continue being a politically, socially and economically traumatic affair.... Like a salve on open sores, the region welcomed neo-structuralism's new discourse promising social harmony with open global markets and flows. (Leiva 2008: 1–2)

Neo-structuralism soon became the dominant ideological paradigm of post-neoliberalism, informing the political projects of putatively post-neoliberal regimes in countries such as Chile, Brazil and Uruguay. In scholarly analyses of post-neoliberalism in Latin America, a division is typically established between such 'pragmatic' regimes and the more radical experiments then under way in Bolivia and Venezuela, with Ecuador invariably grouped with the latter. Correa's political rhetoric encourages this classification, and Leiva himself has framed the Citizens' Revolution as a post-neoliberal alternative that breaks with neo-structuralist orthodoxy (Leiva 2008: 217).
However, this classification overlooks the fact that Correa and the other architects of the Citizens' Revolution were all committed neo-structuralists. For the authors of *Besieging the Impossible*,

gathered around Acosta's dining table, this policy framework constituted the unspoken ideological coordinates of their strategic discussions. In Acosta's own words, 'In the house we didn't debate these things much, because we were in agreement on them.'[6] And as Žižek has observed, 'it is precisely the neutralisation of some features into a spontaneously accepted background that marks out ideology at its purest' (Žižek 2008a: 31). This spontaneous background framed the manifesto of their newly created political party, Alianza Pais, which put Correa forward as its candidate for the presidential elections of 2006. In contrast to Correa's frequent espousal of the Bolivarian project of 'twenty-first-century socialism' in his bombastic speeches on the campaign trail, the small-print of the manifesto included 27 mentions of 'competitiveness' and only one of 'socialism' (Alianza Pais 2006). Following his victory, national development plans were consistently committed to 'a new concept of competitiveness, which permits a less traumatic process of structural change' (SENPLADES 2009: 61), and the concept was even enshrined in the 2008 constitution, which is committed to pursuing 'productivity and systemic competitiveness [and a] strategic insertion into international markets'.[7]

This underlying commitment to neo-structuralism within the inner circle of the Citizens' Revolution was overlaid by a mobilisation of the metaphors of 'night' and 'dream' in official public discourse. The manifesto was presented as 'the crystallisation of a collective dream' (Alianza Pais 2006: 9), which was defined as the 'dream of a competitive nation, in the framework of a systemic competitiveness' (Alianza Pais 2006: 8). And in the run-up to the election, the main campaign poster depicted Correa standing in the darkness, with his face turned upwards towards the light, accompanied by the slogan: 'You decide between the dark past and this beautiful democratic revolution.'[8] As Acosta explains, the discourse of the 'neoliberal night' sent 'a powerful message, because it served to say that what went before was dark and negative', while the manifesto 'was organized on the basis of "the dream". Our idea was to give a positive message. Negative night – positive dream. So that *now we were in the midst of a dream*.'[9]

From the chaotic nightmare of the neoliberal night, to the harmonious dream of systemic competitiveness ... this is the logic of

The Distance Between Two Dreams

the seemingly incongruous injunction to '*Awaken into a dream!*' As Dolar points out, such injunctions are the essence of ideological interpellation: of 'awakening to … an emergence of sense, the retroactive imposition of sense on what didn't make sense' (Dolar 2017: 11). It is at precisely this moment, Dolar argues, that Kafka pulls us back:

> Kafka stops this process on the threshold, just before the fulguration of sense. Something is revealed that is not covered by meaning…. A revelation without meaning…. A wake-up call against wake-up calls, dismantling their logic. It is like interpellation in reverse – the emergence of … a reality that one cannot claim as one's own, a moment where sense and recognition falter, an experience … which, once [it has] come to the foreground, casts a different light on everything. (Dolar 2017: 11)

Let us, then, begin again. But this time we will start from a different place. And this time we will strive to remain upon this threshold.

AWAKENING ONTO THE EDGE

The darkest hour of the neoliberal night came at the turn of the millennium. The Ecuadorian financial crisis of 1999 had defrauded the subaltern classes in the name of saving the banks, plunging the country into a deep recession, and forcing millions to migrate. But neoliberal reforms continued, and transnational capital intensified the extraction of Amazonian crude. At around this time, Donald Moncayo was a peasant farmer, eking out a living amid the oil fields of the Ecuadorian Amazon. One day like any other, he was on his way to the local volleyball court, which had been constructed by one of the oil companies, to gain acceptance from the community for the extraction of oil from beneath their lands. Moncayo was content with this arrangement. 'I wasn't interested in struggles, in what was going on', he recalls. 'I lived a simple life, I didn't have any consciousness.' Suddenly, like one of Kafka's characters, he awoke to the threshold 'of what is neither dream nor reality, but the impossible in-between, where a dream-like Real infringes upon a familiar reality' (Dolar 2017: 2):

> It was in 2000 that *my way of thinking was shaken*. There was an oil spill. I was on my way to play volleyball. We had arranged to meet at the court at 4 p.m. I set out about 3 p.m. And the river was black with oil. The ducks and chickens were catching the fish. Because with the oil, it's like the fish went crazy. They started jumping, and the chickens became like bears catching salmon, like you see on TV. But the ducks were even worse, because they were diving into the water and catching the fish in there…. And at that moment … someone showed up from [the oil company] to compensate the people [for the oil spill]…. There were loads of chickens in the yard. Some of them were already dead. Others … were still moving, but they were covered in oil. And he [the oil company representative] said 'Hey, this one is alive.' And she [a peasant farmer] said 'But no, they are all going to die.' And he said, 'Of course they're not going to die! Wash them with soap and they'll be fine.' Damn it, *and that's when it struck me*. Like 'This son of a bitch, what's his problem? They come here and contaminate our rivers, they kill your animals, and then … they tell you to go to hell over the ones that haven't died yet …' It struck me. And it's like it's still rooted in me now. It's like something that shakes you. And that shook me.[10]

As Žižek (1991: 196) observes, 'We vegetate in our everyday life, deep in the universal lie that structures it, when all of a sudden, some totally contingent encounter … shatters our self-delusion.' For Donald Moncayo, the oil spill functioned as a wake-up call of precisely this kind – the emergence, to repeat Dolar's words, of 'a reality that one cannot claim as one's own … an experience … which, once come to the foreground, casts a different light on everything' (Dolar 2017: 11). Moncayo did not seek to escape from this threshold, back into the phantasmatic coordinates of his everyday reality. Instead, like Kafka's protagonists, he remained 'on this brink … on this this edge' (Dolar 2017: 2). Over the following years, he would play a leading role in a series of blockades and uprisings that spread like wildfire throughout the Ecuadorian Amazon, fuelled by multiple similar moments of awakening, in which a collective fantasy of petroleum prosperity disintegrated into the apocalyptic wastelands of the oil-ravaged Amazon. But these polluted jungle peripheries lacked the ideological state apparatuses required to lull the population back to sleep, and the uprisings espoused no political programme, and possessed no collective vision of the future. In the words of one leader, 'This was not about a political ideology, or the building of a political movement, or anything like that. No ... this was about *unity of thought in the face of urgent necessity*.'[11]

Moncayo and his insurrectional comrades thus remained in the gap between two dreams, and this ideological vacuum 'enabled the impossible edge to invade everything else' (Dolar 2017: 3). Before long, they were organising a series of coordinated blockades of the entire Amazonian oil industry. The largest of these was in August 2005, when the oil wells, stations, roads and airports of the region were completely shut down, ending the flow of petroleum, on which the national economy depended, and forcing Ecuador to suspend oil exports (MPD Sucumbios 2006; Sigcha 2005).

A State of Emergency was called, and the police and military were deployed to crush the blockade, leading to violent confrontations that spread throughout the region. Thousands of people took to the streets. Police vehicles were overturned and torched, and government offices were burned to the ground. The army opened fire on the protesters, who dispatched a defiant message to the nation:

> Nothing can justify the state firing on an unarmed population. We repeat: our struggle is to change the oil politics of our country. So that Ecuador will be a sovereign nation, instead of puppets in the hands of foreign interests.[12]

The conflict was described by one leader as a moment of awakening:

> Now that was it! All against all.... The military opened fire. There were deaths. There were injuries. In that moment, *an immense solidarity was awakened in the people*.... [They] had reached their limit ... they learned to defend their rights.... They threw themselves into the struggle.[13]

'*Unity of thought in the face of urgent necessity*', which is actualised in an avalanche of events that '*awakens an immense solidarity in the people*'. In contrast to the ideological wake-up call of the Citizens' Revolution, this revolutionary sequence began with an awakening into the space between two dreams and remained resolutely within it. This, to quote Žižek again, is 'the true awakening: not only from sleep, but from the spell of fantasies that controls us even more when we are awake' (Žižek 2006: 60). In their liberation from these fantasies, such moments contain a utopian dimension:

> A truly radical utopia is not an exercise in free imagination.... It's something to be immediately enacted when there is no other way.... The point is not about planning utopias. The point is about practicing them. And the point is not 'Should we do it, or should we just persist in the existing order?' The point is much more radical. It's a matter of survival. (Žižek 2003)

This radical form of utopia originates within 'a state between dreaming and awakening, at once lucid and opaque, with which an emergent collectivity can face up to the unbreathable void of a situation' (Bosteels 2012: 192). Despite the absence of a fantasy frame, and in the face of the violence unleashed upon it, an insurgent utopia of this kind possesses an incandescent dimension, which Alain Badiou has called an 'egalitarian passion' (quoted in Hallward 2003: 241), and Walter Benjamin once identified as 'an ecstatic component [that] lives in every revolutionary act' (Benjamin 1978: 55). This was conveyed by those involved in the August Uprising, who recalled it in terms of 'the euphoria of the battles and victories of the people',[14] filled with 'moments of great joy'[15] in which 'people learned to confront power, to equalise themselves. To speak face to face without looking down.'[16] We can now return to the call to '*awaken into a dream*'. This call sounds rather different when heard, not as a cry in the neoliberal night, but as an attempt to avoid a Real awakening.

THE GUARDIANS OF SLEEP

The paralysing of the Amazonian oil industry in August 2005 brought Ecuador to the brink of economic breakdown and threatened to trigger a wider insurrection. This danger was stressed in an open letter to Alfredo Palacio, the president of the time, which warned that: 'It is time that you and your government treated the Amazonian provinces with respect.... Otherwise ... we believe that the conflict in [the northern Amazon] could extend to the rest of the country.'[17] The message of the letter was unambiguous: urgent reform is required in order to prevent a far more radical revolution. And the lead signatory was none other than Rafael Correa, who had resigned from the Palacio administration a few days prior to the uprising, and who, as we have seen, was now regarded by many Ecuadorians as the only politician capable of leading them out of the crisis.

It was at this point that Acosta invited Correa and the other economists to his house in Quito, where they began to formulate the economic and political strategy for *Besieging the Impossible*. And so, we find ourselves back at the moment at which the neoliberal night was first confronted with the call to awaken into a dream. The path that has led us here is reminiscent of the 'temporal loop ... of the psychoanalytic treatment in which, after a long detour, we return to our starting point from another perspective' (Žižek 2000: 18). Returning to the group of economists gathered around the dinner table, we can now see that *the 'besieging of the impossible' had already taken place*. Not in texts but on the streets, and not in the elite suburbs of Quito, but in the impoverished backwaters of the Amazon. Yet these struggles are strangely absent from the pages of *Besieging the Impossible*. In his chapter, Correa argues that 'another agenda is possible ... that gives priority to the poorest and the weakest' but makes no mention of the uprising that had just brought the government to its knees (Correa 2005: 70). In the discourse of the Citizens' Revolution, the supplications of the poor and weak thus replace what one leader of the uprising recalls as the 'euphoria of the battles and victories of the people'.[18]

What, then, was the long dark night from which the people were called on to awaken? Did its darkness symbolise the despair of a population crushed by the brutality of neoliberalism, or did it throw a cloak over the spontaneous vitality of an insurgent utopia? Were the people really asleep, or had they already awoken? Was the dream of the Citizens' Revolution a utopian dream of a radically different future, or was it an attempt to impose the continuity of sleep, and to retroactively close the distance that had emerged between two dreams? We should not forget Freud's famous words: *'Dreams are the guardians of sleep, and not its disturbers'* (quoted in Nagera 1969: 18).

The rift forced open by the August Uprising recalls the iconic image of the overthrow of the Ceausescu regime in Romania in 1989, in which rebels wave a national flag with the star cut out, leaving a gaping hole at the centre. For Žižek, this image captured:

> the open character of a historical situation in its becoming … this hole, not yet hegemonized by any positive ideological project; all ideological appropriations entered the stage afterwards and endeavoured to 'kidnap' the process which was originally not their own. (Žižek 1993: 1–2)

Such ideological strategies are critical to the establishment of new social orders, which relegate their foundational moment to the status of a 'vanishing mediator … the moment of "openness" which, once the eruption of the "event" is institutionalized into a new positivity … becomes literally *invisible*' (Žižek 1991: 188).

Confronted with this manoeuvre, the majority of the Amazonian population abandoned their struggles and became willing accomplices in their own historical erasure. During his election campaign in 2006, Correa travelled to the Amazon with an ambitious development programme for the region. Key figures in the August Uprising recall him being celebrated as 'a god who had come to save the region', promising 'a great utopia', and generating 'a fever of hope' in the people, as the one 'who could change the situation, without blockades, without strikes, without any of those things'.[19] Like Kafka's protagonists, the Amazonian population had been exhausted by their seemingly endless persistence in the space of a Real awakening. When Correa finally arrived, they embraced his wake-up call for what it really was: an invitation to finally get some sleep.

THE REAL OF THE DREAM

Correa was elected by a landslide and assumed the presidency in 2007. His first term in office coincided with a commodities boom, which facilitated the renegotiation of oil contracts, and the global financial crisis, which enabled a renegotiation of the national debt. The result was a vast increase in state revenues and public investment, which Correa directed toward the production of social and economic infrastructures throughout the country, including the Amazon. This strategy promised to produce the integrated national space demanded by the neo-structuralist ideology of systemic competitiveness, and to meet the demands of the August Uprising. Indeed, many of these relatively modest demands were realised on a hallucinatory scale. The demand for road infrastructure was met with an interoceanic corridor; the demand for schools and hospitals was met with the construction of entire towns; and the demand for higher education was met with a university specialising in biotechnology and staffed with international scientists (Wilson and Bayón 2015). This was *the state as dream machine*, funnelling up emancipatory energies and expressions of popular discontent, and regurgitating them in extravagant 'utopias of spatial form' (Harvey 2000).

In Freud's words: 'The dream is already a compromise structure. It has a double function; on the one hand ... it serves the desire to sleep; on the other hand, it allows ... the hallucinated fulfilment of a wish' (quoted in Nagera 1969: 18). This is precisely what the Citizens' Revolution attempted through its utopias of spatial form. Initially, these projects were met with jubilation by the Amazonian population. It really did seem to be the case that 'Dreams are converted into reality with the Citizens' Revolution!' But as Dolar has noted, '*there is something in the dream's own logic of wish fulfilment that tends to run amok*' (Dolar 2017: 8, emphasis added). Dolar is referring here to the dream of the burning child first interpreted by Freud: A child has died. After the funeral, the exhausted father tries to catch some sleep, leaving an old man to maintain the wake. In his dream, his child appears at his bedside, and whispers 'Father, can't you see I'm burning?' The father awakens in horror, and finds that the old man has fallen asleep, and the dead child's sleeve has been ignited by the candle at his bedside. According to Freud's theory of the 'double function' of dreams – as wish fulfilments and as sustaining sleep – the dream fulfilled the father's wish that his son was still alive, while seeking to sustain his sleep by distracting him from the fire in the next room (Freud 1997: 353–4). But as Dolar points out, paraphrasing Lacan's reinterpretation of the dream:

> There is a paradox: the dream, in its endeavour to shield the dreamer, creates a Real from which one then tries to escape…. So, we could say that first we dream in order to be able to sleep, protected from the external intrusion, and then we wake up in order to be able to continue to sleep, protected from the intrusion produced by the dream itself. (Dolar 2017: 8)

This is precisely what happened in the case of the Citizens' Revolution. The dream machine of the post-neoliberal state had functioned to depoliticise the Amazon. Its success in this regard, however, was premised on the promise of its utopias of spatial form. These projects ended in dramatic failure, both in terms of delivering their promised social benefits, and in terms of achieving systemic competitiveness (Wilson and Bayón 2017a, 2017b, 2018). Furthermore, their production had relied upon the accumulation and mobilisation of oil rents, which in turn necessitated an expansion of the Amazonian oil industry – the social and economic consequences of which had catalysed the original uprising. The costs of sustaining the Citizens' Revolution increased exponentially over time, leading to the opening of new mineral frontiers in the southern Amazon, and the concession of gold and copper mines to foreign capital (Purcell and Martinez 2018). This accumulation strategy was destined to intensify the conflictual politics of accumulation by dispossession that have long characterised the region, resulting in a series of violent confrontations between impoverished communities and security forces, which were widely judged to have been even more repressive under Correa than during the 'neoliberal' period. In the words of one of the original leaders of the August Uprising:

> Ten years have passed [since the election of Correa]…. Ten years in which we have been unable to struggle for our rights. Ten years in which the people have been afraid to take to the streets. Ten years in which we have borne witness to the brutalization of our people…. Instead of the friend we supported to win the presidency,

this government has been among the worst butchers [*de los peores verdugos*] of the Amazon.... For us, this government has been a nightmare.[20]

Like the dream of the burning child in relation to the dreaming father, the dream of the Citizens' Revolution had sought to sustain the slumber of the Ecuadorian Amazon. But through its dependence on intensified resource exploitation, it had produced a Real more traumatic than the reality from which it had promised an escape. Just as the father returned to reality to escape the Real announced in his dream, so the population of the Amazon responded to this Real by seeking to escape from the dream machine of the post-neoliberal state. But the depoliticisation of the region in the intervening decade implied that there was no longer any positive alternative to return to. Faced with the Real of his dream, the father's only choice was to return to the reality of his son's death. Equally, the Amazonian population's only choice was to return to the reality of neoliberalism. And this is what they chose. In the 2017 elections, Alianza Pais narrowly scraped to victory, although Correa himself was not eligible for re-election. But five of the six Amazonian provinces voted against Correa's party, in favour of a millionaire banker and ex-finance minister, who had played a central role in the neoliberal night. Since then, Correa's self-appointed successor, Lenin Moreno, has abandoned the post-neoliberal discourse of the Citizens' Revolution, and has embraced a programme of neoliberal reforms imposed by the IMF (Becker and Riofrancos 2018). This outcome was inscribed into the Citizens' Revolution itself, which challenged neoliberalism at the level of policy, but reproduced its underlying faith in the possibility of a capitalism cleansed of its constitutive antagonisms. As Žižek concludes: 'If we change reality only in order to realise our dreams, without changing these dreams themselves, then sooner or later we will regress to the former reality' (2008b: 79).

BEYOND HOPE?

How are we to respond to this closure of the distance between two dreams? How, under such circumstances, can we follow Kafka's injunction 'to persevere on the edge; not to give up on the threshold'? (Dolar 2017: 6). How are we to avoid the conclusion that this threshold will only ever amount to 'a fleeting "vanishing mediator" between two orders ... a transitory moment of liberation, the suspension of social authority, which unavoidably gives rise to the backlash of an even more oppressive power?' (Žižek, quoted in Bosteels 2011: 203). Under such circumstances, it may be tempting to follow the utopian Marxist, Ernst Bloch (1986), in appealing to the 'principle of hope', based on a faith in 'a hidden dimension of reality that inhabits the present one: the *not yet*' (Dinerstein 2014: 23). But it is precisely such a 'glimmer of hope' (*resquicio de esperanza*) that was offered in *Besieging the Impossible* (Ponce 2005: 13). It was Correa's ability to unleash a 'fever of hope' that first swept the Citizens' Revolution to power. And it is to hope that he ultimately appealed when confronted with its failure. In Correa's words, as he was leaving office: 'They can rob us of everything, but they will never steal our hope! (*¡Que nos roben todo, menos la esperanza!*).'[21]

It is hope itself, in other words, that is the ultimate ideological lure, the last gambit of a dream struggling to prolong an increasingly restless sleep. As we saw in the case of the Amazonian uprising, it was precisely the loss of hope that triggered a Real awakening. Indeed, several of the movement's leaders have described this moment in terms that are expressive of this last-ditch utopian impulse: 'The people were desperate and they couldn't take it any more';[22] 'The situation was brought to the point of total rupture';[23] 'There were many, many problems, and we could see no way out.'[24] This suggests that, for those committed to revolutionary change, hope is a temptation to be resisted, and replaced by what Žižek has called 'the courage of hopelessness':

> In our historical moment, even the most pessimistic diagnosis as a rule finishes with ... some version of the proverbial light at the end of the tunnel. The true courage is not to imagine an alternative, but to accept the consequences of the fact that there is no clearly discernible alternative: the dream of an alternative is a sign of theoretical cowardice, functioning as a fetish that prevents us from grasping the deadlock of our predicament. In short, the true

courage is to admit that the light at the end of the tunnel is probably that of another train approaching us from the other direction. (Žižek 2015: 248)

From this perspective, the principle of hope is just another utopian fantasy, in which the promise of the 'not yet' operates to disavow the true 'deadlock of our predicament'. Instead of succumbing to such temptations, we should maintain fidelity to the radical utopian potential of the distance between two dreams. In the words of the Invisible Committee (2009: 23): 'From whatever angle you approach it, the present offers no way out. This is not the least of its virtues. From those who seek hope above all, it tears away every firm ground.' Or, to quote an ancient Zen text: 'If you really want to pass this barrier, you should feel like drinking a hot iron ball that you can neither swallow nor spit out' (Mumon 2000: 95).

NOTES

1. I would like to thank Mladen Dolar for generously sharing a draft of the introduction to his manuscript. This remarkable text has provided much of the inspiration for the present chapter.
2. Ricardo Patiño, a close ally of Correa, quoted in Harnecker (2011: 15).
3. Alberto Acosta. Author interview, 11 September 2016, Quito, Ecuador.
4. Alberto Acosta. Author interview, 11 September 2015, Quito.
5. Alberto Acosta. Author interview, 11 September 2015, Quito.
6. Alberto Acosta. Author interview, 11 September 2015, Quito.
7. See Article 284 of the Ecuadorian Constitution of 2008, available at: https://www.ministeriodegobierno.gob.ec/wp-content/uploads/2015/04/CONSTITUCION-DE-LA-REPUBLICA-DEL-ECUADOR1.pdf (accessed 20 January 2020).
8. This image can be seen here: http://abrebrecha-thisisit.blogspot.co.uk/2012/04/tu-decides-entre-el-oscuro-pasado-o.html (accessed 3 May 2017).
9. Alberto Acosta. Author interview, 11 September 2015, Quito (emphasis added).
10. Donald Moncayo. Author interview, 15 June 2016, Lago Agrio, Ecuador (emphasis added).

11. Enrique Morales. Author interview, 2 June 2016, Coca, Ecuador (emphasis added).
12. Comite del Paro, 'Boletines de Prensa 13-28', 16 August 2005: http://llacta.org/organiz/coms/2005/com0357.htm (accessed 21 September 2017).
13. Angel Sallo. Author interview, 16 June 2017, Lago Agrio (emphasis added).
14. Enrique Morales. Author interview, 22 June 2016, Coca.
15. Pablo Gallegos. Author interview, 22 May 2016, Coca.
16. Angel Sallo. Author interview, 16 June 2017, Lago Agrio.
17. 'Carta abierta al Presidente de la Republica sobre la represión a los pueblos Amazonicos', http://www.llacta.org/organiz/coms/2005/com0369.htm (accessed 22 September 2017).
18. Enrique Morales. Author interview, 2 June 2016, Coca.
19. Author interviews: Humberto Piajuaje, 14 June 2016, Lago Agrio; Pablo Gallegos, 1 June 2016, Coca; Donald Moncayo, 15 June 2016, Lago Agrio.
20. Enrique Morales. Author interview, 22 June 2016, Coca.
21. 'Enlace Ciudadano 508 desde Rumiñahui', https://www.youtube.com/watch?v=eMDEk9BiZd8 (accessed 16 December 2018.
22. Donald Moncayo. Author interview, 15 June 2016, Lago Agrio.
23. Author interview with Angel Sallo, 16 June 2017, Lago Agrio.
24. Author interview with Julio Gonzalez, 18 June 2016, Lago Agrio.

REFERENCES

Acosta, Alberto and Fander Falconi Benitez (2005) 'Otra política económica, deseable y posible', in Albero Acosta and Fander Falconi (eds) *Asedios a lo imposible: Propuestas económicas en construcción*. Quito: FLACSO, pp. 17–38.

Alianza País (2006) *Plan de Gobierno del Movimiento PAIS 2007–2011*. Quito: Alianza País.

Becker, Marc (2011) *Pachakutik! Indigenous Movements and Electoral Politics in Ecuador*. Plymouth: Rowman and Littlefield.

Becker, Marc and Thea N. Riofrancos (2018) 'A Souring Friendship, a Left Divided', *NACLA Report on the Americas* 50(2): 124–127.

Benjamin, Walter (1978) 'Surrealism: The Last Snapshot of the European Intelligentsia', *New Left Review* 108: 47–56.

Bloch, Ernst (1986) *The Principle of Hope*, vol. 1. Cambridge, MA: MIT Press.

Bosteels, Bruno (2011) *The Actuality of Communism*. London: Verso.
Bosteels, Bruno (2012) *Marx and Freud in Latin America: Politics, Psychoanalysis and Religion in Times of Terror*. London: Verso.
Correa, Rafael (2005) 'Otra economía es posible', in Albero Acosta and Fander Falconi (eds) *Asedios a lo imposible: Propuestas económicas en construcción*. Quito: FLACSO, pp. 69–78.
Dinerstein, Ana Cecilia (2014) *The Politics of Autonomy in Latin America: The Art of Organising Hope*. London: Palgrave Macmillan.
Dolar, Mladen (2017) 'Introduction. Awakening' (unpublished manuscript).
Freud, Sigmund (1997) *The Interpretation of Dreams*. Ware: Wordsworth.
Gerlach, Allen (2003) *Indians, Oil and Politics: A Recent History of Ecuador*. Lanham, MD: Rowman and Littlefield.
Hallward, Peter (2003) *Badiou: A Subject to Truth*. Minneapolis, MN: University of Minnesota.
Harnecker, Marta (2011) *Ecuador: una nueva izquierda en busca de la vida en plenitud*. Quito: Abya Yala.
Harvey, David (2000) *Spaces of Hope*. Berkeley: University of California Press.
Invisible Committee (2009) *The Coming Insurrection*. New York: Semiotext(e).
Leiva, Fernando Ignacio (2008) *Latin American Neostructuralism: The Contradictions of Post-neoliberal Development*. Minneapolis, MN: University of Minnesota Press.
Lucero, Jose Antonio (2001) 'Crisis and Contention in Ecuador', *Journal of Democracy* 12(2): pp. 59–73.
MPD Sucumbíos (2006) *Las valerosas jornadas de los pueblos del Nororiente Ecuatoriano*. Lago Agrio: Ediciones Opción.
Mumon (2000) 'The Gateless Gate', in Paul Reps (ed.) *Zen Flesh, Zen Bones: A Collection of Zen and Pre-Zen Writings*. London: Penguin, pp. 89–131.
Muñoz, Francisco et al. (2014) *Balance crítico del gobierno de Rafael Correa*. Quito: Universidad Central.
Nagera, Humberto (1969) *Basic Psychoanalytic Concepts on the Theory of Dreams*. London: Allen and Unwin.
OSAL (Observatorio Social de América Latina) (2005) 'Ecuador: cronología mayo–agosto 2005', *OSAL* 17: 177–185.
Perkins, John (2005) *Confessions of an Economic Hit Man*. London: Ebury Press.
Ponce, Javier (2005) 'Un libro para los escépticos', in Albero Acosta and Fander Falconi (eds) *Asedios a lo imposible: Propuestas económicas en construcción*. Quito: FLACSO, pp. 11–14.

Purcell, Thomas F. and Estefania Martinez (2018) 'Post-neoliberal Energy Modernity and the Political Economy of the Landlord State in Ecuador', *Energy Research and Social Science* 41: 12–21.

SENPLADES (2009) *Plan Nacional Para el Buen Vivir 2009-2013 versión resumida*. Quito: SENPLADES.

Sigcha, Amparo (2005) 'Sucumbíos y Orellana: Un paro que se enfrento al imperialismo', Available at: http://www.voltairenet.org/article127239.html (accessed 22 September 2017).

Stites, Richard (1989) *Revolutionary Dreams: Utopian Visions and Experimental Life in the Russian Revolution*. Oxford: Oxford University Press.

Wilson, Japhy and Manuel Bayón (2015) 'Concrete Jungle: The Planetary Urbanization of the Ecuadorian Amazon', *Human Geography* 8(3): 1–23.

Wilson, Japhy and Manuel Bayón (2017a) 'Fantastical Materializations: Interoceanic Infrastructures in the Ecuadorian Amazon', *Environment and Planning D: Society & Space* 35(5): 836–854.

Wilson, Japhy and Manuel Bayón (2017b) 'The Nature of Post-neoliberalism: Building Biosocialism in the Ecuadorian Amazon', *Geoforum* 81: 55–65.

Wilson, Japhy and Manuel Bayón (2018) 'Potemkin Revolution: Utopian Jungle Cities in the Ecuadorian Amazon', *Antipode* 50(1): 253–254.

Žižek, Slavoj (1991) *For They Know Not What They Do: Enjoyment as a Political Factor*, 2nd edn. London: Verso.

Žižek, Slavoj (1993) *Tarrying with the Negative: Kant, Hegel and the Critique of Ideology*. Durham, NC: Duke University Press.

Žižek, Slavoj (1999) *The Ticklish Subject: The Absent Centre of Political Ontology*. London: Verso.

Žižek, Slavoj (2000) *The Art of the Ridiculous Sublime: On David Lynch's Lost Highway*. Seattle: University of Washington Press.

Žižek, Slavoj (2003) 'The Reality of the Virtual', lecture, available at: https://www.youtube.com/watch?v=RnTQhcrno (accessed 1 May 2017).

Žižek, Slavoj (2006) *How to Read Lacan*. New York: W.W. Norton.

Žižek, Slavoj (2008a) 'Use Your Illusions', *London Review of Books* 14 November, available at: https://www.lrb.co.uk/2008/11/14/slavoj-zizek/use-your-illusions (accessed 30 April 2017).

Žižek, Slavoj (2008b) *Living in the End Times*. London: Verso.

Žižek, Slavoj (2015) *Trouble in Paradise: From the End of History to the End of Capitalism*. London: Penguin.

Afterword: Living in the Catastrophe
Adam Fishwick and Nicholas Kiersey

We began this book with a critical view on catastrophe. All crises are not catastrophic, we argued, but instead provide the material grounds upon which capitalism reconstitutes – through new patterns of accumulation, new modalities of exploitation, and new subjectivations of our selves. To be clear, we argued *against* a catastrophist reading of crisis as a pathway to the end of capitalism.

And then catastrophe happened.

The global pandemic of Covid-19 and the governmental responses to it since February 2020 have opened a new phase of crisis and a new process of crisis-driven capital accumulation. McKenzie Wark (2019) in her latest book offers a vision of capitalism that has already ended – a new world of 'vectoralism' in which the labour relation is no longer the driving force of accumulation, but data. Scheidler (2020) paints a similar picture when he describes what he terms the end of 'the global megamachine'. The upshot is that we may be witnessing the birth of a new, impersonal mode of power. The billions accumulated by tech capitalists like Jeff Bezos and Elon Musk even as economies around the world 'locked down' and millions lost their jobs seem to indicate a new – or consolidated – reordering of the capitalist class. But, at the same time, Covid-19 has not only made clear that technology – and control over data – is key to new patterns of accumulation, but also that, in many ways, this new data-driven modality of accumulation is dependent on the same, intensifying dynamics of labour exploitation that are all too familiar. The workhouses of Amazon Fulfilment Centres and the food processing plants of Europe and North America, staffed often by migrant labour, have become hotspots of infection at the same time as work rhythms and conditions have worsened. The surveillance technologies of the state, too, have intensified – many of which are borrowed from or directly operated by the private sector, with firms such as Google or Serco at the forefront of capturing, monitoring and managing our lives.

More than this, the everyday crises of life and living have intensified. For many, beyond the wealthiest few, the very ability to survive is threatened as jobs fall away, government support teeters on the brink of collapse, and our ability and opportunity to move and interact with one another is curtailed beyond recognition.

These worsening conditions have been facilitated by an unprecedented crisis – a catastrophe not seen for generations – and they have empowered the powerful and destabilised the lives of the rest of us. The pandemic of Covid-19 is destructive, and has killed in unimaginable numbers, but the struggle to manage this catastrophe pales into insignificance compared to the struggle of how we re-emerge.

A CRISIS OF HOPE

To begin, we might interpret the present catastrophe as a crisis of hope. Arundhati Roy, towards the beginning of these events, described the pandemic as 'a portal ... a gateway between one world and the next'. The uncertainty it brought and the responses of care, mutual aid and grassroots community support, seemed to hint towards a new set of possibilities that reconnected individuals in new ways. The pandemic, and our responses to it, are an opportunity to see and act on the world differently, in ways that abandoned the baggage of past and present, equipping us with new ways to reimagine the future. In a widely cited passage, she suggests:

> We can choose to walk through it, dragging the carcasses of our prejudice and hatred, our avarice, our data banks and dead ideas, our dead rivers and smoky skies behind us. Or we can walk through lightly, with little luggage, ready to imagine another world. And ready to fight for it. (Roy 2020)

The uncertainty of the global pandemic, the uncharted territory that had not been experienced for more than a generation, raised hopes that there was no possibility of a return to normal. The climate-destroying, inequality-producing, life-sapping constellations of the international political economy were surely no longer sustainable – not in the sense of 'sustainability', but in the sense that now the question could be asked as to whether a return to the status quo was even possible. For a fleeting moment, as the crisis accelerated, the hope of social transformation was rekindled.

In several of our contributions to this volume, the concept of hope has been central – it is the critical foil for Wilson's thinking on the moment of waking into the dream; it is the radical uncertainty that is central to Bailey's vision of alternative trajectories from capitalism; it is the starting point to Fishwick's unravelling of the ruptures necessitated by and for social change. The challenge for thinking with hope in the current moment, though, is both locating it in the uncertainty of the moment and the uncertainty of its usage. In theorising hope and hopefulness, it is its uncertainty that is most radical – we do not know the exit from a given crisis and so we can craft and struggle to make it anew. However, the unfolding of today's crisis lays bare the idea that, rather than an uncertainty, we are facing an unknowable certainty. The constellation of forces in front of us combine the old and the new modalities of oppression and exploitation, perhaps in unforeseeable ways, but in a manner that belies the possibility of a hopefulness in uncertainty.

What is clear is that the crisis certainly will – beyond its short-term effects – deeply exacerbate the multiple, intersecting inequalities that persisted in preceding years. Already, research has shown that the impacts of lockdowns and school closures have fallen heavily on women, who again pick up the burden of childcare and housework, while, simultaneously, the effect of job losses has also disproportionately affected women as part-time, lower-wage work in the service sector has been stripped away (Power 2020; Mantouvalou 2020). At its barest, the racial inequalities of pre-pandemic political economies are being foregrounded as the right to life has been extinguished across black and minority ethnic communities – who are being killed by government neglect at disproportionate rates in those countries that, for now, are most starkly affected by the pandemic, most notably the US and UK (Meer et al. 2020; Freshour and Williams 2020). The failure to address this disparity in mortality across diverse populations is likely to prove one of the greatest scandals of the pandemic in these and other countries.

Beyond the immediate impacts, global hunger and poverty are also very likely to continue to worsen in the current context, with disruption to food supply networks and global supply chains that provide jobs. Estimates show that poverty is likely to revert back to levels not seen since the late twentieth century (Sumner et al. 2020). With hunger, annual crop productions go to waste as those kicked out of the labour market struggle to afford the basic commodities that continue to circulate via online retailers. In the garment sector, workers at the bottom of huge global supply chains suddenly find themselves either discarded or pushed into working increasingly long hours in more and more dangerous conditions to meet the demands of locked down consumers with nothing to do but idly enrich the largest global brands. This is one of the clearest illustrations of the interlinked Covid catastrophes across the Global North and South, which combine the exploitation of racialised minorities, the massive impoverishment and exclusion that persists, and the digitally enhanced practices of mass consumption that are being maintained via the webs of intense exploitation that underpin the global political economy. Workers in Leicester and Dhaka share common experiences of violent exploitation, within dangerous and highly contagious workplaces, that are being exacerbated by a negligent or complicit state.[1]

Stretching out into the growing failures of global health systems, the large, emerging economies of India and Brazil appear to be amongst the worst hit countries, as the combination of authoritarian right-wing governments with the stark inequalities that permitted the countries' rapid growth provide the perfect breeding ground for Covid-19. Conspiratorial messages on the causes of the pandemic intersect with fake cures that are promoted by authoritarian leaderships desperate to maintain a semblance of legitimacy as mortality rates skyrocket and death tolls mount (Harris 2020).

The Covid crisis is a global catastrophe and one that continues to evolve before us. There are long-term effects that will resonate for years, if not decades, to come. Beyond the unequal effects of impoverishment that will certainly persist throughout the world, our capacities to resist are being slowly eroded. While at the beginning of the crisis the upswell of mutual aid and community organisation breathed new hope into the possibility not only that a return to the status quo was impossible but also that a new normal might resonate with the demands of social movements and the left, the persistence of the crisis and its unfolding has steadily undermined this collective potential. Locked away from meaningful social interaction, communities and workers across the globe are faced by an inability to reconnect and engage in the kinds of solidarity practices that – in better (and worse) times – have enabled the building of collective organisations to resist and rebuild anew from previous crises. Importantly, this crisis has coincided with another historic defeat for the organised left, with electoral defeats for Jeremy Corbyn in the UK and Bernie Sanders in the US occurring just months before this pandemic took hold. How different the responses in these two countries – both deeply affected by the crisis and the intersecting inequalities it has savagely brought to light – would have been is something about which we can only speculate as we see the consolidated power of the right.

THE HOPE OF CRISIS

It might be worth pausing here, as we reach the book's final pages, to reflect on how Covid-19 relates to the horizon of emancipation amid multiple crises that has defined the trajectory of this book. One of the most high-profile intellectual debates of this first year (at the time of writing) of the Covid-19 era concerned a number of commentaries by Giorgio Agamben (2020). Agamben despaired that the coronavirus might occasion an expansion of the state, or sovereignty, and its various technologies of control. Living in Italy, one of the first Western countries to be hit in a substantial way by the virus, the zenith of the country's first wave and the state's effort to suppress it seemed to pose a natural connection with his long-standing thesis. Namely, that since the terrorist attacks in New York in 2001, government has essentially become a permanent state of exception. Yet, alongside this analysis came an altogether more perplexing layer of argument:

> It is blatantly evident that these restrictions are disproportionate to the threat from what is, according to the NRC [National Research Council], a normal flu, not much different from those that affect us

every year.... We might say that once terrorism was exhausted as a justification for exceptional measures, the invention of an epidemic could offer the ideal pretext for broadening such measures beyond any limitation. (Agamben 2020)

Now, we are not epidemiologists. That said, according to the *New York Times*, the typical death rate among those contracting the seasonal flu is 0.1 per cent, at least in the US. Whereas publicly available statistics at the time Agamben was writing suggested that the death rate among those contracting Covid-19 in China varied between 1.4 per cent and 2.3 per cent, with South Korea reporting a rate of 1.7 per cent (Grady 2020). With this in mind, it does not seem unreasonable to infer that Agamben was trivialising the matter to an irresponsible, or even negligent degree.

Agamben's work generated vociferous debate on the left, but two early responses were of particular relevance to the debates raised by contributors to this volume. First, in a piece published on the blog *The Philosophical Salon*, on 16 March, Žižek rebukes Agamben for reducing the politics of the disease to a mere case for his long-standing thesis, that modern society is dominated by 'a mixture of power, exercise of social control and elements of outright racism' (Žižek 2020). This is a mistake, says Žižek, because it downplays the seriousness of the disease and the necessity of a socially coordinated response. However, Žižek insists, Agamben's folly should not be taken as an excuse to argue for its opposite and pursue the return to some kind of idealised authoritarianism. To the contrary, says Žižek, our demand must be for a new, democratic form of communism. Whatever the successes of China in combating Covid-19, he notes, we should be clear that the old communist model of that country encourages corruption. The real challenge of Covid-19, says Žižek, is to create an adequate theory of collective action that recognises the need for expertise in the face of complexity while simultaneously embedding this expertise in transparency, coordination and collaboration.

The second response we wish to draw attention to is perhaps more controversial but extends Žižek's provocation. It's a piece by Panagiotis Sotiris (2020), called 'Thinking Beyond the Lockdown: On the Possibility of a Democratic Biopolitics'. Now, it's not always

Afterword

easy to grasp the difference between governmentality and biopolitics, and there's an intimate relationship between the two of them. For Foucault, however, the political project of governmentality precedes biopolitics. And it is clear, if we read Foucault's *The Birth of Biopolitics* (2010), that where governmentality presents us the basic question of how states can arrange the conduct of their populations 'without a sting', so to speak, biopolitics is the subsequent proposition marking the advent of liberal political theory, that optimal social behaviours can be achieved by means of *market-based* tools. That is, for example in neoliberalism, that changes to behaviour can be achieved by incentivising subjects to develop certain relations with their own 'human capital' through changes in various marketplace dynamics: interest rates, bankruptcy laws, smoking bans, various legal punishments that involve jail time, or don't, and more.

As the cases of neoliberal government examined in this volume indicate, the history of biopolitical government as a way of regulating the conduct of social action offers little to redeem it. At its core, biopolitics is a social technology for cajoling from subjects a way of being that is optimised for capitalist markets. And, critically, we were never asked if we wanted to live this way! Yet, what if there were a way of conducting our conduct that could be decided upon, democratically? What if there was a rationale for a democratic people to create their own machinery of behavioural control? For Sotiris, the Covid-19 crisis has given this question a certain urgency. As he puts it, what we are talking about here is the need for 'behaviour modifications ... from below' (Sotiris 2020).

As an example of democratic biopolitics, he offers the case of the ACT UP movement: that is, the political coalition formed by gay men in the 1980s, in the struggle against HIV, which achieved a certain mastery over the disease through advocacy for behavioural change based on better data.[2] Crucially, for Sotiris, the movement did not restrict itself to self-government. It also appealed to the forces of state hegemony, for new public policy in the regulation of relevant segments of the market. Against Agamben, then, Sotiris concludes, such histories point to the need for the use of 'state power (and coercion) being used to channel resources from the private sector to socially necessary directions'.

As we have argued, it is likely that the viral vectors of global capital will long outlive those of Covid-19. Yet, as activists and scholars anxious to steer humanity towards a brighter post-capitalist future, we may wish to ponder if this debate on the left about Covid-19 can offer us any useful lessons. One avenue for reflection might simply be that, while liberalism may have invented biopolitics, we do not necessarily have to grant it the final word. Neoliberal governmentality uses biopolitics to modify behaviour undemocratically, and in a manner that prioritizes the prerogatives of capital. But this is not to say that the notion of an emancipatory biopolitics should be understood as a contradiction in terms! Indeed, in a recent blog post about organising on the left, Amelia Davenport offers an interesting provocation on this score. Too frequently, she contends, borrowing from Taylorist management theory, the left succumbs to an 'initiative and incentive' model of organising. The problem with this approach is that it tries to maximise the extraction of effort from its activists, without due attention to their bodily limits:

> It doesn't matter whether it's the top-down orders of the leadership or democratic vote by the group; activists are tacitly encouraged to take on an unsustainable load, leading to burnout. (Davenport 2020)

Leftist organisers rely on this model with the best of intentions, she notes, yet the result is often inefficient, and harmful to its volunteers. Therefore, as she puts it, we need something like a 'democratic scientific mass line'. That is, the collaborative creation of democratic systems for activating and orienting ourselves, in our socialist strategy.

In this book that has sought to embed the multiple crises of the endings of capitalism in the theoretical framework of international political economy, social struggle remains the wild card element of the equation. Fragmented and beset by internal disagreements, 'the left' may not be able to stop the slide into a darker post-capitalist future. Together with the other contributors to this volume, however, we remain convinced that the left must win and the crisis that has accompanied the publication of this volume makes that task more urgent than ever. We are entering into a period where deep structural crises of capitalism – and its relationship to nature and human life – are likely to expand and proliferate. The Covid-19 pandemic has also been accompanied, in the summer of 2020, by worsening environmental crises – crises that have long consumed the lives of those across the Global South, but which were exemplified in news media by images of wildfires that burned across California. At the same time, mobilisations of near unseen magnitudes, including the global spread of Black Lives Matter, massive farmer strikes in India, and anti-government protests in Nigeria and Chile, to name a few, continue to reflect the deepening and intersecting crises of capitalism that Covid-19 has exemplified. The urgency of considering the pathways to a post-capitalist future is more pressing than ever. And we hope – hope within a time of real crisis – that this volume will contribute to those discussions we all must now have.

NOTES

1. The Clean Clothes Campaign runs a live, daily updated blog covering the daily abuses faced by garment sector workers across the world, collating reports of mistreatment, hyper-exploitation and worse: https://cleanclothes.org/news/2020/live-blog-on-how-the-coronavirus-influences-workers-in-supply-chains
2. A similar though more trivial example of the democratic use of markets can be found in Peter Frase's discussion of parking spaces, in *Four Futures* (2016).

REFERENCES

All URLs checked on 15 December 2020.

Agamben, Giorgio (2020) 'The State of Exception Provoked by an Unmotivated Emergency', *Positions Politics*, 26 February 2020, available at: http://positionspolitics.org/giorgio-agamben-the-state-of-exception-provoked-by-an-unmotivated-emergency/

Davenport, Amelia (2020) 'Organizing for Power: Stealing Fire From the Gods', *Cosmonaut*, 19 November, available at: https://cosmonaut.blog/2019/11/19/organizing-for-power-stealing-fire-from-the-gods/

Foucault, Michel (2010) *The Birth of Biopolitics: Lectures at the Collège de France, 1978–1979*. Edited by M. Senellart. New York: Picador.

Frase, Peter (2016) *Four Futures: Life after Capitalism*. London: Verso.

Freshour, Carrie and Brian Williams (2020) 'Abolition in the Time of Covid-19', *Antipode Online*, 9 April, available at: https://antipodeonline.org/2020/04/09/abolition-in-the-time-of-covid-19/

Grady, Denise (2020) 'How Does the Coronavirus Compare with the Flu?', *New York Times*, 25 August, available at: https://www.nytimes.com/article/coronavirus-vs-flu.html

Harris, Bryan (2020) 'Spread of Fake News Adds to Brazil's Pandemic Crisis', *Financial Times*, 13 July, available at: https://www.ft.com/content/ea62950e-89c0-4b8b-b458-05c90a55b81f

Mantouvalou, Katerina (2020) 'COVID-19 and Gender-blind Responses: Key Policies Adopted across the UK and EU Put Many Women at Risk', *British Policy and Politics at LSE*, 2 April, available at: https://blogs.lse.ac.uk/politicsandpolicy/covid-19-gender/

Meer, Nasar, Kaveri Qureshi, Ben Kasstan and Sarah Hill (2020) 'The Social Determinants of COVID 19 and BAME Disproportionality', *Discover Society*, 30 April, available at: https://discoversociety.org/2020/04/30/the-social-determinants-of-covid-19-and-bame-disproportionality/

Power, Kate (2020) 'The COVID-19 Pandemic Has Increased the Care Burden of Women and Families', *Sustainability: Science, Practice and Policy* 16(1): 67–73.

Roy, Arundhati (2020) 'The Pandemic Is a Portal', *Financial Times*, 3 April, available at: https://www.ft.com/content/10d8f5e8-74eb-11ea-95fe-fcd274e920ca

Scheidler, Fabian (2020) *The End of the Megamachine: A Brief History of a Failing Civilization*. Alresford: Zero Books.

Sotiris, Panagiotis (2020) 'Thinking Beyond the Lockdown: On the Possibility of a Democratic Biopolitics', *Historical Materialism*, 1–35. doi: 163/1569206X-12342803.

Sumner, Andy, Chris Hoy and Eduardo Ortiz-Juarez (2020) 'Estimates of the Impact of COVID-19 on Global Poverty', WIDER Working Paper 2020/43, April 2020: 1–14.

Wark, McKenzie (2019) *Capital is Dead: Is this Something Worse?* London: Verso.

Žižek, Slavoj (2020) 'Monitor and Punish? Yes, Please!', *The Philosophical Salon*, 16 March, available at: https://thephilosophicalsalon.com/monitor-and-punish-yes-please/

Notes on Contributors

Gorkem Altinors is an Assistant Professor at Bilecik Seyh Edebali University, Turkey. He holds a PhD in Politics from the University of Nottingham. His research interests include critical IPE, MENA politics, and migration. He is the author of *Minarets and Golden Arches: The Political Economy of Islamic Neoliberalism* (forthcoming, Brill).

David J. Bailey is a Senior Lecturer in the Department of Political Science and International Studies at the University of Birmingham. His research focuses on the critical political economy of capitalism, and especially the role of protest and other forms of dissent.

Paul Bowles is a Professor in the Department of Global and International Studies and the Department of Economics at the University of Northern British Columbia, Canada. He has been researching and writing on the political economy of China's reforms for three decades. He has also written on globalisation and Asian regionalism.

Adam Fishwick is a Reader in International Political Economy and Development Studies and a member of the Centre for Urban Research on Austerity at De Montfort University. His research focuses on the labour and social movements in South America, with an interest in alternative and grassroots organising and its impact on economic development in the region.

Catia Gregoratti is Lecturer in Politics and Development at Lund University, Sweden. At Lund University she is also the co-convenor of an advanced study group on social reproduction. Her research focuses on feminist resistance to corporate power and feminist alternatives to capitalism.

Laura Horn is Associate Professor in the Department of Political Science and Business at Roskilde University, Denmark. Her work is situated within critical political economy perspectives. Laura also has a keen interest in imaginaries of, and strategies for alternatives to capitalism, for example in the sphere of science fiction.

Nicholas Kiersey is a Professor in the Department of Political Science at the University of Texas Rio Grande Valley. His research addresses austerity, biopolitics, and the crises of the neoliberal capitalist state. He is currently working on a book about socialist governmentality, and the cultural political economy of the end of capitalism.

Jonathon W. Moses is Professor of Comparative Politics at the Norwegian University of Science and Technology in Trondheim (NTNU), Norway. His most recent books include *Eurobondage: The Political Costs of Monetary Union in Europe* (ECPR Press, 2017); and *Workaway: The Human Costs of Europe's Common Labour Market* (Bristol University Press, forthcoming).

Bryant William Sculos, PhD, is a visiting Assistant Professor at Worcester State University and founding curator of *LeftHooked*, a monthly review of contemporary socialist writing, published by the Hampton Institute, where he is also a contributing editor. Bryant is also the co-editor (with Mary Caputi) of Teaching Marx & Critical Theory in the 21st Century (Brill 2019/Haymarket 2020).

Henry Veltmeyer is Senior Research Professor with the doctoral Development Studies program of the Universidad Autónoma de Zacatecas in Mexico. He is also Senior Research Fellow with the Research Centre of Advanced Latin American Studies (CALAS) at the Universidad de Guadalajara. He has written extensively on development in the Latin American context.

Japhy Wilson is an independent scholar and Honorary Research Fellow at the University of Manchester. His work explores the entanglement of space, power and ideology in the transformation of social reality under conditions of global capitalism. He is the author of

Reality of Dreams: Post-Neoliberal Utopias in the Ecuadorian Amazon (Yale University Press, forthcoming).

Owen Worth is Head of the Department of Politics and Public Administration at the University of Limerick. He writes in the wide areas of International Political Economy and International Relations and is the author of *Hegemony, International Political Economy and Post-Communist Russia* (Ashgate, 2005), *Resistance in the Age of Austerity* (Zed Books, 2013), *Rethinking Hegemony* (Palgrave, 2015) and *Morbid Symptoms: The Global Rise of the Far Right* (Zed Books, 2019).

Index

Accumulation by dispossession, 95–6, 197, 200–1, 232
Adverse incorporation, 202–3
Alienation, 53, 59, 61–2, 75, 81
Alternative models of development, 89–91, 99, 104
Alternative social relations, 176, 179, 181, 210
Amin, Samir, 38
Analectical moment, 209
Anderson, Perry, 111
Anti-capitalism, 52, 68, 109, 114, 176, 182
   scholars of, 7; Islamic, 20, 110, 120, 122–3
Anti-capitalist Muslims, 108–9, 116–19
Argentina, 102, 191–2
Artificial uterus, 67, 69–71, 76
Austerity, 8, 38, 115, 192
   anti-, 9, 37, 177–8; Greece, 145
Authoritarianism, 7, 8, 56, 94, 116, 242
Automation, 15, 133, 136–7, 138–9, 199

Bastani, Aaron, 136–7
Benanav, Aaron, 138–9, 143–5
Bhattacharya, Tithi, 6
Bieler, Andreas and Adam Morton, 8–9, 10
Black Lives Matter, 2, 10, 58, 247
Blyth, Mark, 9
Bourgeoisie, 35, 48, 53–4, 133

Bruff, Ian, 8, 10
Buen Vivir, 91, 99–101, 104
Burak Tansel, Cemal, 8, 10

Capital mobility, 154–5, 164–5
Capital strike, 126, 131, 142, 144, 164–5
Catastrophe, 2, 166, 222, 239, 242
   ecological, 75, 128, 138
Catastrophism, 3–5, 18, 91, 141
Central planning, 97
Chicago Boys, 39
China, 90–1, 92–8
Ciccariello-Maher, George, 21, 207–11
Class struggle, 6, 30, 52, 102, 132–3, 186–7, 211
Cohen, Benjamin, 28
Commons, 17–18, 174, 205, 207
   global commons, 103–4
Communization, 131, 143
Cooperativism, 91, 99, 101
Counterpowers, 183
Covid-19, 2, 58, 127, 239–40, 242, 243–4, 247
Critical Development Studies, 20, 86–9, 90
Crisis, 1–2, 3–4, 6–7, 16, 30, 67, 87, 90, 127, 165–6, 196, 239–41
   collapse, 4, 5, 196; contestable, 68; everyday, 6, 240; ecological, 87, 92; financial, 8, 13, 87; globalisation, 87; multidimensional, 90, 246–7; recomposition, 6–7;

refugee, 145; social reproduction, 74, 202–3
Cyberfeminism, 72

Dardot, Pierre and Christian Laval, 14
De Angelis, Massimo, 17–18, 205, 207
Decolonisation, 88, 188–9, 190
Decolonising dialectic, 21, 197, 207–11
Democracy, 8–9, 60–1, 98, 103, 128, 132, 143, 152–3, 166, 168
  democratic alternative, 49; democratic autonomy, 153; democratic biopolitics, 244–5; democratic control, 20–1, 137–8, 152, 167–8; democratic post-capitalist transition, 50, 54; direct democracy, 177–8; social democracy, 38–9, 126, 181
Depletion, 202
Developmental state, 93–4, 98
Dictatorship of the proletariat, 35, 181
Dikeç, Mustafa, 197
Dinerstein, Ana, 36, 205, 206
  Dinerstein, Ana and Frederick Harry Pitts, 16, 18, 207
Disruption, 10, 18, 37, 175, 191, 207–8, 212
  disruptive resistance, 16, 183; disruptive subjectivities, 17; technological disruption, 136
Dolar, Mladen, 216–18, 225, 231–2
Dreams, 216, 224, 229–30
  awaken into a dream, 228; state as dream machine, 231

Dystopia, 2, 75
  feminist, 73; science-fiction, 63
Dussel, Enrique, 209–10

Economic integration, 156–7, 158–60
Ecuador, 217
  Besieging the Impossible, 221, 223–4; oil blockades, 226–7; Citizen's Revolution, 218, 232–3; Confederation of Indigenous Nationalities of Ecuador, 219–20; Rafael Correa, 220–1, 224, 229, 231; financial crisis, 226; neoliberal reforms, 218–19, 233
Emancipation, 26–7, 30, 34–6, 41–2, 71, 87, 96–7, 135, 197–8, 231, 243
  biopolitics, 246, multidimensional, 62; poverty, 86
End of History, 26–7, 33, 42
Eurocentrism, 20, 88, 108–9, 110–11, 113–14
European Union, 9, 143–4
Exclusion, 196–7, 199, 209
  exteriority and, 209–10; political economy of, 199, 200–4, 212; racialised, 174, 200, 241
Extractive capitalism, 79, 89, 98
  extractivism, 201; neo-extractivism, 100

Fanon, Frantz, 188–91, 208
Federici, Silvia, 6, 78, 79
Feminist science fiction, 68, 71–3
Firestone, Shulamith, 72–3
Fisher, Mark, 6, 17, 59
  Capitalist Realism, 131, 142–3, 146–7

Foucault, Michel, 10–12, 129, 146
  biopolitics, 245; governmentality, 11, 245; socialist governmentality, 129–31, 146–7
Folk politics, 16, 75, 178, 180
Frase, Peter, 47–8
Fromm, Erich, 19, 47, 55–63
  productive social character, 59; psycho-social critical theory, 58–9
Full surrogacy now, 19, 68–9, 75–7
Fully Automated Luxury Communism, 128–31, 136–41

Gago, Verónica, 191–2
Gestational communism, 76
Gezi Park, 116
Gibson-Graham, J.K, 17
Gig economy, 13
Global migration, 163–4
Global poverty chains, 202
Globalisation, 153
  anti-, 176
Graeber, David, 177
Gramsci, Antonio, 19, 112
  war of movement, 32, 146; war of position, 19, 27, 31–4
Greece, 144–5
Green New Deal, 140

Hall, Stuart, 33
Haraway, Donna, 69, 75
Hardt, Michael and Antonio Negri, 16, 131–2, 179, 183, 193
Harvey, David, 1, 40
Hegemony, 31–3, 37, 40, 42, 117, 145
  counter-hegemony, 31–2; post-, 34, 146–7; neoliberal hegemonic order, 38–9;
  state-oriented hegemonic strategy, 16–17, 129–31, 137, 178–9
Hester, Helen, 68, 74
Historical Materialism, 69, 98
Holloway, John, 36, 175–6
Hope, 16, 68, 73, 92, 175, 184, 240, 247
  crisis of, 240–1; limits of, 1–2, 234–5; pessimistic hope, 62; hopelessness, 190, 234
Horizontalism, 75, 128–30, 141, 176–7, 178–9
Hybridity, 91–2, 95, 103–4
  hybrid property forms, 97–8

Industrial Workers of the World, 177
Inequalities, 241–2
International labour mobility, 163–4
International Monetary Fund, 219–20
International political economy, 1, 114, 116, 212, 240, 246
  critical, 28–30, 32–3, 115; feminist, 202–3
International trading regime, 162

Jameson, Frederic, 3

Laclau, Ernesto and Chantal Mouffe, 34
Latin America, 91, 98–103
Lazzarato, Maurizio, 13, 203
Le Guin, Ursula, 71–2
Lebowitz, Michael, 205
Left-wing convergence, 17, 178
Legitimacy, 12
  legitimisation, 10

Lewis, Sophie, 76, 68
Liberation, 75, 184
  reproductive technologies, 78; of women, 81
Lilley, Sasha, 1, 3-5
Lordon, Frédéric, 12-14
Lorey, Isabel, 6
Luxemburg, Rosa, 19, 21, 184-8
  dialectical materialism, 19, 27, 34-7, 39; mass strike, 185, 187; spontaneity, 37

Maoism, 95
Marx, Karl, 30, 38, 62-3, 95 133-4
  alienation, 59; *The Communist Manifesto*, 52, 132; cookshops of the future, 135; concept of power, 11; and Engels, 52-4, 132, 174; gravediggers, 50-1, 132; *Grundrisse*, 133; modern capitalist state, 51
Marxist feminism, 69, 80-1
Mason, Paul, 15, 27
McNally, David, 6
Micro-dialectics, 208, 211
Mirowski, Philip, 9, 40
Multilateral agreements, 154
Munck, Ronaldo, 200

Neoliberalism, 6, 14, 123, 135, 142-3
  actually existing, 9; anti-, 123; crisis of, 30; alternative to, 42; authoritarian, 8-11, 14-15, 88, 115; common sense, 41; intellectual development, 39-40, 142; neoliberal governmentality, 246; neoliberal night, 224; post-, 99, 191, 223-4
Neo-structuralism, 222-3

Non-capitalist property relations, 92
Non-capitalist space, 204
Nordic Common Labour Market, 169

Occupy movement, 127-8, 176, 216

Patrimonialism, 109
People's regime, 157, 169
Piercy, Marge, 73
Piketty, Thomas, 167
Post-capitalism, 15-17, 27, 47-8, 58-9, 74-7, 93, 95, 128, 131, 167, 174-5, 181-3, 189-90, 197-8, 205, 211-12, 246-7
  Eurocentrism and, 88; feminist, 67; political economy of, 2, 3-4, 6, 15, 18; post-capitalist property relations, 90, 95-6, 103; social reproduction and, 68; socialist, 60-1, 147; subjectivities, 192, 203; and technology, 15-16, 27, 67-8, 69, 71, 74-5, 77, 129, 133-4, 143, 239; uncertainty, 174-5, 180, 241; Western-centrism, 197
Political economy of the working class, 205
Populism, 152
  decolonised, 209-10; left, 21, 129, 180, 198; populist Marxism, 147; right-wing, 27, 56
Post-development, 34, 100
Post-work, 15-16, 136, 207
Prefiguration, 16, 21, 176-7, 205-6
  prefigurative politics, 128, 177
Precarity, 6-7, 117
  gendered, 67, 79
Primitive accumulation, 7, 201

Re/decomposition of capitalism, 1, 6, 13–14, 200
Reform versus revolution, 35, 180–1
Reproductive freedom, 80
Resistance, 31, 64, 89, 92–3, 99, 184, 186, 191
  anti-capitalist, 88, 103, 114–15, 123; everyday modes of, 16–17; experimental acts of, 184, 192; survival and, 192
Robinson, Kim Stanley, 2, 63
Roy, Arundhati, 240

Self-management, 91, 102–3, 192
Slobodian, Quinn, 8
Social and solidarity economy, 101–3
Social democracy, 38
Social reproduction, 7, 19, 67–8, 71, 174, 200, 241
  socially reproductive labour, 79
Socialism, 30, 36–8, 49, 54–5, 58, 126–8, 130, 140
  democratic, 127; Islamic, 121; parliamentary, 35; socialist alternative, 36, 41, 49; socialist post-capitalism, 60–1; state, 28, 88, 93–4; twenty-first century, 104, 224
Socialism or barbarism, 19, 47, 48–50, 128
Sotiris, Panagiotis, 244–5
Srnicek, Nick and Alex Williams, 15, 27, 75, 177–8, 198–9

Streeck, Wolfgang, 4-5, 17

Techno-optimism, 71, 77–80, 81, 131, 197–9
Tooze, Adam, 5
Trade-based integration, 159–60
Trump, Donald, 8, 9
Turkey, 115–23
Twentieth-century socialism, 38

Uneven development, 88
Universal Basic Income, 16, 61, 137–8, 139, 198, 207
Urban rage, 203–4
Utopia, 1–2, 16, 19–20, 33, 68–9, 72–3, 128, 131–2, 205, 207, 212, 228–9, 234
  concrete, 205, 206; dangerous, 73; feminist, 77; insurgent, 228; socialist, 128; yin, 81

Violence, 57, 188–9, 201, 203, 227
  everyday, 204; and rupture, 208–9

Wark, McKenzie, 48, 138, 196, 239

Xenofeminism, 19, 68–9, 73–5
Xenofeminist Manifesto, 74

Zapatistas, 36, 101, 176
Žižek, Slavoj, 222, 228, 230, 234–5, 244

The Pluto Press Newsletter

Hello friend of Pluto!

Want to stay on top of the best radical books we publish?

Then sign up to be the first to hear about our new books, as well as special events, podcasts and videos.

You'll also get 50% off your first order with us when you sign up.

Come and join us!

Go to bit.ly/PlutoNewsletter